INTIMATE
INTRUSIONS

INTIMATE INTRUSIONS

WOMEN'S EXPERIENCE OF MALE VIOLENCE

ELIZABETH A. STANKO

Routledge & Kegan Paul
London and New York

First published in 1985
Reprinted 1985 twice and 1986
by Routledge & Kegan Paul Ltd
11 New Fetter Lane, London EC4P 4EE

Published in the USA by
Routledge & Kegan Paul Inc.
in association with Meuthen Inc.
29 West 35th Street, New York NY 10001

Set in Linotron Ehrhardt
by Input Typesetting Ltd, London
and printed in Great Britain
by Billing & Sons Ltd, Worcester

Library of Congress Cataloging in Publication Data

Stanko, Elizabeth Anne, 1950–

Intimate intrusions.
Bibliography: p.
Includes index.
1. Women – Crimes against. 2. Victims of crimes – Great
Britain. 3. Victims of crimes – United States. 4. Violent
crimes – Great Britain. 5. Violent crimes – United States
6. Sex discrimination in criminal justice administration –
Great Britain.   7. Sex discrimination in criminal justice
administration – United States. I. Title.
HV6250.4.W65S73   1985   362.8'8   84–9765

British Library CIP data available

ISBN 0–7102–0069–2 (pbk.)

To Kitty Britt, my mother, and
in memory of my father, George Stanko,
both of whom taught me courage:
and to Ximena Bunster B, who taught me
the meaning of the word 'basta'

Contents

Preface

When I tell others I am writing a book on women's experiences of men's threatening, intimidating and violent behaviour, I am struck by the comments I receive. 'Don't you have a hard time finding women who have had such experiences?' some ask. 'Certainly these things don't happen as much as you are led to believe by alarmist feminists,' others add. 'And tell me,' the liberal-minded remark, 'what are they really like?' I think of my women friends, relatives, students, colleagues, acquaintances and I reply, 'They are just like me. They are all women.'

During my adult years, I've worked as a store clerk, a waitress, a secretary, a researcher, and a university teacher. My experiences in all these positions have taught me that regardless of job category I am, above all else, a woman. As part of my professional training and work over the past ten years, I have examined the American criminal justice system and begun to familiarise myself with the British systems. I've ridden in American police squad cars, observed American prosecutors making decisions about serious crime, lectured to police in both the US and England, visited American prisons and observed many a court room in America and Britain. The more I observed the criminal justice process, the more I began to see that women were treated differently; after all, women who were complainants, offenders or professionals were 'just' women. Seven years ago, my personal commitment turned to finding ways of assisting women who experienced male violence. The more I worked with raped and battered women, the more I discovered the gap between women's experiences of male violence and the understanding of those experiences to others, and more significantly, to others in positions of power to intervene on women's behalf. Yet it was my own experiences which ultimately clarified my own understanding of this gap. For four years, I was involved in my own struggle against sexual harassment.

I owe a great debt to many people who have been emotionally and intellectually supportive of my work over the years. For their assistance during this particular task, I have to thank: Kitty Britt, Lois Burwell, Mike Collison, Barbara Goodwin, Kathy Hobdell, Janet Holland, Eileen Langbant, Anne Mahoney, Gloria Miraskind, Jill Radford, Andrew Sanders, Carol Smart, Jenny Temkin, Fran Wasoff and Lynn Wolfe. Cynthia Enloe and Jalna Hanmer provided invaluable encouragement and support during all stages; Philippa Brewster just assumed a book would emerge, and I appreciate her confidence. And to Tony Green, who has promised to read the manuscript now it is complete, for his personal support throughout the most frustrating and frightening times during the writing of this book, my special thanks.

Acknowledgments

The author and publishers are grateful to the following for permission to reproduce copyright material: extracts from *Kiss Daddy Goodnight*, copyright © Louise Armstrong, 1978, published by E. P. Dutton Publishers Inc.; material from *Conspiracy of Silence*, copyright © 1978 by Sandra Butler, published by Volcano Press, 1982, San Francisco, CA, USA; material from *Battered Wives*, copyright © 1976, 1981 by Del Martin, published by Volcano Press, San Francisco, CA, USA; 'The confusion between sex and rape', letter to the editor, 22 October 1979, reprinted with permission of the *Village Voice*, copyright 1979; André Deutsch and Charlotte Sheedy Literary Agency Inc. for an extract from *The Women's Room* by Marilyn French; McGraw Hill for material from Lin Farley, *Sexual Shakedown*; 'Two Rapes' by Jane Doe, 28 August 1982, © 1982 by The New York Times Company, reprinted by permission; an extract from *The Shame is Over: A Political Life Story* by Anja Meulenbelt, translated from the Dutch by Ann Oosthuizen, The Women's Press, London; an extract from 'Sexual harassment in schools', letter to the editor, *Spare Rib*, issue 131, June 1983; material from 'The meaning of rape', article in *The Sunday Times*, 10 January 1982, © Times Newspapers Ltd.

Chapter 1

Introduction

This book is about women's lives in contemporary Britain and the United States. It focuses on the commonness of their lives through an understanding of their experiences of men's behaviour – behaviour women themselves perceive and/or experience as intimidating, threatening, coercive or violent. The brutal rape, the sexually harassing comments, the slap on the face, the grab on the street – all forms of men's threatening, intimidating and violent behaviour – are reminders to women of their vulnerability to men. Try as they might, women are unable to predict when a threatening or intimidating form of male behaviour will escalate to violence. As a result, women are continually on guard to the possibility of men's violence.

Women, in fact, are specialists in devising ways to minimise their exposure to the possibility of male violence. Some hesitate going out on the street alone after dark (even in their own neighbourhoods). Some buy cars so that they can feel freer, and safer, as they travel about. Some quit jobs. Some leave violent husbands. Some alter their lifestyles or their appearance to avoid drawing attention to themselves.

Specialists in survival through avoidance strategies, women *know*, consciously or unconsciously, what it means to be vulnerable to sexual and/or physical male intimidation or violence. Old and young, rich and poor, white and black, no woman is immune from men's intimidating, threatening or violent behaviour. If one is young, poor or from a minority, though, chances of being affected by different forms of male violence are increased; resources for avoidance strategies – owning a car, living in a 'nice' neighbourhood, being employed in daytime employment – are much more limited. (While the focus of this book is

1

on the effects of being female, feelings of vulnerability are significantly compounded when women are poor or minority or poor and minority.)

Linked with women's subordinate position *vis-à-vis* men, women's survival strategies include observing men's behaviour because it affects what women have to do to avoid male violence. (In contrast, states William Goode, men do not often observe women's lives because their behaviour is not affected by them.)[1] Women, for example, monitor footsteps behind them or sexualised comments or glances directed from men because they must devise strategies in case the encounter moves in a direction not of their own choice. Certainly, in many instances, but unpredictably so, the footsteps or the glances could be characterised by women to be men's perfectly 'innocent' behaviour. This characterisation, however, only arises after there has been 'no trouble'. As long as women do not feel coerced by men's behaviour, then women feel safe, or feel that at least this time they are not immediately threatened.

Being on guard for women, though, is not paranoia; it is reasonable caution. Many women have encountered men's threatening, intimidating or violent behaviour at first hand. As children, many women have had experiences of sexual abuse, either from male relatives or from male strangers. Quite likely, female children are even taught to be on guard for male strangers who wish to offer them candy or money to do something unspeakable (unspeakable, because, of course, few of us were ever told why male strangers might wish to offer us goodies). Female adolescence too is a time of learning what it means to be on guard. As soon as women begin pubescent development, they actually begin to see men's behaviour toward them change. Adolescent women are met with comments, glances, whistles, admiration for the visible development of their sexuality. At the same time within their peer group, sexual experimentation starts. Fending off male sexuality, much of which is initially welcomed, the young woman learns that she cannot always control sexual encounters she engages in. She also learns that if anything 'happens', she is to blame. As adults, then, women have acquired, as part of their maturation, an idea of how men respond to them as sexual beings. They are also aware that they are less physically powerful than men, that much of their surrounding world rewards them for their feminine appearance, and that men – young and old – make sexual advances toward them. It is not uncommon that, by the time women are adults, they have experienced some form of coercive, threatening, intimidating or violent behaviour from men. It is no wonder that, as adults, women are on guard.

Awareness of the commonness of physical and sexual exploitation of women by men is not new. It was a major focus of nineteenth-century feminists.[2] Despite the contradictions and middle-class bias of the 'sexual purity' campaigns in both the US and Britain, nineteenth-century feminists were aware that behaviour that men considered 'typical' was in fact exploiting many women, particularly poor and working women. One major contradiction centred on the belief that somehow 'respectable' women could avoid men's sexual and physical exploitation. Newspaper coverage of the Jack the Ripper murders in London in 1888, for example 'blamed "women of evil life" for bringing the murders on themselves, but elsewhere warned that "no woman is safe while this ghoul's abroad".'[3] Even more interesting, nineteenth-century English men's reactions to the Ripper murders took different forms, 'from conscious intimidation and impersonation of the Ripper to a more latent identification with the criminal and subtle exploitation of female terror'.[4] Judith Walkowitz includes the following story in her 1982 article.

> James Henderson, a tailor, was brought before the Dalston
> Magistrates for threatening Rosa Goldstein, an 'unfortunate',
> with 'ripping' her up if she did not go with him and for striking
> her several hard blows with his cane. Henderson was let off with
> a fine of forty shillings, on the grounds that he had been drunk –
> despite the fact that the severely injured Goldstein appeared in
> court 'with surgical bandages about her head' and 'weak from the
> loss of blood'.[5]

Regardless of the hope of nineteenth-century feminists that female respectability would grant women immunity from male violence (respectability which stemmed from being middle-class and white as well), the Ripper murders exposed deep-seated antagonisms of men toward women.

Across the waters in the United States, nineteenth-century American feminists too recognised the importance of female respectability. They also recognised women's obstacle in complaining about men's sexual and physical exploitation: the male-dominated criminal justice system. In 1885, for example, the Chicago Women's Club was established to offer legal aid to women who experienced sexual molestation, rape, wife beating, incest, and so forth. Staffed by women, agency members also appeared in court on behalf of raped women because 'they believed that the presence of respectable women helped create a moral atmosphere and in order to encourage the victim to testify in a courtroom dominated by men.'[6] The Chicago Women's Club was an exceptional agency; few other such agencies existed. Around this same time, feminists in various cities both in the US and Britain also sought to have women hired in the police departments.[7] This move too was a recognition that women's complaints of male violence were not being heard by the male police forces. None the less, most women were unassisted by this wave of feminist intervention into male violence. As respectable women turned their efforts to gaining the right to vote, they virtually abandoned their efforts to stem the tide of male violence.

The double bind of nineteenth-century women is still with us: to maximise women's safety from male violence, women are to remain 'pure'; this purity, however, is no guarantee that any woman will not encounter male violence. Yet it was the nineteenth-century feminists who provided us with valuable information: *typical men's behaviour, particularly their sexual behaviour, can be violent, intimidating, coercive, indeed damaging to women.* Women, however, still bear the blame for men's 'indiscretions', which are the result, many believe, of women's 'unrespectable' behaviour.

Understanding what it means to be female within contemporary British and American societies is understanding the meaning of male violence in women's lives. Many women's lives, in fact, revolve around strategies to avoid men's threatening, intimidating, coercive or violent behaviour. Contemporary feminists, not unlike their nineteenth-century sisters, have uncovered widespread experiences of male violence among women. Efforts to assist women affected by rape, incest, wife battering, or sexual harassment have led these feminists to see the endemic nature of men's threatening or violent behaviour in many of women's everyday interactions with men. Yet there is a stony silence surrounding incidents of male violence. It is because women who encounter men's threatening, intimidating, coercive or violent behaviour are suspected of being 'unrespectable'.

The purpose of this book is to explore how male violence against women remains a problem of women's respectability, not men's behaviour. Part I examines women's experiences of men's threatening, intimidating, coercive or violent behaviour and their typical reaction, silence. Women's silence demonstrates a recognition of their untenable position: blamed for men's behaviour, women seek an explanation for male violence in their own 'unrespectability'. So too do those to whom women complain about men's potentially threatening or violent behaviour (if, indeed, they complain at all). Part II explores the inquiry process where individuals in official capacities – police, judges, prosecutors, or personnel managers – handle women's complaints of men's 'indiscretions'. Not surprisingly, they do so with an eye to women's 'respectability'.

Part I
Ordinary experiences

Elli is raped when she accepts a lift from a truck driver, her own fault, a woman can't hitch on her own. A girl comes crying into the woman's house. Raped by an Angolan with whom she had been talking in the pub about the liberation movement in the Third World and when he asked would you like to come home for coffee because we are having such a good talk she thought don't be paranoid there are some nice men. Own fault, she shouldn't have gone with him. Francine was attacked in a lift, threatened with a knife, abducted and raped, afterwards allowed to go. Own fault, you know that you mustn't stand in a lift at night alone with a man. Her woman friend, who thought rape only happened after twelve o'clock, had the same thing happen to her a week later during the day. I don't even dare talk about it, says Francine, it was a black man and there are all the disgusting things said about blacks that I always challenge when I hear them. I understand they don't have an easy time here and that they are discriminated against and that they must then take out their aggression somewhere, but why should it be taken out on women? What must you do, start a discussion about us both being oppressed?

While he has his hands in your pants.

While we talk we continually find more stories to tell. The usual stuff, pinching our tits as we walk past, hands on our cunt on the tram, being pulled off our bicycle, pushed against a wall by a gang of drunken adolescents. Normal experiences. And then, naturally, the remarks. Don't look so grim, otherwise I'll stuff a broomstick up your cunt. Now, girl, if your cunt is as sloppy as your tits you're in bad shape. Shall we get her, men? I remember the opinions I held before. Women who don't want it aren't raped because he has only two hands. And:

perhaps the woman to whom it happened asked for it a little. At least I haven't been raped really, I say in the group, and then immediately I realise it isn't true. Toni, I remember, wasn't that rape, he only stopped when I scratched his skin to draw blood. And afterwards the forced fucking to buy my freedom. Why didn't I see that, I say. You were married, says Francine, that doesn't count as rape, that's called normal. And then we investigate what that means for us, for all women, not only those to whom it happens. We don't walk alone along the street at night, if we do we look straight in front of us, big steps, hands balled into fists, and our buttocks tight. No strolling, no looking in shop windows, walking round groups of men, getting into a panic if you hear steps behind you, making a detour not to go through a dark street, being careful not to look anyone directly in his face because eye contact, by accident, is already an invitation.

Ordinary, daily fear. We don't even notice it any more, so ordinary. It's not about if it happens to you – it's about our living in a society where it *can* happen, we are all outlawed.

Anja Meulenbelt[1]

Chapter 2

Ordinary experiences

To be a woman – in most societies, in most eras – is to experience physical and/or sexual terrorism at the hands of men. Our everyday behaviour reflects our precautions, the measures we take to protect ourselves. We are wary of going out at night, even in our own neighbourhoods. We are warned by men and other women not to trust strangers. But somehow they forget to warn us about men we know: our fathers, our acquaintances, our co-workers, our lovers, our teachers. Many men familiar to us also terrorise our everyday lives in our homes, our schools, our workplaces.

Women's experiences of incest, battering, rape and sexual harassment become the sources for documenting all women's actual and potential experiences. Physically and/or sexually assaulted women speak in similar voices; much of what they say describes what it means to be female: the child who finds she is treated as sexually available at 9, the battered woman who is embarrassed by her black eyes, shamed by her failed marriage; the raped woman who is grateful to survive, only to live with nightmares; the sexually harassed woman who is humiliated by the pornographic pictures she finds every day on her desk. In each case, a woman endures an invasion of self, the intrusion of inner space, a violation of her sexual and physical autonomy.

Cast in a mould constructed within male-dominated society, women's experiences of sexual and physical violation take on an illusion of normality, ordinariness. Through an assumption of normality, many characterise male physical and/or sexual aggression as linked to biological make-up, sparked by an innate, at times uncontrollable, sexual drive. After all, boys will be boys, we sigh. While we acknowledge that not all men publicly display this uncontrollable biological predisposition, we further believe its display is generally aroused by deserving, provoking women. We consequently ignore what is assumed to be typical male behaviour directed toward provoking women. At the same time, though, we recognise that some male aggression is not sparked by provocative women. These, we reassure ourselves, are the rarest of situations. Above all, we retain traditional assumptions about women who experience sexual and/or physical assault; some women are alluring, masochistic and provoke the uncontrollable responses of some men, and some women are pure, proper but unfortunately come across some men who are uncontrollable. When we try to account for women's experiences of male violence, explanations of it centre around the naturalness or unnaturalness of male aggression in relation to women's behaviour.

As a result, women's experiences of male violence are filtered through an understanding of *men's* behaviour which is characterised as either typical or aberrant. If it is considered typical, men's physical and sexual aggression toward women is left, to a large extent, unfettered. The sexual advance by a male professor toward a young female student, the 'rough sex', the slapping of one's wife, the wolf whistle on the street, the comments about women's physicality, the man's brushing up against a female secretary's body in the xerox room (and on and on) are, most people accept, natural expressions of maleness. These expressions are assumed to be non-threatening to women, even, some would say, flattering. The vicious rape, the brutal murder of a woman, the cruel physical torture of a girlfriend are, we feel, the aberrant examples of maleness. These examples, most would agree, are threatening to women. In the abstract we easily draw lines between those aberrant (thus harmful) and those typical (thus unharmful) types of male behaviour. We even label the aberrant behaviour as potentially criminal behaviour.

What becomes lost, though, in this commonsensical separation between 'aberrant' and 'typical' male behaviour is a woman-defined understanding of what is threatening, of what women consider to be potentially violent. Often, women themselves are confused – sometimes defining male behaviour as typical, other times as aberrant – but none the less feel threatened by some displays of either. Women who feel violated or intimidated by typical male behaviour have no way of specifying how or why typical male behaviour feels like aberrant male behaviour. Essentially, the categories *typical* and *aberrant* are not useful for understanding women's feelings about, and thus women's experiences of male intimidation and violence. Confusing though they may be, women's experiences point to a potential for violence in many of women's ordinary encounters with men. One important study, that by Jalna Hanmer and Sheila Saunders, surveyed a Yorkshire, England community querying women about their experiences of male violence.[1] Of the 129 adult women interviewed, 59 per cent reported some form of 'threatening, violent or sexually harassing behaviour' toward them in the past year. It is unlikely that women, when threatened, wait to categorise potentially threatening behaviour toward them as either typical (thus unthreatening) or aberrant (thus threatening) male behaviour. Women not only define a whole variety of male behaviour toward them as potentially violent, but male behaviour toward other women is seen as potentially threatening as well. The interviewed women of Hanmer and Saunders's study also reported incidents of male violence they witnessed or overheard happening to other women. Hence, the *daily* possibility of being threatened by male behaviour is one message women constantly receive.

A common theme throughout the women's descriptions of everyday encounters with men, report Hanmer and Saunders, is powerlessness: women are unable to predict, and thus unable to control, men's behaviour or anticipate when it might lead to violence. It doesn't matter whether men themselves read their own behaviour as typical or aberrant. Women read a great deal of male behaviour as threatening. For example, while many think 'flashing', exposure of the male genitals, is a non-threatening event, the women who were interviewed interpreted these events as potentially violent. 'Exposure of the male genitals . . . to a woman on her own in an isolated part of an open space or deserted street,' state Hanmer and Saunders, 'may engender fears of injury and death because of the uncertainty about what may happen next.'[2] Women's uncertainty, their inability to predict what is supposed to be typical (and thus not threatening) or what is aberrant (and thus threatening) male behaviour opens up an ever-present fear and makes women uneasy about their safety on the street, in the home, or in the workplace. Women's fear reflects a recognition of their vulnerability *as women* to men's behaviour and thus to the possibility of male violence.

In what have come to be called criminal victimisation studies, evidence of women's fear has in fact been found in studies focusing on the incidence of crime. Conducted in both the United States and

Britain, these surveys attempt to measure the prevalence of criminal behaviour and the extent to which these criminal incidents are reported to the police. (Not surprisingly, not all criminal incidents are reported to the police. In fact less than one half of all serious incidents come to police attention in both US and Britain.) Researchers also ask whether the interviewed person feels safe walking alone at night in their own neighbourhood. Women's fear about their safety on the street, according to these surveys, is *overwhelmingly* higher than men's fear.[3] According to these same surveys, women are less likely than men to be subjected to serious criminal incidents. Why is there such a difference between women's reported fear and women's reported experiences of criminal behaviour? Why are more women than men afraid to walk alone in their own neighbourhoods after dark? It is the Hanmer and Saunders study which provides the clues. First, women's experiences of threatening or sexually harassing male behaviour, feeding directly into their inability to predict when male intimidating behaviour will lead to violence, remind women that they are vulnerable. Second, as we shall see in detail later, many women are reluctant to report criminal incidents when they feel they should have predicted when a man would act violently toward them. Consequently, women's fear stems from their powerless and precarious position: being vulnerable to men's threatening, sexually harassing or violent behaviour and unable to predict when the threatening behaviour will turn to violence.[4]

Vulnerability, also commonly assumed to be an inherent gender trait of women, has connotations other than those related to the probability of criminal attack. Women's vulnerability takes on additional meaning; for women, it is, above all, sexual vulnerability. As Catharine MacKinnon correctly recognises, 'Vulnerability means the appearance/reality of easy sexual access; passivity means receptivity and disabled resistance, enforced by trained physical weakness; softness means pregnability by something hard.'[5]

It is women's vulnerability that makes women's sexuality and the everpresent potential for sexual violation a 'material reality of women's lives, not just a psychological, attitudinal, or ideological one'.[6] This reality rings clear in account after account of women who experience sexual and/or physical assault. Its potential reality is experienced by many other women. Those women whose houses have been burgled, for example, where there is no confrontation between assailant and the woman, report feelings of sexual violation.[7] The reality of physical and/or sexual vulnerability is part of women's experience of being in the world.

Yet vulnerability for women has another, more insidious side. It also has connotations about the 'invitation' to be physically and/or sexually violated. Any attempt to label men's behaviour as threatening or sexually harassing raises additional myths surrounding women's sexuality as the *cause* for men's actions. 'She asked for it', 'she considers it flattery', as the myth goes, the woman is to blame. A woman who labels behaviour as sexually harassing, for instance, is accused of reading into 'perfectly innocent' behaviour. Or she is accused of encouraging men's behaviour in the first place. It is assumed a woman's very presence is what introjects sexuality into the workplace or street – an assumed asexual territory. So, too, women are expected not to acknowledge any advances as sexual for fear they might be suspected of being 'wise' to all other forms of sexuality.[8] Suddenly, it is the woman who is misinterpreting the event, according to traditional thinking, only 'whores' can recognise the street cues of sexualised behaviour, and the responsibility for 'sexualising' encounters rests solely with the woman.

Not surprisingly, academic as well as legal orientations toward women's experiences of sexual and/or physical violence incorporate a concept of vulnerability into general explanations of criminal violence. In the last forty years, within American and European criminology, there has emerged a focus on the 'victim' of crime, a focus which theoretically includes an explanation for women's experiences of male violence. (Keep in mind that criminal violence involves what becomes labelled 'aberrant' male behaviour toward women, behaviour for which men can be legally punished or sanctioned. I will look at this more closely in Part II.) Victimology, often deemed to be a separate discipline in its own right, explores the relevance of victims to the phenomenon of crime. The term 'victim' is applied by various theorists to those who experience traditional crimes, such as murder, rape, assault, robbery, burglary and so forth, as well as to groups of individuals who experience high rates of or distinct forms of crime, like, for example, physically boundaried communities or the elderly. In applying the term 'victim', though, one implicitly separates victim from non-victim. Accordingly, victim characteristics are then explored by theorists for their contribution to patterns of criminal behaviour.[9] Women – as a special group – are considered worthy of study; men are not.

Women and their vulnerability fit neatly into the theoretical focus

of victimologists.[10] Suspicions regarding a woman 'victim's' behaviour
– what led the man to attack the woman? – have foundations in the
assumptions about typical and aberrant male behaviour. A woman
'victim' is thus seen as separate from women who are not victims of
male violence.

Benjamin Mendelsohn, who in 1956 proposed the term 'victimology', studied the victim-criminal relationship, essentially to examine
the 'potential of victimal receptivity'. He established victim typologies
along the lines of victim 'culpability'. Categories such as the
'completely innocent victim', 'victim with minor guilt' due to 'ignor-
ance', the 'provoker victim', or the 'simulating victim' (one who feigns
victimisation in order to punish another person) are included in Mendelsohn's list.[11] These particular categories were constructed so as to
be applicable to both male and female victims. When, however, these
categories are placed within the context of many traditional
assumptions about women, we can see how certain categories can be
more readily applied to women as a whole. Pointing to the probable
participation of women in their own sexual and/or physical violation,
traditional characteristics of women match those of a 'victimised'
populace. Some of these – that women are passive, easily led, vulnerable, sexually unmanageable, impulsive, unpredictable – continue to
have power over the way women who have experienced male violence
are viewed by criminal justice decision makers (see Part II) and how
'victimised' women are viewed by their neighbours and relatives, all
of whom make judgments about the nature of male violence to women.
From these traditional characteristics, we get the idea that women are
by nature 'victims'.

Von Hentig, the influential European theorist, in his 1940s analysis
of sexual crimes, did just that. 'The female', one of von Hentig's types
of victims, places women in the 'born victim' category. Being female,
according to him, is yet 'another form of weakness';[12] women have
less strength, thus are easy prey to men. Furthermore, women occupy
a biologically determined status in sexual crimes. Von Hentig's typology is rather blatantly rooted in assumptions about women. I am not,
however, arguing that women have the same strength as men and that
is why von Hentig's typology is faulty. It is more a problem of omission:
what does women's weakness have to do with 'sexual' crimes? Should
not the inquiry be directed to the reasons why women, who are
physically weaker than men, are subjected to attack from them? The
1960s theorists in victimology, who began to question biologically

based explanations, did not address this question. Instead, they constructed another, perhaps more subtle process of categorisation, one that focuses on 'victim' responsibility for criminal behaviour. Some victims precipitate or provoke criminal behaviour. It is not difficult to characterise women as 'precipitative' or 'provocative' in situations of men's sexual and/or physical aggression. Both these categories focus attention on the woman's behaviour, away from that of the male aggressor.

Just as women are, according to some theorists, biologically predisposed to being 'victims', their experience of male violence, according to another group of theorists, becomes rooted in social explanations derived from 'independent' assessments of women's provocation and participation. Precipitative victims are those

> who have done nothing specifically against the criminal (as opposed to the provocative victims), but whose thoughtless behaviour instigates, tempts, or *allures* the offender to commit a crime against the enticing victim ... *an overly revealing dress of a female may allure to rape.* Naturally, a perfectly socialized person [if there is such a thing at all] is not supposed to be tempted or enticed to the extent of violating the rules of the criminal law. . . . Yet, the characteristics of the criminal's personality are often bent by the characteristics of the victim's behaviour toward committing the crime.[13]

Here we see how the typical male becomes an aberrant male: women cause it. (This thinking does not work in reverse. Just for a moment imagine why an over-revealing pair of trousers doesn't allure a woman to rape a man. Sexual precipitation or for that matter sexual provocation means women arouse men.) Provocative victims, on the other hand, have done something to incite the aggressor; the responsibility for any criminal action is heavily shared by both offender and the abused woman. (I'm not sure which category is better for women: born victims or socially responsible victims. Each are equally insidious, easily rooted in a male view of women's behaviour, and equally important, a male view of men's behaviour. Once biology is challenged as an explanation for behaviour, it seems, behaviour becomes socially learned. In both, however, females are targets of male violence. Regardless, traditional stereotypes just carry on in another form.) These typologies – victim as provocative or as precipitative – fit neatly with existing stereotypes about women: they are sexually unmanageable and thus they 'ask for' it; they are nagging and thus they deserve the punch in the mouth.

In essence, Western criminologists have adopted theoretical explanations characterising women's experiences of male violence through what Kathleen Barry terms the 'rape paradigm'.[14] In many ways, academics and policy makers do not merely passively incorporate traditional stereotypes about women; they frequently create new forms of them. Rather than look to any explanations of male violence in social forces or in masculinity, academics, criminal justice decision makers, and men and women alike look instead to women's supposed behaviour – before, during and after men's actions. As we examine in more detail women's own reactions to male behaviour which they experience as violent, we see that it too rests in seeing women themselves 'as driven by their own needs into abusive situations and enslavement'.[15]

Creating a category 'victim' is one way of dealing with women's experiences of male violence. The role and status of 'victim' is separate from that of all women. 'Victimism', the practice of objectifying women's experiences of male violence, serves to deny the commonality among sexually and/or physically assaulted women and their oneness with all women.[16] (As we will see in Part II, this category 'victim' is important for the work of the decision makers who assess the parameters of criminal behaviour. It is here that the 'legitimate' victim is separated from the 'deserving' victim.) We can then easily separate victims from all women. We even have academic and institutional explanations to assist us.

Yet women *know* to read situations as potentially threatening, sexualised, or violent. It is a form of protection, a way of hoping to avoid the blame placed upon them for any sexual and/or physical attack. Comments, glances, physical touching can be felt as either sexual or not. Sometimes those comments, glances or touching are acknowledged, some are returned willingly, but many others, unwelcomed, serve as intrusions. It is assumed, at least from a male point of view, that men honour or flatter women by acknowledging their sexuality, and that women are to trust that men will protect them from threatening behaviour. And sexuality – tacitly understood as heterosexual sexuality – is, after all, a taken-for-granted part of life, purportedly pleasurable, welcomed at all times – at least from a male point of view.[17]

For women to label male behaviour as 'aberrant' – that is to report

sexually and/or physically violent male behaviour to the official authorities (in most instances women call the police, the authority invoked
is the authority of the criminal law) – is to characterise it outside the
parameters of typical, normal or inevitable. Many women too believe
that men's aberrant (thus criminal) behaviour is supposedly distinct
from men's typical behaviour toward women. The category 'crime' –
the only official category which exists within society to define aberrant
behaviour – emerges as the standard against which women have to
measure aberrant male behaviour toward them. It is a standard which
does not arise from women's experiences of male violence. 'As
women's experience blurs the lines between deviance and normalcy
(aberrant and typical), it obliterates the distinction between abuses *of*
women and the social definition of what a woman *is*.'[18] To be a woman
is to be potentially sexually and/or physically assaulted by men. Is
there a difference between typical and aberrant male behaviour? Is
there a difference between women who have experienced male violence and those who have not? How do we, as women, distinguish
between typical male physical and sexual aggression (thus not
harmful?) and aberrant male aggression or between women who have
experienced male aggression and those who have not? We must turn
to women's experiences to find the parameters or to find that the
parameters are not really distinguishable.

Women do define instances of male behaviour as abusive,
threatening, violent or potentially violent – many more than we have
ever known before. But because women experience the world through
male perceptions of it, they question their own feelings and perceptions of the world. Their voices crack of qualification and self-doubt
because they know, a powerful lesson of growing up in a male-
dominated world, that their private assessment and the public assessment of their experiences of sexual and/or physical violation are likely
to be at odds.[19] Women also learn to define their worlds and thus
their experience as less important than men's. In the social hierarchy
of value, they are less. Women therefore internalise and silence many
of their experiences of sexual and/or physical intimidation and violation. That is why many of their experiences do not show up in
surveys counting criminal incidents. Only 'bad' girls get hurt, we've
been told. Rather than being exposed as 'bad', women stay quiet. As
a consequence, women feel shame, humiliation, and self-blame for
men's sexual and/or physical aggressive behaviour toward them.
Women's experiences of physical and/or sexual intimidation and of

male violence and their own reactions to it are thus welded to male dominance in Western society which rests upon women's secondary position.

To understand women's experiences of men's physical and/or sexual intimidation and violence is also to understand that society allows for, and on many levels encourages, male intimidation and violence to women, and, in particular, intimidation and violence which is directed at women as sexual beings.

By separating women's experiences of sexual and/or physical assault from women's experiences of sexual and/or physical intimidation, as many are likely to do, we see each assault as an aberration or a random occurrence – a 'personal' problem. Alternatively if we link them together, we can create new information on the overall treatment of women by men. What emerges is not random or isolated. What emerges is a flood of common experiences. Women are likely to experience some form of men's intimidating or violent behaviour in their lifetimes, often many times over. It is irrelevant to women whether this behaviour is, for men, conscious or unconscious, intended or unintended, typical or aberrant.[20] It is experienced by women as intimidating, harassing and violent.

Women, no longer afraid of their feelings, of sharing those daily instances of humiliation, and of hearing women speak of physical and sexual assault, break the pattern of men's intimidation and violence. It is a way of gaining power over our awareness of our condition as women. At its very heart, says Susan Griffin, is that

the whole issue [of understanding men's power over women seems] . . . to revolve around whether or not one could trust a woman's word; and behind this questioning of our word, whether one could trust a woman's being, whether we could *trust our own being*.[21]

In the following chapters I will explore four areas which, as the result of feminist-initiated research and action, document an important feature of women's experiences as women: incest, rape, wife battering, and sexual harassment. In each of these, men's physical and emotional intimidation and violence is directed at women and their sexuality. In each of these, women are surrounded by stereotypes and beliefs which point to women's responsibility for men's violence toward them.

I explore these incidents through the voices and experiences of women themselves, women in both Britain and in America. Sexually and/or physically assaulted women speak of their pain in much the same way; they speak of the factors which have silenced them and many others from recounting their experiences aloud. Throughout the discussion I argue that in general, women, as part of growing up in a world which operates from a male point of view, are not taught how to resist men's intimidation and violence. At the same time on the street, in the home, or in the office, women try to avoid unpredictable confrontation with men. The office pass, the sexualised remarks on the street or threats of violence, the double messages, the random battering at home keep us virtually in a constant state of awareness about the ever-presence of men's power over women's physical and sexual autonomy. Experiences of threatening or violent male behaviour become powerful lessons in themselves: they essentially are examples that women can be and in fact are subject to physical and sexual intrusion by male strangers as well as intimates.

Women do resist, persistently and tenaciously, the effects of male violence. Women are survivors. They have done so for hundreds and hundreds of years. Many have developed scar tissue, but survive they do and continue to struggle for autonomy. Women are not, as some would have us believe, masochistic, addicted to violence, prone to seeking it out, or in any way defeated by violence directed toward them. Our survival is our strength, our experiences the reminders that there is much more work to do.

Understanding the process of women's responses to men's intimidating, threatening, or violent behaviour can enable us to uncover the reasons why women remain silent. This silence, contrary to popular thinking, does not mean tacit acceptance. Silence is a way for the powerless to cope with very real situations.

Silence is a *declaration*. Factors such as concern for others, situational helplessness, fear and terror, and perhaps even immobilising depression encourage silence. This exploration into women's experiences with men's intimidating or violent behaviour, then, is meant to articulate the process of making sense of women's lives and the role male violence plays in it. This very discussion breaks the silence and begins to transform it into a deafening roar, for it is through sharing and understanding men's power in our own lives that we also share the courage, laud the resistance, and help other women continue to resist it in their own lives.

Chapter 3

Incest: some of us learn as children

Little girls grow up in a 'pink' world.[1] At infancy, the female child becomes surrounded by Western culture's traditional feminine colour, 'pink', marking not an innate preference for colour tone, but a parcel of information which surrounds the induction of this child into the world. (Have you ever noticed how the congratulatory cards we send to parents have so many variations of pink and fluff in them?) The female child is likely to be attended to by a woman, usually her mother. By age 5 or so, she is also likely to have acquired many of the ingredients which make up the ideal female temperament of a female in today's society which she is expected to exhibit adeptly to others. She trots off to kindergarten 'thoroughly primed' for her feminine role: she is helpful, nurturant, supportive, loving.[2] One basic part in some children's lives, however, can be a source of confusion: as part of the pink world, incestually assaulted children learn that their female role also entails sexual availability to men.

Growing up in the pink world, while at the same time being sexually abused by daddy (or any other adult male figure of authority), is a terrifying experience. As the taboo about the subject of incest is slowly being lifted (due primarily to women themselves who are breaking their silence because they are sharing their experiences), we are gaining insight into what many women experienced as young girls or teenagers. Behind the front doors of too many of our homes, incestually assaulted women learned all too soon what it means to be sexually vulnerable to men, for even their own homes are the places where their sexual intrusion occurs.

Terror, according to many incestually assaulted women, is the result of a constant state of anxiety, coupled with the inability to predict when, where and in what form sexual intrusion will occur. It is having to be continually aware of the movements of the assaulter. To understand what it means to live under such terror, we must listen to women who themselves experienced incestuous assault. Elizabeth speaks first about her encounter with her father, a single encounter that had profound effects on her life.

It was quite normal to get into bed on a Sunday morning with my parents and have a cuddle, and it was just a continuation of that. I was ten or eleven when it happened. My mother had got up to make breakfast, and my father and I were just lying there, chatting, I suppose. I can't remember things very clearly – I'd have been wearing pyjamas or a nightdress. I don't remember exactly, and he was in his pyjamas – I'm pretty sure he kept them on. I picked up that something was different from the way he was talking – I had a sense this wasn't the usual Sunday morning cuddle even before he began to hug me and ask me if I knew where babies came from. I remember thinking, he knows quite well I know all about that – my mother had told me a couple of years before – so why is he asking me, and why is he getting hold of me like this? He wouldn't drop the subject, he kept on about it even after I told him I knew, and he was rubbing himself up against me. He had his arms around me – it was an extension of a father cuddling a child in bed – but it got beyond that and I was aware of his genitals. . . . I think if I'd just *seen* him naked with an erection I'd have been rather shattered, but to be in bed and to feel this is a very bewildering experience: you've no terms of reference to deal with it.[3]

Jenny's experience, while differing in the form of assault, illustrates again the terror, and the confusion accompanying experiences of incest. Most of all, for Jenny as well as Elizabeth, silence is the response.

Early childhood by most standards was pretty ideal. Raised in the midst of an old established family, we had a fairly traditional upbringing. It was very clearly child-centred, and our world was protected to the point of being sheltered. We all had our own childhood battles to fight, but it was safe, and we never doubted that we'd win.
Basic background stuff included prominent lawyer father, a

college professor mother, and three younger brothers. We all did the private day school, summer camp, and boarding school number. I have just finished my third year at a small, liberal arts, women's college.

The times are hazy. But Daddy had always come by to kiss us goodnight. At some point I woke up and realized he was sitting on the side of my bed and had pushed my nightgown up and was just touching me, more or less all over. I foxed sleeping and after a while he left. These visits grew more frequent and longer. He always came in long after I was supposed to be asleep and never spoke. I was always awake when he arrived although I was pretending to be asleep (I wonder now if he knew). These encounters were obviously clandestine, and there were a whole other set of visits, right at bedtime, that were actively physical, but in some ways more pressured. At these points, Daddy would ask me to do something for him and would be displeased if I balked. In some ways they bothered me more than the other visits, because I was awake and he knew it and I felt therefore responsible.

During this time, Daddy and I were fighting like cats and dogs – tooth and nail, which at the time I did not connect at all with our evening encounters. By the time I left for boarding school, I couldn't wait to go. Until that time I was deadly afraid of becoming pregnant, because then everybody would know. I never told anybody, but fought with the world – my grades dropped for the first time in my life; I hated my teacher (although that was legitimate in and of itself); I hated school, friends – everything. It took me years to connect all this stuff with Daddy with the time period. Mom says I arrived home from school every day in tears (and that she dreaded it).

Until about a year ago I had no awareness that any of it had happened. I had completely removed it from any form of consciousness. Until that point I had not come near to having a relationship even as close as a best friend.[4]

Elizabeth and Jenny voice many of the experiences, the fear, the fighting to keep themselves alive by blocking out many of the memories that other incestually assaulted women voice. They tell of confusion, shame, humiliation, powerlessness. Freud would have termed these stories fantasies. For the most part, it was his orientation that established the professional view towards reports of incest: it should be treated as a normal fantasy of developing female children.[5] Even Elizabeth and Jenny wished it would be so; they too questioned the reality of what had happened in their lives. Their memories might be hazy, but their experience is not. It is locked away, yet constantly intruding on their present lives.

Incest is real; it is physical and psychological sexual intrusion many women have experienced while growing up. Sandra Butler would use the phrase 'incestuous assault' in describing Elizabeth and Jenny's experiences rather than incest. The term 'incest' merely describes sexual relations between people related to each other. Sexual relations, however, connotes consent at least within our typical thinking about male/female sexual relationships; it is a connotation which Butler explicitly challenges. The phrase 'incestuous assault' is useful, Butler states, because it implies the dynamic involved in *non-consensual* (essentially coercive) behaviour. She goes on to define incestuous assault as

> any manual, oral or genital sexual contact or other explicit sexual behaviour that an adult family member imposes on a child, who is unable to alter or understand the adult's behaviour because of his or her powerlessness in the family and early stage of psychological development. This type of incest is non-consensual because the child has not yet developed an understanding of sexuality that allows him or her to make a free and fully conscious response to the adult's behaviour.[6]

The forms of sexual intrusion vary – it is not always genital, nor always physical; none the less, the female child is likely to be affected by various forms of sexual intimidation. The father who fondles his genitals while he stares at his daughter as she undresses invades his child's feelings of security or safety. The father who progresses from fondling to intercourse uses a pattern of intimidation and control. It is the father who rapes his daughter that is most likely to be viewed by others as violent. In all these situations, an adult male, be it father, stepfather, grandfather, uncle or brother-in-law, asserts his rights over a child's sexuality, his power and right to use the child sexually, as he pleases. The source of this power is located in adult emotional and physical experience and in the trust male adults automatically receive within the family unit. On the other hand, the female child is powerless: her position in the family structure (as child, not adult), her lack of life experience (who could expect a 6- or 7-year-old to negotiate sexual relations with an adult male?) do not often give her the structural or emotional power to fend off sexual advances; her femaleness is powerlessnesss. As such, incestuous assault is perhaps the most glaring example of men's power over women and women's sexuality.

From what we know so far, incestuous assault has patterns:

- in over 90–97 per cent of the cases, the offender is male;
- in over 87 per cent of the cases, the assaulted is female;
- incestuous assault is coercive, but not always violent; coercion exists within the structural positions of the offender and the assaulted;
- the assaulted suffers emotional trauma; the longer the behaviour had been going on, the deeper the trauma is likely to be;
- incestuous assault, like other forms of violence against women, is steeped in myths about the seductiveness, and consequently the blameworthiness of the assaulted;
- the incidence is grossly underestimated.

What official figures do exist, exist in an historical vacuum. They are likely to be American figures. Judith Lewis Herman, in her detailed examination of five American surveys about incest conducted from 1940 to the present, illustrates not only the consistency in the findings, but the stony silence surrounding their publication, at least until the recent work of the American, David Finkelhor, in 1979. (Even now, it is primarily feminists who are shouting.) These surveys tapped women's experiences of childhood sexual encounters, querying predominantly middle-class women, most of whom tended to be young (some of the surveys were conducted with college-aged students) and considered to be of 'normal' mental health. The results:

> One fifth to one third of all women reported that they had some sort of childhood sexual encounter with an adult male. Between four and twelve per cent of all women reported a sexual experience with a relative, and one woman in one hundred reported a sexual experience with her father or stepfather.[7]

Few respondents had reported these incidents to anyone, indeed one of these reported studies revealed that only 6 per cent of the respondents had previously reported the incident to authorities and one in five had never informed anyone about the incident at all. (It is not likely that even if the incident had been reported there would have been anything done about it.) As Herman points out, the climate for assessing the significance of these figures just didn't exist. What did exist was an attempt to open up the whole issue of sexuality in people's everyday lives and experiences. While that goal might be laudable for that particular historical period, we are more aware now that opening up the issue of sexuality means *men's* sexuality. Obscured were the elements of power and coercion felt by women. Of focus is 'free sexual expression', relying upon assumptions that both men and women have equal access to sexuality and sexual pleasure – which they should, as long as it is free of coercion as well.

Even as today's climate is beginning to take different views of women's childhood sexual experiences – that they are more likely to be incestuous assault than 'innocent' play – the figures are far from complete, leaving us with more a sense of the unknown than the known. Butler, in alerting us to the widespread nature of childhood sexual abuse, reminds us that three of four reported cases of childhood sexual abuse are committed by someone the child knows and trusts.[8] As we know from other types of assault among intimates – rape and battering in particular – reported cases are far fewer than the estimates of incidence. Silence about intimate assault, including childhood sexual abuse, remains the norm. So much so that David Finkelhor has remarked that, in his opinion, the vast majority of children never tell anybody about incestuous assault. He estimates that 75 to 90 per cent of the incidents are never discovered.[9]

They are never discovered because women continue to remain silent. While the women's movement is creating a climate for many women to state their experiences aloud (the 'personal' is indeed the 'political'), women's socialisation and the lack of understanding of (or perhaps refusal to give credence to) the long-term effects of incestuous assault on women's lives are powerful silencers in themselves. The female child who suffers from incestuous assaults over time (and we are only beginning to understand how many) is at first unable to comprehend what is happening to her, particularly if she is very young at the time the assaults begin. By the time she is old enough to understand or at least to know that something is seriously wrong, the feelings of guilt, self-blame and humiliation may be well entrenched. Even if she is successful at stopping the incestuous assaults (as she grows older she may learn techniques such as threatening to tell others about her assaulter), she is left with the scars, reminders of the humiliation. Researchers have found that incestually assaulted women report feeling 'frightened' or 'upset' years later and state that the experience was 'unpleasant' or 'extremely unpleasant', in effect, over-whelmingly 'negative'.[10]

In listening to incest survivors tell of their incest experiences, one picture clearly gels, a picture which exposes the incest survivor's agony on the one hand, and the disadvantages she faces from her femaleness on the other. The pattern of incest, its documentation, emerges from these experiences: lessons which taught the female child to be helpful, nurturant, supportive, and loving are not advantages to stopping the assaults.

The implied, and sometimes stated, reactions of others point to how others are likely to characterise an incestuous assault. If she hadn't consented, some ask, why didn't she do something to stop it? When this question is asked, it exposes the 'seductive daughter' stereotype and the underlying traditional views about women, women's sexuality, and the assumed equal nature of sexual exchange between men and women.[11]

Judith Herman and Lisa Hirschman describe what might be termed typical features of the relationship between the assaulted and the offender; they are hardly situations involving 'equal' sexual exchange:

> The majority of the victims [in their study] were oldest or only
> daughters and were between the ages of six and nine when they
> were first approached sexually by their fathers or male guardians
> [9 fathers, 3 stepfathers, a grandfather, a brother-in-law, and an
> uncle]. The youngest girl was four years old; the oldest 14. The
> sexual contact usually took place repeatedly. In most cases the
> incestuous relationship lasted three years or more. Physical force
> was not used, and intercourse was rarely attempted with girls
> who had not reached puberty; the sexual contact was limited to
> masturbation and fondling. In three cases, the relationship was
> terminated when the father attempted intercourse.[12]

It is quite likely that the aggressors themselves use sexuality in such a way as to maximise the ambiguity of the encounters. Short of sexual encounters, the aggressors can assault with impunity without the ire brought by the knowledge that the assaulter has 'raped' a child. From what evidence we have, the encounters are not always what others would imagine as rape or forced encounters; they may take place over years, sometimes with the children receiving 'rewards' for sexual favours. yet all the while the element of coercion and intimidation exists, and quite powerfully so. If the assault falls short of intercourse, then the consequences are assumed to be less harmful than violent rape. The prescription for silence is thus found in what is believed to be sexually harmful: defined from a male point of view, anything short of a vicious rape is not considered that harmful.

An incestually assaulted child's silence is also fostered through illusions about the existence of an ideal social world. That ideal, fed by stereotypes of 'real' life in the media, is moulded in terms of the family unit, and female roles within that unit. Roles within the family descend upon the child – mother, father, sisters, brothers, and other members of an extended family network. A child learns the process of interpersonal interaction through her family; her security, her emotional self is grounded in those relationships. When a male family member with authority within the family network suddenly changes his behaviour, he introduces interpersonal behaviour that results in feelings of terror or confusion. Everyone on television seems to be having no problems with adult men; why is she? Account after account of incest points to this strange *feeling* female children had about the sexualised behaviour toward them. As Elizabeth stated, 'I couldn't explain it to myself ... I couldn't understand it.' These children, lacking a frame of reference, know only their feelings. (They are left with what, as adult women, we are left with in terms of our own experiences. We feel them, but we often cannot articulate them.) And those feelings fill them with anxiety, shame, guilt (just as they do for adult women!).

The change in the offender's behaviour, moreover, means a loss; her father or father figure, who was once a source of comfort and love, is now a source of pain and anxiety. The ideal happy family comes crashing down. States one woman:

Here is this wonderful man who is the most important person in your life, whom you idolize and trust, and he's betraying your trust. Part of you is *angry*, but another part is saying, maybe it'll stop, maybe it'll go away. I'd keep thinking, this is going to be the last time, praying that it was and that he'd look at me and say 'you're my baby, I love you, let me hold you'. My mother never held me, never loved me – when my father wasn't being sexual he'd love me the way I wanted to be loved, hold me right, and I must remember that when I was little he did this. He was all I had! How could I help but hope somehow he'd miraculously change?[13]

Father becomes 'male', and male behaviour thus becomes suspect for its coercive and sexual overtones. Is this 'typical' male behaviour? This categorisation isn't useful to the incestually assaulted female child. As Herman and Hirschman note:

> the daughter who has been molested is dependent on her father for protection and care. . . . She has no recourse. She does not dare express, or even feel, depths of her anger at being used. She must comply with her father's demands or risk losing the parental love that she needs. She is not an adult. She cannot walk out of the situation (though she may try to run away). She must endure it, and find in it what compensations she can.[14]

This hope, mixed with anger and humiliation, also mixes with self-blame, another silencer. Many victims feel, as Jenny did, responsible for the behaviour of their assaulters. Responsibility, for girls, means '*doing* what others are counting on her to do regardless of what she herself wants'.[15] If she has learned her world correctly, she, to her own detriment, feels responsibility for the male sexualised behaviour exhibited toward her. She finds herself dragged into a situation that she has no control over – sometimes even without knowing the words, let alone the concepts, for the behaviour in which she is 'participating'. How could a 5-year-old possibly understand sexuality or sexual intercourse? Or a 12-year-old? (I know too many 40-year-olds that still don't understand!)

Female incestually assaulted children suddenly become 'wise' to sexuality and are out of step with their peers; they already know the 'facts of life' too well. Barbara speaks directly about the shame felt by her experiences of incestuous assault and how it affected her relationships with her peers:

> I couldn't bring myself to wear make-up or earrings like the rest of the girls; I didn't want to be sexy or look like a woman. Worst of all, I never really had any peers. They thought I was aloof, whereas I simply didn't know how to relate to them. How could I join in their conversations about boyfriends and first kisses when I was having sex with my father? I never felt like a part of that teenage world because I never was. I could only relate to older boys who were two or three grades ahead of me. The boys talked about sex a lot, and at least that was something to which I could relate. The other girls thought I was a slut because I only hung

around with older boys, but none of those relationships was sexual. I never knew how to explain it to them, so I always felt left on the outside.

I always skipped classes that required close contact or focused attention on me. I couldn't stand up in front of a class; I was afraid they would see something, or if I opened my mouth, everything about my father would come pouring out. I never asked any questions for the same reason and for fear of sounding stupid.[16]

Perhaps more overwhelming, it is the daily intimidation and terrorism that also silences. Women describe living within an environment that is 'unsafe', 'dangerous', or 'frightening'. Their helplessness, their rage continues to grow. Evelyn, another survivor, states:

Much of the anger I carry around inside me about my parents is directed at the world because I cannot understand. Somewhere deep inside me I'm furious that the world would have let my father and my mother betray me. There's a real anger at the unfairness that people I saw every day, who heard what went on through the windows, didn't try to help. And because it was never vented out, it's still with me. But it's not just rage, though. It's sadness. I just haven't been able to say, 'Well, that's the way life is. People suffer.' There's this sad place inside that says, 'It didn't have to be that way.'[17]

Silence too is reinforced by self-doubt, the internalisation of the confusion. As the behaviour continues – sometimes over years – the assaulted women no longer know whether their perception of the situation is 'real'. If it is, why don't others see it? Why don't others stop what is happening to them? Perhaps outsiders too are blinded by the ideal, for if they see something other than that fragile reality, they might have to question their own reality as well. Evelyn continues:

It was so hard when I was a kid, not being able to ask for help, not being able to get it from a world that just didn't care. But I feel a real sense of responsibility to other people now who have suffered the kind of pain and loss that I have. Because I know what it feels like. It's sort of like a deal that I made. Okay, God, get me through this and I'll be good. You know? And I do feel like I have to help people. Because if I don't, maybe I'll kill them. But that pain is human pain. What made my parents do what they did to me? And what made the neighbours not listen? And what made the teachers not answer? Were all the people running from that pain?

I know that I explain and rationalize and defend because there have been so few people, when I was young, when I was growing up, or even now, that have been able to give me some simple human comfort, kindness or help. Sometimes when I'm quiet or if I'm meditating, there surfaces the sound of a scream. The feeling of the scream is one of horror of all the stuff that's locked up inside me that I'm so driven to unlock.[18]

What of the long-term effects? Part of these effects is the result of years of smothering terrifying experiences of the most intimate invasion. Perhaps the most insidious, the deepest violation, is the intrusion into the female child's sexual being. As a result of incestuous experiences, research indicates, some women develop various forms of 'sexual dysfunction', some may fall prey to other forms of sexual or physical violation, still others, with the help and support of friends and lovers, come to terms with the assault.[19] Some female children, as Jennifer James has noted, have their concepts of themselves as sex objects strengthened; she found evidence that some child prostitutes' first sexual experiences come from their home environments.[20] Maggie, below, articulates how her self-image was affected by some of the abuse to which she was subjected:

And my father would call me all sorts of names and would storm around saying, 'You're no goddam good. You're a whore. You're a nothing. You're this and you're that. You're bad through and through.' Just the whole verbal abuse that he heaped on me. They would turn even the most innocent relationship [with a man] into a really dirty thing.

It's hard to know which was worse abuse, I think that the 'you're no good, you're a whore, you're nothing' – that constant theme was almost or as bad as the sexual abuse because it was constant. But the *big* thing was sex. It was the sexual thing that made me so crazy for so many years. And I felt that the only way that I could have relationships with men was on a sexual basis. That that was the only way I could be accepted – if I put out. That was the only tool I had. Nothing else.

But they're constantly calling me a whore – so therefore I am. So therefore I can go to bed with anybody. It's a vicious cycle.[21]

Being labelled a 'whore' is perhaps one of the most powerful accusations that can be hurled at a woman/child. Whore implies sexuality; sexuality implies impurity; impurity implies badness/worthlessness. A woman's sexuality is a marker for her worthiness. To allude to a woman's sexuality is to imply that whatever happens to her she is likely to have caused herself. In essence, if a woman's sexuality is publicly displayed, it becomes her stigma ('the sexualized woman').[22] Just as Hester Prynne was forced to wear the Scarlet 'A' for her adulterous behaviour, contemporary women are similarly labelled for their improper sexuality – any sexuality which is conducted outside of marital bonds. Our scarlet letter, although invisible, seems as visible as Hester's.

Incestually assaulted children learn this as well: some women, as a response to incestuous assault, may learn what it means to be a sexual object, some may block out their sexuality altogether, avoiding sexuality, yet still others struggle with both extremes. Carmen, quoted below, chose to block out her sexuality.

My weight still is the central physical manifestation of my incest experiences. All that extra flesh is the separation I need between myself and my sexual feelings. I don't trust my feelings, and if I can keep myself fat and unattractive, I don't need to deal with them at all. I'm smart, funny and people like me. I have decided that will simply have to be enough. My weight also is the source of my power and protection against feeling small and vulnerable, like I was as a skinny little kid of eleven.

I do have some relationships with men. Usually the men are older intellectuals, where there are few sexual expectations. Sometimes they are gay men, and infrequently they are bisexual men whose own sexual confusions preclude their making any demands on me. That way I can enjoy the company of men but don't have to deal with the sexuality inherent in having intimate relationships with them.

I suppose the hardest part for me, still, is trying to talk openly with my mother about the incest. When I try to bring it up, she begins to cry and blame herself for it having happened. She feels that she chose him, and whatever he did is her responsibility. What I keep trying to make her understand, and what is still unresolved, is that my mother and I shared this experience together. I don't want us to be separated by any feeling that what happened was her fault or mine. It wasn't. It was his fault, and until we can both accept that, we can never have the kind of relationship we had together before he came into our lives.[23]

The fact that the overwhelming proportion of offenders are male, and their targets, female, shows how incest, as a phenomenon, reproduces the power and control men hold over women in society at large as well as within the family unit. Explaining incest in terms of the 'dysfunctional family', the dominant explanation at present, ignores this fact.[24] We really cannot expect female children to have sexual autonomy until their adult sisters do. Evelyn, below, expresses the remnants of her experiences of incestuous assault – remnants which serve as reminders of men's intimidating control over women's lives.

I participate now, somewhat marginally, in a therapy group for incest victims, and I watch myself and my response to the other women's stories. I hear myself think a lot, 'How horrible!' or 'How could you have let that happen?' and I understand that the response I have to others is the internal response I have to my own childhood, my own experience that's much less available to me.

My hunch is that any person who has been violated by a parent must have a response of horror, because somehow if you can't be protected in so basic a way by your parents, then some basic need is betrayed. Even as a young child I understood that I had to protect and help them because they were so clearly unable to put controls on their own behaviour. But there were no outlets or comfort for me.

I feel sometimes that I've grown up to be poison. If I let my power out, my meanness out, I will contaminate other people. That directly relates to the feeling of being this bad little girl who didn't use her power correctly to stop her father from assaulting her.

Somehow I felt that I was responsible for my father's life. That it was me who caused his migraines and his ulcer. In a sense, it's not too far from true. Because if I had not been who I was, he might not have been tempted to lose control and suffered the consequent guilt I presumed he suffered through these migraines and ulcers, which he did not have prior to his sexual acting out. It's a tricky issue, my child's notion of power and responsibility.

Sure, I was just a little kid, but I did feel I had some responsibility for what happened.

My father reinforced my feelings as a child that I had no power to stave off his assault. But he also reinforced the notion that I had a lot of power, because if I hadn't had a lot of power, I wouldn't have seduced this grown man into sexually acting out. And somehow the experience with him exaggerated my child's sense of omnipotence. So from that time on, I grew up with a very distorted imbalance between feeling I had no power and feeling I had tremendous power.

But when I try as an adult woman to let some of that power, vitality, strength out, it gets misinterpreted by the world – the world of men. I am called angry, hostile, overbearing, etc. I remember being in a group in New York City where you had to learn to deal with a lot of things on a street level. I remember learning at a young age that if you walk through the streets smiling and feeling happy, you had better be prepared for a sexual come-on from guys that see you. So you learn how to veil your eyes and convey the message that you're not interested. On a practical level, you learn how to deceive and to inhibit your feelings. On a larger level, I have learned that if I let myself be, I will not be misunderstood. And that hurts in a very deep place. People tend to get threatened by their own unresolved stuff, and the feedback I get is, 'You come on like a bulldozer.' Somehow it's too much power. I see this as being related to issues of sexism, of my being a woman and of my options for expressing my power being culturally limited. Somehow, for women to express their power is alright only if that power is used in the service of helping men.

I hold it all in now, because for me to let out my power would also mean to let out the anger, the hurt, the memories of assault, and the fear of letting all that out . . . means that I would die.[25]

Chapter 4

Rape: the ever-present terror

Letter to the Editor, *The Village Voice*, October 22, 1979

Dear Editor:

I would like to offer a few comments on Molly Haskell's 'Rape in the Movies: Update on an Ancient War' (*Voice*, October 8). As a rape victim, it seems to me that most people, male and female, even those who are sympathetic toward the victim, do not fully understand the nature of forcible rape.

I believe that most view this crime as forced sex or intercourse, in the sense that this intercourse does not differ much in a physiological respect from that of consensual intercourse. Hence, 'men seem incapable of understanding what rape means to women.' Forcible rape is not in any normal sense intercourse. In most cases, the lubrication of the vagina required for normal completed intercourse does not exist, since petting has, more often than not, not occurred. As a result of this crucial aspect, as well as the fact that the victim is usually in a traumatized state immediately preceeding the rape and, thus, the muscles at the entrance to the vagina are not relaxed, penetration cannot either easily or immediately occur. What does happen is that the rapist repeatedly batters with his penis in the very delicate and sensitive features lying *outside* the vagina, causing the tissues to tear and to bleed. When the force of the thrusting eventually results in the penis entering the vagina, it enters usually no more than a few inches, and again the tissues (this time, the lining of the vagina) are repeatedly, with each thrust, ripped and torn.

As can be imagined, forcible rape is traumatically painful. I believe that it is the most physically painful ordeal that an individual can undergo and still live afterward. When I was being raped I felt as though I were being repeatedly stabbed with a knife in one of the most sensitive areas of my body. Near the end, I was in shock. I felt numb and could feel no pain, but I knew that the rapist was tearing me apart inside. Hours after the attack, the pain returned, and I felt as though I had been set on fire. Although I bled for only a few days, the pain lasted for weeks.

'What harm does it do?' Some of the flesh of my external genitalia has been battered away. It simply does not exist anymore. Other areas are torn and snagged. Some of the flesh can be pulled apart. Most of my hyman has been obliterated, with a ragged circular edge of tissue left in its place. Inside my vagina, the muscles at the entrance are damaged and I fear that this will adversely affect any future sexual intercourse that I engage in. Polyps have developed immediately before and at the entrance to my vagina. Also, the tissues of the lower part of my vaginal walls remain ripped. Thus, not only do people fail to comprehend the severe pain involved in a rape, or the length of time that the victim must suffer, they also do not understand that the physical damage done to the genital organs does not repair itself with time and that rape is a mutilating, disfiguring crime.

Haskell states that 'the integratedness with which a woman experiences love and sex and herself is what makes rape devastating', but this is not the whole truth, because there is no 'sex' in rape. There is only pain – traumatic, physical pain – and I believe that this is what makes rape devastating.

Perhaps her theory best explains the rampant fear of rape as experienced by the majority of women who have never been and will never be raped, and who, therefore, do not anticipate having their vaginas ripped and torn for 15 minutes, but rather some sort of sex.

I have listened to many women say that it is probably better to submit to rape than to endanger one's life by resisting, all the while knowing in my heart that they had no idea as to the kind of hell they would be in for. I presumed they felt that they would be submitting to sex. I, myself, could not have imagined what rape was really like until it happened. I think this confusion between sex and rape is largely responsible for the male fantasies of it as being pleasurable for the victim, for its glorification in the movies as such, and for the relatively light sentences imposed by judges on convincted rapists, as well as for Haskell's interpretation. (Name withheld[1] Philadelphia, Pennsylvania)

Why is there such confusion between 'sex' and 'rape'[2] Does the presence of sex preclude the occurrence of rape, or vice versa? Should we separate 'sex' from 'rape', as the woman above suggests, in order to clarify the horror of women's experiences?

Despite a movement in the 1970s to characterise rape as a violent act, confusion about rape and its meaning within male/female sexuality remains. Spurred by Susan Browmiller's treatise, *Against Our Will*, many discussions turned to emphasise the violence of rape as opposed to the sex in rape. The fact that many rapes are planned, that in many weapons are involved, that many women (though not all) sustain additional bodily injury, that raped women suffer short- and long-term trauma served to underscore the violence of rape and downplay the 'sex'.[3] However, the assumption underlying this understanding of rape as violence is that it is somehow easily distinguishable from sex.

Many of the traditional assumptions about women and men's sexuality, however, continue to hold a powerful grip on our understanding about rape. We stand less of a chance of understanding the fear, intimidation, coercion, even the physical pain involved in rape because its form is tied to what is assumed to be pleasurable. Many raped women are thus stigmatised for being a temptress, alluring, provocative, ignorant of where and how to draw the line, or being uncontrollable sexually. At the same time, men are assumed to be naturally sexually aggressive, easily overcome by biological mating urges each time they see women walking down streets wearing miniskirts. Yet the stereotype of the true rapist is entrenched in that of the sexual pervert who stalks his prey behind bushes only to release his aberrant sexual urges.[4] While seemingly commonsensical, the distinctions between which men are acting typically and which are acting aberrantly are not drawn through women's experiences; moreover, they continue to focus on women's behaviour as an explanation for men's behaviour.

This confusion between sex and rape gets carried into our efforts to gain a wider view of rape. When we try in any social scientific sense, for example, to establish incidence of rape (and at the same time, document the reality of rape in women's lives) we find large gaps between the counting of rape as a criminal offence by police – the legal view of rape – and the counting of rape as women experience it. Reported rapes, that is those rapes that come to the attention of the police, only constitute a small proportion of serious crimes, somewhere around 1 per cent for both America and Britain.[5] While police admit that rape, as a criminal offence, is a grievous crime, they treat it as a narrow, legally defined experience. Further, as a result of the heightened awareness fostered by the women's movement and the subsequent establishment of rape crisis centres in the 1970s in both the US and Britain, we know that most rapes are *not* reported to the police. We are thus forced to rely on crude estimates as evidence of the incidence of rape.[6]

Victimisation surveys, mentioned in Chapter 2, shed some, albeit hazy, light on reluctance of women to report rape. In the US, these victimisation surveys indicate that approximately 68 per cent of rapes are reported to the police, but these figures are incomplete: they only reflect rape as committed by strangers. Researchers found while attempting to verify information collected by their interviewers that only about one in every two incidents of rape by non-strangers was ever reported to them. In addition, they found the figure on rape by strangers was undercounted as well: only about 84 per cent of incidents of rape by strangers were reported to their interviewers.[7] Quite likely, their verification checks on the reporting of rape incidents is also an undercount. The recent British Crime Survey, in their study of 11,000 households in England and Wales, found only one instance of attempted rape![8] Thus, victimisation surveys, the best 'official' figures on criminal incidence, while perhaps indicating a proportion of the gap between reported and non-reported rape, miss any close estimate of the incidence of rape. Other sources of information, such as data from rape crisis programs in the US and Britain, indicate that as many as 75 per cent of rapes never come to the attention of the police. In one study in Canada, researchers speculate that there are somewhere between 2.5 and 25 rapes not reported for each reported rape.[9] Two major reasons for not reporting rape, according to a US government study, are women's 'fear of treatment by police and prosecutors' and the feeling that 'nothing can be done'.[10]

Women themselves remain the best source for documenting rape experiences. Recently, Diana Russell's survey seems to have come closer to capturing an incidence of women's experiences of rape and attempted rape.[11] In a random sample of adult women in the United States, Russell unmasks rape as a common phenomenon in women's lives. Not only did she find, in her interviews with 930 women, that

44 per cent of the women reported that they had experienced at least one attempted or completed rape in their lives, but one in seven women reported having been raped by their husbands. Russell's figures are overwhelming reminders that, on the whole, women are at risk; typical or aberrant, male sexual aggression has far-reaching effects on women's lives. This conclusion was already noted in 1980 by Allan Griswold Johnson who concluded:

> It is difficult to believe that such widespread violence is the responsibility of a small lunatic fringe of psychopathic men. That sexual violence is so pervasive supports the view that the focus of violence against women rests squarely in the middle of what our culture defines as 'normal' interaction between men and women.[12]

'To be *rapable*, a position which is social, not biological, defines what a woman *is*,'[13] states Catherine MacKinnon. The experiences of raped women and the awareness women have about sexual intimidation are diffused into all women's everyday existence; we feel vulnerable, while at the same time, experience doubt and even denial of our feelings of vulnerability.[14] Women's own silence, at least in terms of bringing their assaults to official attention, reflects their position as women. Life-threatening, humiliating, degrading, being raped has long-lasting effects on a woman's life; the fact of rape has long-lasting effects on all women's lives.

In terms of women's experiences, then, what is rape? Why is it such an enigma? Surely few would deny that rape exists, yet, when faced with specific instances of rape, people (and this includes authorities charged with enforcing criminal statutes) are quick to make judgments about which incidents are 'real' and 'not real' rapes. Clearly, woman-defined experience is overlooked; male definitions of what constitutes rape prevail.

Two concepts, I believe, often add to the confusion and obstruct our ability to *hear* women's experiences. These two concepts also appeared in our discussions of incestuous assault. They are the nature of 'force' and the nature of 'consent'. Each have a life in the legal world as well as in our everyday worlds; for rape, each has been constructed through male understanding of these in terms of women's *sexuality*, not men's *coercion*.

To understand women's experiences of rape we must reconstruct these concepts. Force, for example, is understood differently by women who are not only physically smaller than men, but who also have differential access to verbal power, fighting power, or intimidation power. We are surrounded by advisors who suggest ways about 'how to say no to a rapist and survive'. But we cannot be told how to predict behaviour that cannot be predicted. Assuming women can predict their rapists' behaviour sets up a situation where sexually assaulted women are blamed for not avoiding what these advisors suggest could have been avoided. 'If only you had run, screamed, fought back . . .' and so on. We must be reminded that the ingredients for avoiding rape require that women are not disarmed by terror, confusion or lethal weapons. But many are. The very uncertainty of the outcome renders many women vulnerable. It is the suddenness, the violence, the fear of death or physical mutilation, the physical restraints, the realisation that the lack of physical prowess or the reluctance to risk the possibility of escalating an already explosive situation that is behind the power of force. Women, faced with a life-threatening situation, act to minimise their injury or prolong their lives, and in doing so, they risk being accused of 'co-operating' or worse, 'consenting' to being raped.

So, too, we need to examine the notion of consent, another concept wrapped within the blanket of male presumptions about women's behaviour, and look to women's experiences for our understanding. Lack of consent *means* against women's will. Not 'no' means 'yes'. The typical male presumption is that women need convincing and cajoling to participate in what men feel women want. In addition, because the understanding about rape remains fixed on male-female sexuality – heterosexual intercourse – the notion of consent is assumed to be related to harmless 'sexual game playing' in order to 'convince' women to participate in sexual activity. By widening the definition of rape, as many feminists have been so successful in doing in the US, to include other forms of sexual violation – oral and anal rape as well as forced 'digital penetration' (objects or fists violently thrust into women's bodies), the discussion can then focus on the violence aimed at sexually intruding upon and humiliating women.[15] To be raped now implies submission to traditional 'pleasurable' sexuality.

The legal definition of rape, both in the UK and in the US, sharpens this focus on a woman's consent rather than on a question of force as a primary element in establishing a legal 'fact' of rape. In doing so, the focus remains on women's sexuality, that which is rarely women's own. With the primary conceptualisation of rape rooted in traditional male-female intercourse, vaginal-penile penetration, any understanding of rape as women's experience is clouded by a male point of view about 'sex'. In the UK, in fact, rape is solely defined as a crime in which a man, through the threat or actual use of force, commits penetration of a woman's vagina with his penis. Violation through fear, sexual violation through coercion and physical force or threat of force, becomes obscured behind discussions of what, today, constitutes what is assumed to be appropriate sexual exchange between women and men.

Yet women know (and Russell's data shows) that sexual intrusion is an ever-present threat to women's physical and sexual autonomy. Its occurrence is unpredictable; its aggressors, be they husbands, friends, acquaintances, fathers, or authority figures – are equally as unpredictable. We turn now to raped women speaking of their experiences. Here we see more clearly what rape actually means to women who are raped and to all women who are potential targets of rape. When, as the woman below describes, a woman is suddenly faced with the possibility of rape, it is a shock.

[The cab driver] didn't look at me, though, when I told him he had taken the wrong fork in the road. He didn't even answer me. If we took the next turning on the left, I told him helpfully, we could get back on the road again. But he took a right turn instead and I groaned, knowing that particular road to be a cul-de-sac.

Even when he stopped the car and got out, muttering to himself in some unrecognizable language, I was more annoyed than alarmed, suspecting some mechanical fault.

It was only when he got into the back of the car, pulling at the same time at his trouser belt to unbuckle it, that I realized in an instant of the purest clarity what was about to happen. I opened my mouth to scream as I edged away, but no sound came. I couldn't believe it. Surely I could *scream*, at least. And then it was too late. His hand was over my mouth and I was being forced down on to the floor of the car. All I could register, as the belt was pulled around my neck like a noose, was that the name of the car was 'Avenger'.

I shall spare you the details of what followed, mainly because I prefer to spare myself. Suffice it to say that I was raped orally and anally as well as vaginally and under the continuous threat of the noose being pulled tighter. I submitted, if submit is the word, because I realized I would rather be alive than dead.[16]

No warnings, no preparation. While women have an awareness that rape is possible at any time, they may not immediately react, lest they be accused of being paranoid. Rape often occurs in ordinary situations that have, at least until this encounter, proceeded upon already understood grounds. Women raped by friends, acquaintances, lovers, boyfriends, husbands have a history – an accumulated body of knowledge of which rape is not a part, at least until the first rape occurs. What was once 'typical' behaviour suddenly becomes 'aberrant'. When a woman is raped, she, like Karen, might question her own behaviour first.

Karen was hitchhiking, as she had often done for short distances around the city. But this driver pulled a gun on her, drove her to an isolated area and raped her, keeping the gun in his hand throughout the entire ordeal. She was sure he intended to kill her.
   She called us a month later, in tears because the rape still dominated her thoughts and gave her nightmares. She had come to believe that she could have avoided being raped, and that having missed the chance to get away from her attacker, she must have wanted the rape. When queried about her opportunities to escape, she replied, 'We were on the interstate, and the car slowed down to about forty because of the traffic. I put my hand on the door handle to try to jump out, but he put the gun up against my head and said, "Don't try that or I'll kill you." 'I should have gone ahead and jumped.' While she agreed that logically such a move would have been foolish and perhaps fatal, she still felt that if she were innocent, she would have jumped anyway.[17]

Raped women's own feelings reflect feelings similar to incestually assaulted women; self-blame for not escaping an inescapable situation. (I'm constantly reminded as I write this book about the young saint who jumped from a window rather than be raped. The story was told consistently throughout my Catholic grammar school education.) Ann Burgess and Lynda Holmstrom, in their research about raped women's reactions to and recovery from the rape experience, suggest a pattern of reaction exhibited by raped women. Initial reactions, the acute phase, include shock, disbelief, physical trauma, restlessness, and mood swings – from an emotive to a controlled emotional state or vice versa. Further, the whole general routine of a woman's life is disrupted by the rape. Appetites, sleep patterns, lifestyles, relationships, all undergo some alteration, some of it radical.[18]

As one woman explained her initial reactions:

> I stayed in bed for the next 36 hours, telling my children that I was ill. They brought me cups of tea and cigarettes. I smoked and smoked and wept and wept, hardly sleeping and hardly thinking, yet desperately needing to do both. I cursed myself for my stupidity and naïveté, I cursed my husband for not being with me. I didn't answer the phone. Periodically I got up to go to the lavatory and to wash. Once I had got rid of the blood, and it had stopped flowing, I felt cleaner – or, rather, less dirty.[19]

Contrary to her own experience, a raped woman makes sense of sexual violation through a backdrop of common sense; she too struggles against blaming herself, for not jumping out of the window or the car before the rape. Saints and 'good' women do. Perhaps most important about Burgess and Holmstrom's research, I believe, is how it illustrates women's struggles against powerful stereotypes about rape which, in the abstract, blame them for causing the rape in the first place. Self-blame, reinforced by myths about rape and sometimes by the reactions of those around her, is a common reaction of raped women. As one woman stated:

> I kept wondering maybe if I had done something different when I first saw him that it wouldn't have happened – neither he nor I would be in trouble. Maybe it was my fault. See, that's where I get when I think about it. My father always said whatever a man did to a woman, she provoked it.[20]

And another:

> I am having problems with my husband. He doesn't want me around his family. He told his mother on Sunday and said he was ashamed of me. He said I shouldn't have been working there [where it happened], that it was my fault that I had been working there.[21]

In both the above instances, raped women, as part of the making sense of their physical violation, use common sense which does not match their experience but affects how they themselves make sense of their experience. They articulate the contradictory expectations that 'femaleness' means in Western society. Being raped, it seems, automatically raises questions about a woman's respectability.[22] As one woman remarked:

> I felt like I'd brought out the worst in these men just by being an available female body on the road. I felt like if I hadn't been on the road, these men would have continued in their good upstanding ways, and that it was my fault that they'd been lowered to rape me.[23]

Feeling personally responsible is another typical reaction of raped women, and another example of how again the onus for men's behaviour is placed again on women. As noted earlier in our discussions on incest, women learn to be responsible for the behaviour of others, particularly the behaviour of men. Social respectability is bound in many ways to the conduct of women's sexual life. Together with the myths surrounding rape – that only women who ask for or who wish for sexual relations are raped – women's untenable position reproduces itself in raped women's emotional responses, as both women who spoke earlier noted: raped women are told directly that whatever happened to them is a commentary on their behaviour. Questions about why rape occurs, why *men* rape women, become lost in the emotional turmoil surrounding the rape experience. Time and time again, one hears statements from women like the following:

> I felt guilty. I felt that it was my fault because I had been drinking. I felt angry at myself for not having fought or screamed louder. I thought that I was really strong and that I could fight and was tough. But the violence that was coming from this man really frightened me. He really paralyzed me. Now I actually view men with suspicion. All men I see as potential rapists and violent. I have since talked about it to friends who have had similar experiences.[24]

Raped women speak of being guilty on the one hand and on the other hand, they speak of being 'really frightened', even 'paralysed'. Contrary to popular belief, though, many women resist their rapists. According to data from the US victimisation surveys, four out of every five rape victims take some self-protective measures, either by trying to summon help, using physical resistance, or using some verbal tactics.[25] While some women, in their attempts to thwart rape, escape, others may receive even greater injuries. Threats of force, however, are powerful deterrents to self-protective measures, especially if weapons are present. A woman, raped by a stranger, reported her rapist's threats as follows:

> I've raped three other women and killed them and that's what's going to happen to you [waving a knife at her]. Undress. If you don't hurry, I'll kill you. If you're not quiet I'll kill you [poking knife at her nose and eyes]. Maybe I'll take off your nose too.[26]

Threats are disarming, even if weapons are not present. As Hanmer and Saunders found in their study of community violence to women, women are afraid of what might happen, *especially if their·life is being threatened* – typical of rape incidents.[27] Russell's recent work on wife rape sheds more light here on conceptions of force. How, as many still believe, is it possible for a husband to forcibly rape his wife? Mrs Stanley, one of Russell's respondents, was 21 years old when her husband first raped her:

> We had a fight and I went to some friends' house. I returned and was taking a shower. I was still upset, when he came into the shower. He started touching my body. (Breasts?) Yes. (Genitals?) Yes. He was trying to patch things up. I said, 'I don't want anything to do with you right now!' He grabbed my face and forced me to go down on him. I tried to fight him off but he grabbed my arm, and forced me out of the shower. I begged him to leave me alone, but he wouldn't. He then threw me on the bed and forced intercourse on me unwillingly. (Force?) He had me pinned down with his elbows on top of me while he had intercourse.
>
> Othertimes when I wouldn't cooperate, he would hit me across the face or put a pillow over my head. I felt like he was going to choke me. I think I felt most helpless in the shower. I was really scared.[28]

Force, perhaps the most crucial factor of raped women's experiences, has many forms but its effect is much the same. Physical or verbal threats are demands, not invitations. Women are reminded, quite blatantly, that they are the available 'body', whether in situations with strangers, lovers or husbands. Many women then search for ways to survive rape.

Chris has been on her way home from a peace demonstration in Chicago, and was in high spirits, thinking she had done something good, and having had a good time. After the demonstration, she and some friends and a teaching assistant at the university had gone out for a pizza and a couple of beers. Chris's apartment was in a fairly safe neighbourhood, and she walked home from the subway. Her legs were tired and she was wearing bad shoes – they had high wedges and thin straps around the ankles. She was a few doors from her apartment, walking along the sidewalk, when a boy leaped out at her from behind two parked cars. He had leaped, not stepped, and he stood directly in her path. She was instantly terrified and thought about her rotten shoes. There was no way she could run fast in them, and no way she could slip them off her feet. He asked her for a cigarette. She gave him one, and tried to pass coolly by him, but he grabbed her arm. 'What do you want?' she shouted. 'Match,' he said, wiggling the cigarette at her. 'Let go,' she said, but he didn't, 'I can't get a match unless you let go.' He let go of her arm, but moved his body so that again he stood directly in front of her. Behind her, she knew, were the two empty blocks back to the subway. It was only about nine thirty, but there were no people on the street. She handed him the match book, her mind whirling. The apartment buildings rose darkly around her. She did not want to scream. Perhaps he was just trying to frighten her – her scream might frighten him, turn him violent. People were killed every week on Chicago streets. She decided to play cool. She asked him to get out of her way, then tried to walk around him. He grabbed her and pulled her off the sidewalk; he had one hand over her mouth. He pushed her down in the street between the two parked cars and held his hand over her mouth. He leaned down toward her ear and said softly that in the last months he had killed three people along these very blocks, that if she screamed, he would kill her. She did not see a weapon, she did not know whether to believe him, but she was too terrified to challenge him. She nodded, and he let her mouth go.

He pulled her pants off and put his penis, which was already stiff, into her. He thrust hard and fast and came quickly. She lay there wide-eyed, unable to breathe. When he was finished, he lay on top of her.

'Can I get up now?' she asked, hearing the trembling in her

own voice. He laughed. She was thinking hard. It was not unknown for rapists to kill their victims. He was not going to let her go easily. Chris searched her mind. She never once thought of the possibility of using physical force to fight him; it never entered her mind that there was any way to get away from him except outwitting him. She tried to imagine what would make a person a rapist. She thought of all the excuses for crime she had already heard, and all those she could imagine.

'I bet you've had a hard life,' she said after a while.[29]

Disarmed by threats, Chris, in the above instance, searches for ways to avoid her rape, and ultimately for ways to stay alive. Such is the experience of raped women. Most women survive; recovery, emotional survival, is the next stage in this experience.

Emotional survival, the process of making sense of the rape experience, as noted earlier, has immediate effects – self-blame, fear and shock are just a few. As the initial reactions wear off, raped women carry the long-term effects of rape with them. No fewer than 87 per cent of the women interviewed by Russell indicated they had some long-term effects; over 30 per cent stated the rape had 'great effects' on their lives; approximately 70 per cent stated they were either 'very' or 'extremely' upset by the rape. The traumatic effect of the rape varied, with women raped by strangers and husbands reporting the most trauma. The effects on women's lives include increased negative feelings/attitudes/beliefs/behaviour toward men in general, negative feelings/attitudes/beliefs/behaviour toward self, change in behaviour specifically associated with rape (such as, not accepting rides, never getting married again, never living alone again) and an impact on her sexual feeling or her perception of her sexuality.[30] Other studies report similar findings.[31] One study in the UK of victims of serious crime found that raped women's recovery took much longer than recovery from other serious crime.[32]

Many raped women also report that they have great difficulty distinguishing between the sex which was rape and the sex which is not rape. 'I had problems with sex, after the rape,' stated one woman. 'There was no way that Arthur could touch me that it didn't remind me of having been raped by this guy I never saw.'[33] If rape becomes indistinguishable from sex, even for a period of time, then the depth of the sexual violation of rape should be recognised as well, along with that of the violence of rape.

Raped women's silence can be understood then as one of the many features of women's survival. Rather than contend with authorities who will in turn judge whether their experience was, after all, a 'real' rape, many women refuse to report rape to police. They also may not tell their family, friends or colleagues in anticipation of what their responses might be. Women's experiences of rape, similar to women's experiences of incestuous assault, point to an atmosphere rife with sexual intimidation and terrorism. Far from being trivial, these experiences should suggest a serious cause for alarm.

Chapter 5

Wife battering: all in the family

More than anything else, the experiences of women battered by husbands, boyfriends or lovers expose the underside of the ideal family or the happy couple. To hear battered women recount these experiences is to hear stories of abuse which are often characterised as 'normal' interaction of intimate couples. Blinded by patriarchal notions about the privacy of family matters, deafened by the rhetoric which maintains these notions, society once again focuses blame on individual women who, because of their assumed weakness, 'choose' battering relationships. Masochistic women, they are called. Battered women live within their own state of siege; they know, to the core of their being, the weight of the contradictory demands of their roles as women.

In a letter to a friend of Del Martin, author of *Battered Wives*, one woman articulates the dilemmas, confusion, and isolation felt by many:

I have learned [from my battering situation] that no one believes me and that I cannot depend upon any outside help. All I have left is the hope that I can get away before it is too late.

I have learned also that the doctors, the police, the clergy, and my friends will excuse my husband for distorting my face, but won't forgive me for looking bruised and broken. The greatest tragedy is that I am still praying, and there is not a human person to listen.

Being beaten is a terrible thing; it is most terrible of all if you are not equipped to fight back. I recall an occasion when I tried to defend myself and actually tore my husband's shirt. Later, he showed it to a relative as proof that I had done something terribly wrong. The fact that at that moment I had several raised spots on my head hidden by my hair, a swollen lip that was bleeding, a severely damaged cheek with a blood clot that caused a permanent dimple didn't matter to him. What mattered was that I tore his shirt! That I tore it in self-defense didn't mean anything to him.

My situation is so untenable I would guess that anyone who has not experienced one like it would find it incomprehensible. I find it difficult to believe myself.

It must be pointed out that while a husband can beat, slap, or threaten his wife, there are 'good days'. These days tend to wear away the effects of the beating. They tend to cause the wife to put aside the traumas and look to the good – first, because there is nothing else to do; second, because there is nowhere and no one to turn to; and third, because the defeat is the beating and the hope is that it will not happen again. A loving woman like myself always hopes that it will not happen again. When it does, she simply hopes again, until it becomes obvious after a third beating that there is no hope. That is when she turns outward for help to find an answer. When that help is denied, she either resigns herself to the situation she is in or pulls herself together and starts making plans for a future life that includes only herself and her children.

For many the third beating may be too late. Several of the times I have been abused I have been amazed that I have remained alive. Imagine that I have been thrown to a very hard slate floor several times, kicked in the abdomen, the head, and the chest, and still remained alive!

What determines who is lucky and who isn't? I could have been dead a long time ago had I been hit the wrong way. My baby could have been killed or deformed had I been kicked the wrong way. What saved me?

I don't know. I only know that it has happened and that each night I dread the final blow that will kill me and leave my children motherless. I hope I can hang on until I complete my education, get a good job, and become self-sufficient enough to care for my children on my own.[1]

Incomprehensible? Untenable? Difficult to believe? We have in the past few years all read account after account of battering situations. These stories still appear daily in the paper, not as ongoing stories of beatings, but as small news stories about murdered women whose husband/lovers/boyfriends dispensed the final, fatal beating. The momentary interest in wife beating as a social problem has come and gone. The select committees, hearings held both in the US and UK, did result in drawing media attention to the issue of battering;[2] feminists spurred on the establishment of shelters for women and their children, and to some extent both instigated some legislative changes.[3] But patriarchy dies hard; women continue to be beaten within their intimate relationships. The situation remains to be seen as 'untenable', 'incomprehensible', particularly as many continue to assume that women's position in society is improving. The continuous violence against women questions the true effect of any 'improvements' in women's lives.

Physical intrusion within intimate relationships reflects a pattern similar to sexual intimidation and violence: women are overwhelmingly the recipients of 'domestic violence'.[4] So too, women are blamed for their powerlessness, and labelled as passive, submissive, even desirous of their own harm. Hence dominant stereotypes of women provide the commonsense information to divide women in two categories, those who are nurturers and caregivers, and those who are nagging, selfish, and in violation of women's expected role. And men's behaviour? Too often, it is seen as 'typical'.

While the stereotype of the blameworthy battered wife remains steadfast, researchers have found that wife beating is perhaps the most under-reported crime. One estimate suggests that only one out of 270 incidents of wife abuse is ever reported to the authorities.[5] When incidents do come to police attention, they compose a significant proportion of assault complaints. Rebecca and Russell Dobash's analysis of 3,020 reported cases of violence in two Scottish cities, for instance, found assault against wives to be the second largest category of assault that comes to police attention.[6] Researchers who examine violent incidents outside police involvement find even higher incidence of wife abuse. Diana Russell's recent random survey on women's experiences of sexual assault revealed that 21 per cent of women who had ever been married reported physical violence by a husband at some time in their lives.[7] Murray Straus, Richard Gelles and Suzanne Steinmetz, in a random survey of 2,143 households in the US, found evidence of 'domestic violence' in 28 per cent of households.[8] It is important to note here, however, that domestic violence and wife battering are different concepts. In one – domestic violence – the researcher assumes that all violence is experienced by men and women alike and that the damage administered by a wife is equivalent to that administered by a husband. In fact, the Straus *et al.* survey found that the incidence of husband battering exceeded that for wife battering. As Russell points out in her critique of these findings, Straus *et al.* 'fail to distinguish between offensive and defensive violence', ignoring strength differences, variation in fighting skills, and the sustained injuries of women and men.[9] The term wife abuse then stresses the social position of women *vis à vis* men. The context of women's position is what needs to be explained, not the 'exchange' of physical abuse. Furthermore wives who fight back might be more severely injured. Women who are beaten either try to defend themselves or remain physically passive: there is no set pattern. What remains a 'social fact', as the Dobashs emphasise, is that violence between adults in the family is directed at women.[10]

Common among women's experiences of physical assault are reports of sexual assault. Approximately 10 per cent of Russell's respondents who had ever been married reported being raped and beaten by their husbands. So, too, Irene Hanson Frieze's research reveals widespread sexual abuse among the battered women in her US study; one of every three women she interviewed had been battered. Of the battered women, one-third of her respondents had been raped, two thirds felt they had been pressured into having sex with their husbands, and 40 per cent felt sex was unpleasant because it was forced. Clearly men's sexual intimidation and violence toward women goes hand in hand with physical intimidation and violence.[11]

Behaviour referred to as wife battering – the violent action on the part of husband against wife – includes forms of pushing, kicking, slapping, throwing objects, burning, dragging, stabbing or shooting. Assaults over time may have cumulative physical effects; severe bruising and all around bodily soreness accompany emotional distress. For example, in answering 'What kind of injuries were inflicted on you?' asked by a member of the Select Committee on Violence in Marriage, UK, one woman replied:

> I have had ten stitches, three stitches, five stitches, seven stitches, where he has cut me. I have had a knife stuck through my stomach; I have had a poker put through my face; I have no teeth where he knocked them all out; I have been burnt with red hot pokers; I have had red hot coals slung all over me; I have been

sprayed with petrol and stood there while he has flicked lighted matches at me. But I had to stay there because I could not get out. He has told me to get out. Yet if I had stood up I know what would have happened to me. I would have gotten knocked down again.[12]

Pat Carlen, in her research on Scottish women in prison, came upon many women's accounts of violent attacks at the hands of men. These attacks included severe beatings, with a range of bodily injuries from the loss of an eye and a tooth to physical mutilation: a carved swastika on one woman's forehead. Women's discussions about their lives eventually focused on the common occurrence of male violence, which some women attributed to 'Scottishness'. (Some American, English, and Welsh women subjected to violence might also attribute it to that which arises from a particular cultural context. The similarities across cultures, however, reinforce the commonness of male violence in both British and American societies.) The 'cult of aggressive and assertive masculinity' is attributed to a Scottish working-class ethos; women's experiences of male violence elsewhere show how this cult crosses class boundaries. Equally important, the cult of aggressive and assertive masculinity is taken by some women to be typical male behaviour.[13]

Ultimately, women's injuries reflect the effects of aggressive masculinity. In the Dobash study, nearly 80 per cent of the battered women reported going to a doctor at least once during their marriage for injuries resulting from attacks by their husbands; nearly 40 per cent stated they sought medical attention on five separate occasions. Dobash and Dobash conclude:

Untreated injuries and vicious attacks often result in permanent disfigurement such as loss of hair, improperly healed bones, and severe scars from cuts, burns, and abrasions. . . . The women we interviewed . . . suffered serious woundings, innumerable bloodied noses, fractured teeth and bones, concussions, miscarriages and severe internal injuries that often resulted in permanent scars, disfigurement and sometimes persistent poor health.[14]

The medical profession too participates in perpetuating wife battering by ignoring women's complaints of physical injury as symptomatic of a pattern of battering.[15] So do those who feel that the sanctity of marriage is, above all, more important than a woman's physical safety.

By late afternoon I still hadn't come up with a specific plan of action. All I knew was that I would have to get away from Florida. Just before dinner my mother said she wanted to talk to me.

'Chuck has been calling all day,' she said. 'I've talked to him a few times now and all I know for sure is that he really loves you.'

'Mother, you don't know what you're talking about.'

'Oh, you never think that I know what I'm talking about,' she said. 'I've been married a good long time, longer than you've been alive, and after all this time I guess I know a thing or two about husbands and wives. You don't want to forget that he's your husband and you're his wife. No matter what little difficulties you've been having, you should be able to work them out.'

'Little difficulties? *Little* difficulties!'

'Chuck has told me everything,' my mother said. 'He told me enough so that I know this is just a lovers' quarrel.'

All day I had been thinking about how I could tell my parents what was going on in my life. I felt that I should break it to them gently. Well, all those plans just flew out the window. I laid the situation flat-out, using the bluntest words I knew.

'Mom, Chuck has beaten me bloody,' I began. 'He has held a gun to my head and made me do awful things. He has forced me to have sex with women and other men. And now he is talking about making me have sex with animals. He has made me pose for dirty pictures and he is turning me into a prostitute. He is always threatening to kill me. He has even threatened to kill you and Daddy.'

'But, Linda, he's your *husband*.'[16]

That women are to blame – the strongly entrenched male point of view often held by many doctors, police, neighbours, parents and so forth – is difficult for battered women to confront. Many women still envision a life of domestic tranquillity. Yet the economic and emotional ties wrap tightly around women's uncertainty about that domestic tranquillity when violence arises. All too often, battered women's responses, similarly to incestually assaulted or raped women's responses end up in self-blame. As the woman quoted below explains in her letter to *Spare Rib*, the English women's liberation magazine, this uncertainty has roots in the male point of view against which her experience continually is at odds.

Dear Spare Rib:

I am writing this letter because there is no way that I can show my gratitude to the Women's Aid Centre in Cardiff; they have helped me so much. I wish to express to them and other groups how thankful I am that they were there to turn to, and how much I owe to them.

I also wish to communicate with other women who have been very cruelly treated by the men they love and live with, and to tell them that they are not alone.

In *Spare Rib* I always feel we see, apart from the interviews with women working under bad conditions, or sacked for bad reasons, women who are already strong; who may have suffered, but know how to stand up for themselves in their personal and political lives. That is a good thing. How many of us can write to you or be part of your movement until we are strong and confident in ourselves? Sometimes it has made me feel inferior, and has made me feel your magazine is for other women who are more together than I am, who are prepared to fight where I am not; but please make room for us who don't know where we are going, or what we are doing, who only feel that we are failing because of the pressure we are under. I want to speak to women who, like me, don't yet have the strength to fight from where they are; who still feel trapped in cruel and brutal situations; who feel humiliated and ashamed at being used as they are, but also feel ashamed of what they are, because they do not know how to be free of it, and still allow themselves to be used and abused, and will again, because we half believe as we have been told, that we deserve no better.

I am like that, and there must be a lot of us. As well as being ashamed of how I am degraded, I am ashamed because I do not have the guts to fight it, and ashamed, because when I was told the way to stop this horror was to go to the police; to go to the law and get an injunction with a power to arrest against my man, I could not do it. I would have let him tear my house apart, rather than shop [sic] him to the law. I am luckier than many. At least it is my house. But even so I would have let him destroy it rather than have him arrested.

I am telling you this because I feel so ashamed of it; failure in his terms and failure in yours! I am beginning to understand that it will come to that, but it has taken two years of this horror; I am sure many women are still in it after thirty or more years.

I am coming to the conclusion that my man must be sick, and must just hate women. I loved him and we had happy times. I guess he'll have put me in hospital before I'll go to the police. But I feel now it's bound to come, and I'm just waiting for it. He doesn't really want me, but he couldn't bear for me not to want him; Women's Aid let me talk to them. They let me sit there when I was too frightened to go back home. They've told me what to do when I have to turn to the law and the police. I know that the refuge is there. I think without them I would have taken my own life. I am still not out of my nightmare, but at least I have admitted to it; maybe that's the first step.

Remember us please,
        Sue
Cardiff.[17]

Like her American counterparts, Sue speaks profoundly to the ongoing experience of battered women and the process whereby they begin to realise that their 'loving' husbands are in fact killing them. Moreover, Sue specifies how women become entangled in a battering situation: the structure of women's lives essentially prepares them for it. 'We half believe as we have been told, that we deserve no better.' We see 'typical' male aggressive behaviour, 'typical' female masochism and no more: wife abuse is seen as just part of being a wife.

The responsibility of wife to husband, as Linda Lovelace was told, entails ignoring abuse. Women themselves report becoming confused when the battering begins, a confusion perhaps connected to not knowing how to reconcile abuse with a vision of the ideal. There is no set pattern as to when battering might occur in a particular relationship. Some battering begins immediately, some five, ten years after marriage, or when the woman becomes pregnant, when supper isn't ready on time, or when the wife overcooks the three-minute egg. Battering may be interpreted by the woman as an indication, not of her husband's problem, but as her failure as a wife. Mortified, ashamed, humiliated, a woman may then remain silent about her abuse to others, fearing most of all that she is ultimately to blame.

I don't know. I kept thinking he was changing, you know, change

for the better. . . . He's bound to change. Then I used to think
it's my blame and I used to lie awake at night wondering if it is
my blame – You know, I used to blame myself all the time.[18]

I was concerned, I didn't do anything to deserve it. I mean, I
never went out. I never went out of the house, you know. I never
looked at anybody.[19]

The feeling of helplessness due to the fact that it was my fault
that I got battered, which I think is common that a woman is blamed
because she provoked him. Certainly my husband immediately
blamed me. 'If you had done so and so; if you hadn't done so
and so.' And the fact that he did almost kill me and threatened if
I said anything to the police he *would* kill me and the destruction
of confidence or any way out. I had no money, I had kids. I
couldn't for years see my way out of this situation, in myself I
didn't have any sense of it. If I left, he'd follow me. He'd take my
kids away. He threatened to do that. I believed all that. Getting
the strength came with my finally deciding that I was dying, and
that if I was going to die, I was going to die fighting, which
meant I had to leave. I could not die this way any longer in this
relationship and if he came after me, damn it, I was going to
give him what he was trying to give me. It was a giving up of his
power over me and my acknowledgement of his power over me
[that] gave me power to move. It was a long time before I was
able to – ten years – get over really being afraid of that man.
I'm just now getting to a point to where I am not afraid of him,
and move forward into my life. My life has always been attached
to this kind of powerlessness. If I do this, what's he going to do.
It's a reaction instead of an action. It's always a reaction instead
of moving with the confidence of no matter what he does I can
somehow manage, maybe get killed in the process. I don't think
that anymore but I did for a long time. And I talk to other women
who have had other experiences like that who have the same
kind of hopelessness and in many instances, without resources,
without the ability to make a living, find a house, to solve all
these terrible problems, these real problems, practical problems.
Where they are as bad as this, it is better than that [the battering
situation], better than going into an absolute abyss of nothing.[20]

For a period of time – days, months, years – many battered women are caught within the web of violence, unable to predict when more violence will occur or to understand why violence is occurring in the first place. During this period, many report symptoms of stress, such as lack of sleep, weight loss or gain, ulcers, nervousness, irritability, and some, even thoughts of suicide. Moreover, depression slows down a battered woman's ability to escape the battering, an act that, by its very nature, is an assertive one. Phyllis Chesler describes women's depression as a 'continual state of mourning for what they [women] never had – or had too briefly – and for what they can't have in the present, be it Prince Charming or direct worldly power.'[21] Battered women have neither Prince Charming nor worldly power: they see themselves as failures, as their husbands treat them. 'When women feel excluded from direct participation in society [and many women, regardless of social position, do], they see themselves as subject to a consensus or judgment made and reinforced by the men on whose protection and support they depend and by whose names they are known.'[22]

Keeping the relationship together, despite the violence, is also important for practical reasons – financial support, shelter, even access to the ability to earn a living many times rest with the husband/boyfriend. Getting out is almost as bad as staying in the relationship. Women often feel inadequate to cope with self-sufficiency; the lack of self-confidence often acts as a trap to keep women within a violent home.

Women stay within battering situations because of the real conditions of their lives within a male-dominated world. Men's power is not an individual, but a collective one. Women's lives are bounded by it. The threat of male violence outside the home, as women currently within violent relationships told Russell, is an acutely intimidating reality of women who endure violence within their own homes.[23] Keeping women in relationships with men, says Adrienne Rich, is a primary 'means of assuring [the] male right of physical, economical, and emotional access.'[24] Having women react instead of act, as the woman stated above, is a response pattern fostered by women's dependence upon men.

Many women do leave violent husbands/boyfriends. In doing so, many women leave, return, leave again, return again, and leave never to return. The process could take years, or it could happen immediately after the first beating.

I went to my parents and of course, he came – I left him because of his hitting and kicking me – and I went home to them, but he came there and I had to go. I went back really to keep the peace because my parents weren't able to cope with it.[25]

[I returned to my husband] because I was sure there was something in me that could make the marriage work. I was quite positive about that.[26]

Reasons for returning are similar to those for staying: hope that the husband will change or, because he has apologised, hope that he will never strike again; concern for the children; worry over financial difficulties; resignation to the 'inevitability' of violence; fear for the safety of others; fear of being outside the home; fear of losing the status of 'wife'; just plain fear – these are but a few of the motivating forces affecting women's decisions to leave or stay.

Like women subjected to incestuous assault, battered women live within their own houses of terror. To both groups of women, men's physical and/or sexual potential and actual violence is ever-present. Its presence is a glaring contradiction to the safety and security of the ideal home protected and headed by men. If, as Russell's work suggests, women living within such atmospheres are more likely to be intimidated by the unpredictability of men's typical behaviour, then the existence of sexual harassment at work or on the street, the next subject for discussion, further encircles women under male dominance.

Chapter 6

Sexual harassment: coercion at work

I needed help with an assignment so I went to the professor's office hours. He was staring at my breasts. It made me uncomfortable and confused. . . . He reached over, unbuttoned my blouse and started fondling my breasts.[1]

Up until the time of our conflict he repeatedly told me that the work I was doing for him was good and that he was pleased with it. During the conflict period I was told the complete opposite: that my work was lousy, that I was lazy. . . . He tried to make me feel inept and incompetent. He then proceeded to prevent me from obtaining another job in the department. When the sexual conflict arose, my position was suddenly terminated and no explanation was given. As an employee and a student in the department my credibility was completely ruined. (For a while, I really worried about the quality of my work, I questioned whether it was good or not, even though I knew it was.)[2]

As I remember all the sexual abuse and negative work experiences I am left feeling sick and helpless and upset instead of angry. . . . Reinforced feelings of no control – sense of doom. . . . I have difficulty dropping the emotion barrier I work behind when I come home from work. My husband turns into just another man. . . . Kept me in a constant state of emotional agitation and frustration; I drank a lot. . . . Soured the essential delight in the work . . . stomach ache, migraine, cried every night, no appetite.[3]

Sexual harassment, assumed to be a minor complaint of moaning feminists, has significant effects on women and women's employment.

Yet another form of sexual intrusion which occurs at the source of women's livelihood, her workplace, it exists in many forms, and, similar to rape or battering, its forms closely parallel what is commonly assumed to be 'normal' behaviour between women and men. Obscured behind the wall of acceptable behaviour, complaints about sexual harassment are quite often treated lightly, its debilitating effects on women ignored.

What is sexual harassment? The reported behaviour includes many forms of unwanted sexual attention that occur in working situations: visual (leering) or verbal (sexual teasing, jokes, comments or questions) behaviour; unwanted pressure for sexual favours or dates; unwanted touching or pinching; unwanted pressure for sexual favours with implied threats of retaliation for non-co-operation.[4] The form of sexual intrusion is often immaterial. Women are as likely to be distressed by persistent 'low-level' harassment – leering, for instance – as they are by more blatant touching. As Polly states:

> When I first joined the laboratory and was working with about
> fifteen other people, three of them male, everything was fine.
> Then two of the men and myself were moved to a department on
> our own with our head of department, a nice bloke of about 29,
> the same age as the other two men. After about another four
> months another young man joined us, and almost immediately,
> he started passing sexual comments to the other two men, talking
> loudly across the lab. It made me feel very embarrassed, but I
> ignored them hoping they would get bored eventually and stop.
> But I started to change. I became very wary and careful of
> whatever I said, because they'd pick it up and turn it round to
> have a double meaning.
>
> Then the comments got worse and were directed at me, my
> body, questions about my private life and my sexual likes and
> dislikes. I just ignored them all. And one day, I don't remember
> how, they got round to the fact that they had decided that I was
> obviously a virgin, but they would make sure that didn't last. They
> began bringing *Playboy* magazine into work and leaving it lying
> around open, and little sexual drawings began appearing scribbled
> on my desk diary. I don't know which one of them was doing it,
> they egged each other on all the time.[5]

Polly's account is interesting, for it illustrates that the relentless comments of her male colleagues resulted in Polly becoming more careful and wary. Being subjected to leering or sexual comments on a daily basis, like Polly, has cumulative effects. Harassed women report becoming nervous and irritable; they feel humiliated; they feel they cannot control the encounters with the harasser(s) and thus feel threatened and helpless. Many develop techniques to protect themselves, through for example, avoidance (particularly difficult if the woman works in the same location as the harasser(s)) or through changing their dress or behaviour (acting 'coolly'). These women describe the daily barrage of sexual interplay in the office as psychological rape. The day in and day out exposure to what many assume to be 'harmless' behaviour produces reactions similar to those of sexually assaulted women. In fact, rape crisis centres receive calls from sexually harassed women who report having similar feelings as raped women.

While the harassing behaviour varies widely, the pattern of the behaviour and its effects both represent a serious violation to women's personal integrity. In each instance, a woman is no longer made to feel like an employee or a colleague; she is immediately transformed into a sexual object. At this point, her gender, her physical being, receives attention from her male colleagues. As we will see later, this transformation has consequences for the woman's own evaluation of her self-confidence and her work performance. Her value is not in her work, but in her use as a sexual being. As one woman stated, 'The whole atmosphere was like a singles' bar. The only thing missing was the piano.'[6]

Sexual harassment is a common working condition for women in the US and Britain. At least until 1976, no one had a name for this collective experience. The earlier US surveys, those undertaken in 1976 by *Redbook* magazine and the Working Women's Institute, provided a foundation for an understanding of sexual harassment. Research in the UK followed in 1981–2.

Surveys of sexual harassment and its effects, conducted in both the UK and US, document the widespread presence of harassment in the workplace. On both sides of the Atlantic, women report experiencing sexual harassment in overwhelming proportions. Ranging from *one of five* to *four of five* women indicating an incident of sexual harassment, survey figures alert us to the widespread, indeed endemic, existence of sexual harassment in the workplace.

In perhaps the most comprehensive US survey to date, the US Merit System's Protection Board (MSPB) queried 23,000 federal employees in 1981 and found an incidence of sexual harassment experienced by respondents within the two years prior to the survey to be as high as 42 per cent.[7] This figure corresponds with a survey of *Harvard Business Review* readers.[8] Of that 42 per cent MSPB survey, 12 per cent experienced what was termed 'less severe sexual harassment' which includes unwanted suggestive remarks or gestures, unwanted sexual teasing, jokes, remarks or unwanted pressure for dates; 29 per cent experienced 'severe sexual harassment' including incidents such as receiving unwanted letters, phone calls, or materials of a sexual nature, unwanted touching or pinching, or unwanted pressure for sexual favours; and *1 per cent experienced actual or attempted rape or sexual assault.*

The women who reported harassment varied in terms of age and marital status. Younger, single women reported a higher incidence of harassment: 67 per cent of women between the ages of 16 and 19 reported being harassed as opposed to 33 per cent of women between the ages of 45 and 54; 53 per cent of the single women as opposed to 37 per cent of married women reported experience of harassment. (The survey only queried whether harassment had occurred within the last two years.) More highly educated women reported more harassment, perhaps because their presence in non-traditional jobs was more threatening to their male peers and/or because of their perception of more forms of men's behaviour to be harassing. These women occupied various positions within the governmental structure, having jobs in professional, technical, clerical, and blue-collar positions.

In Britain, surveys conducted along similar lines as the American ones find comparable figures. In conjunction with their 1981 programme on 'unwanted advances', TV Eye, together with NALGO, the union representing local civil servants, conducted a survey of the Liverpool City Treasurer's Department. Of those who responded, 36 per cent reported experiencing some form of harassment. Alfred Marks Bureau Ltd queried 799 managers and employees of their branches throughout the UK in 1982: 66 per cent of the employees and 86 per cent of the management reported that they were aware of various forms of sexual harassment being present in their office. Moreover, 51 per cent of the females admitted having experienced some form of harassment in their working lives. Carey Cooper and Marilyn Davidson using the format of the *Harvard Business Review* study, found that 52 per cent of the woman managers they studied had experienced sexual harassment.[9]

No matter how common the experience, women who are harassed lose control over the definition of themselves as workers and as women. Sexual objectification – a process over which women have had little, if any, control – permeates the workplace. A woman worker commonly finds herself in a position where she is subjected to her male co-workers' sexual fantasies or sexual advances. The harassed woman may fear that the harassment might escalate (a realistic worry in the light of findings) or that she might lose her job (another realistic concern). Further, within the context of society's propensity to blame women for creating 'sexual atmospheres', she may fear – like the woman who is raped – that she somehow is the cause of the harassing behaviour.

In many situations of harassment, the women are likely to be subordinate to the men who harass them. Frustration, anxiety, nervousness and above all feelings of powerlessness are typical reactions to being harassed. And while the stories may differ, the similarities are striking.

The case of Carmita Wood, stated in the early 1970s appeal to the New York State Unemployment Commission, is but one illustration of how harassment situations develop, grow, and are the sole burden of the women.

When she left her job Carmita had been an outstanding employee who had been working in one of Cornell's laboratories since 1966. She had been promoted in 1971 to the job of Administrative Assistant, the first woman to hold such a post. At this time she became the second woman ever admitted to the Ithaca Management Club and in the glow of all this new-found status and security she felt it was 'safe' to take out a $10,000 loan to remodel her home in Ludlowville.

It wasn't long after her promotion, however, that she moved into a new office which brought her into closer proximity with an extremely high-up Cornell official. He found reasons to visit her office at least once a day. This became a matter of concern to her as almost all her previous contacts with him had resulted in repeated, unwanted touching.

The repeated visits of this man to Ms Wood's office now involved more of the same treatment and became an intolerable source of tension and emotional stress. He would make her feel exceedingly uncomfortable by making sexual gestures, he would often lean against her, immobilizing her between his own body and the chair and desk. He would never look her in the eye but would instead move his eyes up and down her body below the neck. He would also stand with his hands in his pockets as if rubbing his genitals. These actions were persistent throughout the whole time they worked in this proximity.

Carmita complained about his behavior, both towards herself and other women, to her supervisor on several different occasions, but his response was that they 'were very capable women'. He further suggested that 'they try not to get into these situations'. Beyond this, Carmita consciously avoided the man as much as she could, to the point of using the stairs instead of the elevator because she knew of at least one instance in which he had molested a woman in the elevator. She also made a point of wearing slacks in order to avoid the man's staring at her legs and she also told her secretary that she didn't want to be alone with him. Finally, she made a consistent effort to transfer away from the situation; however none of these attempts were successful.

There finally occurred an incident at a Christmas party which she attended because it was part of her job to supervise all social functions for the laboratory. At one point the man asked her to dance; she refused several times because of her past experiences and because she was managing the party. He insisted, however, and yanking her arm he pulled her forcibly onto the dance floor, where he then shoved his hands under her sweater and vest, pushing them up and exposing her back and rubbing her bare skin. Ms Wood was embarrassed and later said, 'I felt I was publicly humiliated,' but she didn't want to make a scene in public so she didn't push him away until he released her at the end of the dance. There were witnesses to this incident, including her supervisor and her secretary; the supervisor again failed to do anything about the situation.

She intensified efforts to obtain a transfer but was frustrated. Finally, unable to cope with her building emotional and physical distress and desperately not wanting to come into contact with this man again, Carmita resigned from her job, although she was fully conscious of the current economic recession and the great risk she was incurring in leaving. Her position was a substantial one and had she stayed there two weeks longer she would have been eligible for a raise.

She stayed in the area looking for another job. Unable finally to find an acceptable job, she applied for unemployment insurance. She was denied insurance benefits because her reasons for leaving her job were termed 'personal' and 'non-compelling'.[10]

The effects of power, coercion, and control tend to be doubly stacked against harassed women. As workers, women are often in positions of the subordinate, with unequal access to the position of the aggrieved party. A boss can complain about a worker's performance, for example, but a worker cannot complain about sexual advances. Work performance is a concern within the workplace; sexual advances, however, are 'private', of no concern in the mediation of public working matters. Sexual 'attraction' is assumed to be mutually desirable, flattery, a 'private' concern. Sexual harassment contradicts these assumptions. The power that is male – to make sexual advances – is laced together with the power that is boss, teacher, supervisor, shop steward and so forth.

Linda, who works in the British film industry, recounts one experience:

The first job I had in the film business was with this producer who had his office at home. My office was down in the basement, and when his wife went out, he'd rush downstairs and start groping me. This went on for about a month, with me fighting him off and him pleading.

Then one day his wife came home while he was trying to kiss me, and he dragged me into the loo and grabbed my hands and clapped them round his erection, whispering 'Don't stop, for Christ's sake.' He wanted me to masturbate him.

I left after that, I just couldn't go back. Anyway, he didn't give me any choice. When I wouldn't do to him what he wanted, he told me I was fired. Now I find filming on location is the worst experience. All the men make sexual remarks and jokes all the time. Some of them are aimed directly at me, as there aren't many other women around, and the ones they go to bed with, they tell everyone what it was like the next day. The real trouble is simply that if you don't sleep with any of them, they go around calling you a mean cow, and if you do, they call you a whore. Either way, you can't win.[11]

Perhaps most frustrating for harassed women is that they confront the stereotypes Linda noted: either women are 'cows' (sexually unco-operative) or 'whores' (sexually co-operative). Either way women are not in control of stereotypes used against them, stereotypes which revolve around women's sexuality. These have already been firmly established; indeed, they have a life of their own. Often coping with sexual harassment involves the fending off on an individual basis, attitudes and thinking which arise from these stereotypes. Assumptions that working women are 'available' to their male counterparts for sexual use or that women 'sleep their way to the top' reflect a male-dominated point of view which in turn affects our views and therefore our treatment of harassed women. Lynn Wehrli notes:

> Since women seem to 'go along' with sexual harassment [the assumption is that] they must like it, and it is not really harassment at all. This constitutes little more than a simplistic denial of all we know about the ways in which socialization and economic dependence foster submissiveness and override free choice. . . . Those women who are able to speak out about sexual harassment use terms such as 'humiliating', 'embarrassing', 'nerve-wracking', 'awful', and 'frustrating' to describe it. These words are hardly those used to describe a situation which one 'likes'.[12]

Diane Williams, who in 1976 sued the US Department of Justice for the 'pattern and practice of sexual harassment', endured a working environment within which her boss made a number of sexual advances toward her. When she did not comply, she was fired. In her discussion with Lin Farley, she noted:

> It [the harassment and her subsequent firing] had a very traumatic effect on me. I found it embarrassing; I was humiliated and very demoralized. I had never been fired, I'd never even known anybody who had been fired. I felt, God, this is the end. You're fired on a Friday; you don't have anyplace to go on Monday except to look through the want-ads on Sunday and start pounding the pavement. Nobody had taken into consideration whether I would be able to get another job, especially after they had said such terrible things about me [the Justice Department had placed in her personnel file a notation that she was fired for making a false, malicious, and slanderous statement], or whether I had any

money saved, or how I was going to pay the rent, or how was I going to buy food – whether I had to go on welfare or stand in the unemployment line. Nobody took that into consideration. It was so ironic too because this is the government agency that is supposed to be enforcing the nation's civil rights laws. . . .

It took a long time to come to grips with the actual facts as I knew them to be and that was that I hadn't done anything wrong, and then I was very much embarrassed to discuss the issues involved in the case. And the fact that this was a black man who had done this to me. I felt embarrassed on that account. You just feel a lot the way sexual assault victims feel. You're the victim but you're the one who's fired or being harassed or you didn't get the job training or you've had to quit. It's demoralizing, and there is this inescapable feeling of being responsible because you are being punished. It finally came to the point where I had to realize I was the complainant, not the defendant.[13]

So often women, like Diane Williams, are made to feel they are the ones to blame, that they somehow 'asked for' their harassment. Recall the many assumptions about women who are raped or battered. Contributory negligence belongs, it seems, to the female gender by fiat.

Sexual harassment affects women's lives. Harassed women respond in different ways to their harassment: many quit or are fired from their jobs, still some others are successful in stopping the behaviour. The next two women speak to these different responses.

What I did was quit. It's one of the hardest things I've ever done in my life. I lost a lot of self-respect because I'm not a quitter. I've never done anything like that but I have to live with it. My family didn't understand, a lot of people didn't understand.[14]

One time I was doing some writing of cases for the director's signature. He called me in to tell me how great one was and then he leaned over and passionately tried to kiss me. I screamed and shouted, 'No, stop.' Well, he tried to explain that he just wanted to show me his approval and I asked if he showed his approval that way to the man who had been doing the same kind of work. He said, 'No, he has a mustache.' I said, 'Well, from now on just think of me as having a mustache.' It always got down to the fact I was a woman. He just never could see me as a professional.[15]

Women who complain about sexual harassment are at times accused of being 'frigid', a 'bad sport', 'unfriendly', or, as Linda earlier, a 'cow'. Such comments effectively dismiss a woman's complaint about men's so-called typical behaviour, and as an additional cause of discomfort, deny women's experiences of sexual intimidation.

Additionally, women's relationships with men outside the particular harassing situation may be affected: 'I became disillusioned and suspicious of people I'd otherwise responded naturally to,' stated one woman harassed by her professor. 'I'm more cautious of male faculty in general.'[16] 'When I come home from work,' stated another, 'my husband becomes just another man.'[17] Experiencing sexually harassing behaviour, 'typical' male behaviour, leads many women to suspect all men's typical behaviour. Relationships with co-workers may be affected as well. In England, Elaine spoke to me about her anxiety about returning to work after taking a complaint to a tribunal. (Her account is covered more fully in Chapter 10.) Many of her fellow workers never knew what happened to her; the only thing they ever knew was that she was transferred out of a job she had had for seven years.

> What worries me is, you know, just the thought of actually going back there, and people still not knowing what went on. I just don't know if I can face it. You know, I want to go in and wear sort of a T-shirt with written on 'I was sexually harassed', this and this happened to me, then this. That's what I want, I want everyone to know. And this is all ok. You know, this can happen to you. I'd like people to know. If people knew, I would feel easier in my life.

As for battered women, exhaustion and humiliation dominate a sexually harassed woman's life. 'It has been a nightmare. I would not wish that anyone would go through what I have gone through,' reflected one woman. Later this same woman looked back on her experiences, now that they were over. In the meantime, she had lost her job, been sued by the harasser for a large sum of money, sued her employer, and settled the case out of court, with the employer eventually implementing a grievance procedure for future complaints about sexual harassment. Her reflections ring true for many harassed women:

In terms of feeling probably the thing that will always remain with me, and probably has made me more human, is this sense of humiliation and oppression. It's such a demeaning [thing]. Women cannot face themselves with a sense of pride because they have had to give in so much. It [the four years of the experience] was so smearing. I felt so powerless. I felt I was confronting a lion. I don't know how we did it. It was a business of survival and stubbornness to show them. But what a price.[18]

Such is the task of confronting men's power to sexually intimidate women. Sheila, a London new programme researcher, recognises this power as well.

I think that being female is a grave disadvantage at work. You have to prove your credibility; you have to work harder. Sexual harassment undermines your confidence and makes your job far more difficult. Every day a woman's confidence at work is on a knife edge because we're programmed to want a man's esteem. We're just conditioned that way, but when a man finds himself confronted by a capable woman he doesn't know what to do. Men in our office seem to think that the secretaries, personnel assistants and researchers, who are nearly all female, are supposed to spend their days doing things for them. They seem to be under some impressions that they're as available as the morning coffee.[19]

Just as women's sexual and physical autonomy is at risk at home or on the street, so too it is at work. Sexual harassment constitutes yet another intrusion, another example that women's treatment, far from encouraging the acceptance of women in public and private spheres, actually promotes further discrimination and exclusion. But, perhaps most important, much of sexual harassment is a result of men's typical, not aberrant, behaviour. To these women, men's typical behaviour turns their everyday working lives into humiliating, frustrating, hostile and sometimes even terrifying experiences.

Chapter 7

Women's lives and male power

What it is to *know* the *politics* of women's situations is to know women's personal lives. (Catherine MacKinnon, 1982)

A twenty-five-year old office worker was seen in the emergency room with an acute anxiety attack. She was pacing, agitated, unable to eat or sleep, and had a feeling of impending doom. She related a vivid fantasy of being pursued by a man with a knife. The previous day she had been cornered in the office by her boss, who aggressively propositioned her. She needed the job badly and did not want to lose it, but she dreaded the thought of returning to work. It later emerged in psychotherapy that this episode of sexual harassment had reawakened previously repressed memories of sexual assaults by her father. From the age of six until mid-adolescence, her father had repeatedly exhibited himself to her and insisted that she masturbate him. The experience of being entrapped at work had recalled her childhood feelings of helplessness and fear. (Judith Lewis Herman, 1981)

Women's experiences of sexual and/or physical intimidation and violence – much of it the result of what is assumed to be typical male behaviour – is an integral part of women's lives. It is so common women would like to take it for granted; instead, we take our fear for granted. Women know about the unpredictability of men's physical and sexual intimidation. We plan our lives around it: finding the right street to walk down when coming home, cooking the eggs the way the husband likes them, and avoiding office parties are examples of strategies designed to avoid male sexual and physical intimidation and violence. None of them are foolproof.

Women's engendered vulnerability to intimidating and violent male behaviour is due to their social position, not their biological position. That physical and/or sexual intrusion can happen, with little or no interference from others (and even, to some extent, encouragement) is a declaration of women's powerlessness.

The physical and/or sexual abuse of women is a manifestation of male domination itself; so often characterised as typical, it has been seen to be a natural right of men. According to women's experiences, much of male sexual and physical aggression toward them is not prohibited; it is regulated.[1] Fathers have the right to use their daughters as they please; husbands, their wives; bosses, their female employees; even men unknown to us act as if they have the right to comment or abuse any woman's body. The fact that all men do not exercise this right is irrelevant to the power afforded to men *as a gender* over women *as a gender*.

If gender inequality is the root of male violence, then the remedy is, of course, its abolition. It would be nice to call upon the Good Witch of the North, who, in a wave of her magic wand, would remove male dominance, its notions, its thinking, and its mechanisms from society. Unfortunately, this is highly unlikely. We are left with the longer route, slow societal change (indeed, the tortoise would win hands down).

Recognising the similarities in women's experiences of male behaviour – considered as either aberrant or typical male behaviour – is one such step in abolishing male dominance. Many of women's experiences take place in private (the private domain, too, is regarded as having secondary importance to the public) and, as a result, many similarities among women's experiences are often lost. No doubt, at least on an abstract level, we know how experiences of rape might be similar to experiences of incest or battering or sexual harassment. When we hear women speaking about those experiences, however, we see the similarities even more clearly. It is even hard to deny them or take them lightly. That an act of rape is different from an act of street harassment is not argued, but in fact each act is a physical and/or sexual intrusion, only the form, the intensity, differs. Many women can and do feel sexually and/or physically intimidated or violated by comments they receive from strangers or acquaintances; these comments serve as ever-present reminders of women's vulnerability to male violence.

The commonality of women's experiences exposes a process

whereby men's physical and sexual intimidation toward women is permitted to carry on with only minimum efforts to curb it. This process, one which significantly contributes to the maintenance of women's powerlessness and subjugation to men, operates on two levels. On one level – that of individual reactions – women's feelings of violation serve as an effective internal silencer for their experiences of men's threatening, intimidating or violent behaviour. Commonly, experiencing male violence makes women feel unrespectable, impure, tarnished, shamed. The wider societal reaction to male violence – the second level – effectively makes women who complain about men's behaviour feel unrespectable, impure, tarnished, shamed. At both levels, male-dominated ideology, one which reflects an engendered (male) view of women and their sexuality, is the looking glass through which women view their own experiences and how those experiences are viewed by others. Both levels ensure silence concerning the detrimental effects of male behaviour on women's physical, sexual and emotional autonomy. Both levels deny the effect of male violence on all women's lives.

Women's own reactions to what they perceive and/or experience as male violence illustrate the effects of powerlessness.[2] Their silence is linked to an understanding of this powerlessness; it is a recognition of the contradictory expectations of femaleness and probable judgments others commonly render about any woman's involvement in male violence. Good women avoid sexual and physical abuse; bad women don't. Women are often right about others' judgments.

As discussed earlier, women, as part of growing up in a male-dominated society, learn that the two genders – male and female – occupy different value positions in society. Men, as men, occupy a higher one. Power, prestige, and credibility too are awarded on a gender basis; men, as men, have greater access to the benefits of power, prestige and credibility. It is likely that female children, as part of growing up in an unequal, thus-gendered position, learn that they are less valued and have less prestige than their male counterparts. In acquiring a gender identity, a little girl *knows* she is a girl; she has been taught about and has observed her world for gender differences and roles. She incorporates a complex set of values and behaviours geared toward becoming and being recognised as a competent female. By the time she enters kindergarten, she has incorporated the feminine roles: she is helpful, nurturant, supportive, loving.[3] It seems too that girls' psychological development takes a divergent path from boys.

While boys may see a world comprised of people standing alone, a world that coheres through a system of rules, Carol Gilligan states, girls see the world comprised of relationships and as achieving coherence through human connection. In essence, then, female children are cultured into a system which teaches them to be supportive, helpful and loving and in turn see the world as an extension of themselves, connected to others. These traits are not as valued, however, as the individuality rewarded in males.[4] Moreover, these traits are interesting with respect to male violence. If females are connected to the world through relationships, and particularly their relationships to men, they are likely to be confused by aggression exhibited toward them within their relationships. Perhaps they aren't giving enough, they might think, perhaps they somehow provoked a typical encounter into an aberrant one. If women are taught to think that the loving and support, while a less valued task in life, hasn't been enough, it makes sense that they would attempt to provide even more love and support – again thinking that perhaps they didn't do it right in the first place. Being female, then, provides the program for teaching women to internalise their 'failure' (noted only by the fact that they encountered male physical and/or sexual intimidation or violence) and for encouraging women to look into their own behaviour as an explanation of male sexual and/or physical aggression.

Additionally, located within our male-dominated world are expectations, indeed prescriptions for being a 'respectable' woman. Central to respectability is woman's sexual purity. This standard, too, is moulded from male terms, ones which value women's sexual purity and men's sexual prowess. As Catherine A. MacKinnon states, sexuality is, for women, 'that which is most one's own, yet most taken away'.[5] Women learn, often at a very early age, that their sexuality is not their own and that maleness can at any point intrude into it. Sexuality, then, is a form of power, and gender, as socially constructed, embodies it, not the reverse. As such, male sexual and physical prowess takes precedence over female sexual and physical autonomy. Enter the dominant stereotypes of women, encapsulated in the stereotype of the 'madonna' and the 'whore', which are foundations for general views of women and their behaviour. The madonna somehow avoids male intrusion; the whore invites it. Documentation of women's experiences however challenges these stereotypes and exposes women's engendered vulnerability to male sexual and physical aggression.

Knowing women's experiences of male violence then is knowing women's position in society, the very social and cultural reality of what a woman *is*. When sexually and/or physically assaulted women speak, therefore, we hear a recognition of the power of the male point of view which acts to undermine women's own assertions of the damage they experience from male behaviour – be it defined by men as typical or aberrant behaviour. In the previous chapters, women themselves point to how the male point of view affects their own recovery and survival from male violence. According to the male point of view, women's lives revolve around women's sexuality and around their relationships to men, men who are often their assailants. Women are, above all, sexual beings. As sexual beings, women intrude into all spaces – the street, the workplace, the home – all of which are assumed to be settings which are not 'sexual' settings. We know from women's experiences that women's sexuality is treated as if it were essentially available to any man within any setting. Women, by virtue of their very presence, are expected to bring forth men's 'natural' sexual urges, yet are blamed for receiving sexual and physical advances from men. That women are wives, part of a couple, identified in relation to the male 'provider' and 'protector', and are responsible for men's and their children's happiness, is yet another important lynchpin in women's lives. Women have a duty to keep together men and children in the same household. As such, women as a gender are not – and in industrial society at least never have been – autonomous from men as a gender – physically or sexually. As connections of men, women have been expected to endure or alternatively have been seen as legitimate, deserving targets of male sexual and physical aggression because that is part of what men *are*. Women, as connected to men, are then violated. The taken-for-granted nature of male violence is extended to women automatically; women, it is taken for granted, put up with it. Ultimately the male point of view reinforces and maintains male power over women's lives and women's sexual and physical autonomy.

Nowhere is that power stronger than men's control over women's sexuality. Women who have experienced male sexual aggression – be it incestuous assault, rape, indecent assault, sexual harassment or battering of women who endure additional sexual abuse – have a hard time recovering their own sexual feelings again, at least for a period of time after the assault.[6] Any sexual advance becomes indistinguishable from an aggressive sexual advance. Women's heterosexual interaction becomes the place where they relive the coercion, the violence, the terror of the sexual abuse over which they had no control. Forced sexuality for women is 'paradigmatic' of their existence within a social sphere of male power.[7] Women themselves note this connection:

> We had sex for the first time several days ago. My husband said that it just wasn't the same. *I didn't want sex, but I couldn't say no.* All I could think of was that guy – it went through my head the whole time. I couldn't relax. My husband thought that I should be the same as I always was.[8]

> I have difficulty dropping the emotional barrier I work behind when I come home from work. My husband turns into just another man.[9]

> It's become clearer to me that the thing with my stepfather has affected me more deeply than even I could have thought, I feel in a certain way like a handicapped person (they should reserve parking for the sexually handicapped) and like I function sexually in *defiance* of the damage – *but it is real damage.*[10]

The real damage is damage to women and as such cannot be realised, felt, understood or legitimated by men who assume consensual sexuality (here heterosexuality) to be always pleasurable. Within a male-dominated world, we do not trust women to make the distinction between what is or is not damaging to them. Instead, that distinction is left to men. Yet how can we trust men to fully understand the real damage of women's experiences of coercive sexuality when they do not recognise the link between consensual and coercive sexuality and how it is welded to their typical, normal, presumed-to-be-unharmful sexuality?

Living in a society which constantly reminds women of the expectation to uphold their roles of womanhood, women often internalise their experiences of male violence which might be interpreted as a failure to maintain that womanhood. Feelings reported by physically and/or sexually assaulted women reflect this internalisation. Feelings of self-blame, of humiliation, of responsibility for men's behaviour, of shame, of loss of self-esteem, of being stigmatised – all of these encourage silence; breaking the silence barrier exposes the woman to judgment from others for her failure to live up to ideal womanhood.

A closer look at women's feelings illustrates how a male point of view commonly seeps into women's own reactions to male violence.

A woman's self-blame, one such feeling, becomes a way of looking within her own behaviour, finding fault with herself as being individually accountable for her aggressor's behaviour.

[Self blame] relates to this feeling of being this bad little girl who didn't use her power correctly to stop her father from assaulting her.[11] (Incestually assaulted woman)

I kept wondering maybe if I had done something different when I first saw him that it wouldn't have happened – neither he nor I would be in trouble.[12] (Raped woman)

Then I used to think it's my blame and I used to lie awake at night wondering if it is my blame.[13] (Battered woman)

I just thought I was doing something. It's like the whole thing just puts doubt in you and stays with you for a while.[14] (Sexually harassed woman)

Feeling responsible for the aggressor's behaviour, similar to self-blame, corresponds to the traditional myth about women's uncontrollable sexuality. Women 'ask for it', we have learned so well.

In some ways they [the visits from my father] bothered me more than the other visits, because I was awake and he knew it and I felt therefore responsible.[15](Incestually assaulted woman)

I felt like I'd brought out the worst in these men just by being an available female body in the road . . . and that it was my fault that they'd been lowered to rape me.[16] (Raped woman)

You're the victim but you're the one who's fired or being harassed or you didn't get the job training or you've had to quit. It's demoralizing, and there is this inescapable feeling of being responsible because you *are* being punished.[17] (Sexually harassed woman)

Moreover, women feel shame and embarrassment, another indication of the power of commonly available knowledge about women and how they (as respectable women) should feel when they arouse men.

To me it [my body] was always dirty and ugly and a source of shame.[18] (Incestually assaulted woman)

As well as being ashamed because of how I am degraded, I am

ashamed because I do not have the guts to fight it.[19] (Battered woman)

I felt embarrassment, shame and disgust. And I felt guilty because I felt I shouldn't have gone out with anybody except my boy friend. And hate. I hated the guy.[20] (Raped woman)

It [the sexual comments] made me feel very embarrassed.[21] (Sexually harassed woman)

These feelings of shame, self-blame and responsibility all point to feelings of being set apart from 'proper' women, in essence, feelings of being stigmatised.

I always felt that everyone was laughing at me or talking about me behind my back. I felt that they somehow knew about my father, so I attributed most of these feelings to my looks.[22] (Incestually assaulted woman)

[My husband] doesn't want me around his family. He told his mother on Sunday and said he was ashamed of me.[23] (Raped woman)

I never went out of the house, you know, I never looked at anybody.[24] (Battered woman)

The real trouble is simply that if you don't sleep with any of them, they go around calling you a mean cow, and if you do, they call you a whore.[25] (Sexually harassed woman)

Internalising the 'other', separating oneself from women who, these women feel, have never experienced male violence or intrusion, encourages women's silence. Mobilising against it is often a solitary act, left to the woman alone; the incestually assaulted woman may leave home, the harassed woman her job, the battered woman her husband. Leaving the situation is one form of resistance. Before she leaves, however, the woman may try good old-fashioned 'hope' that things will just change. This hope is also fostered by dependence and helplessness.

First, hope.

Here is this wonderful man who is the most important person in your life, whom you idolize and trust, and he's betraying your trust. . . . How could I help but hope somehow he'd miraculously change?[26] (Incestually assaulted woman)

I don't know. I kept on thinking he was changing, you know, change for the better. . . . He's bound to change.[27] (Battered woman)

I ignored them [my co-workers] hoping they would get bored eventually and stop. But I started to change.[28] (Sexually harassed woman).

Perhaps, dependence and helplessness are the truer ingredients of hope.

I thought that I was really strong and that I could fight and was tough. But the violence that was coming from this man really frightened me. He really paralysed me.[29] (Raped woman)

Where would I go? My college education was interrupted to marry and have a large family. I was a suburban housewife, a wife of a successful businessman and well versed in entertaining and dressing to fit the right occasion. None of these qualities are sought on the job market. . . . So the trap is built – stay in the marriage, make the best of it and gradually lose not only your identity but your self-respect.[30]

It is important at this point to comment about women who, over the course of their lives, find themselves experiencing male violence time and time again. To posit that women who are violent in their own lives or only establish relationships with violent men because they are addicted to violence, as Erin Pizzey and Jeff Shapiro have done recently in *Prone to Violence*, is to be blinded to the social context within which women experience sexual and/or physical assault.[31] It is easier for Pizzey and Shapiro to conclude, it seems, with an individually based, chemically rooted theory of violence than to address the entrenched, male-dominated conditions in which many women have no recourse but to be part of a couple, and no resources to change patterns of behaviour that fit neatly in grooves carved not by their own hands.

A violence-prone woman can tell you in all honesty that she really does want to get away, and does not want any more violent relationships. Yet she then often goes straight back to her violent partner, or to an equally violent man. At the time though, she is not lying. On one level, an intellectual level, she means what she says: she desperately wants to get out. But on another level, the chemical level, she is powerfully addicted to the amount of violence in their relationship, and cannot help but go back to it. Having been reared on violence, she will only feel *alive* and satisfied in a situation of great danger, so she often deliberately provokes a man to the point where he will hit her. Then in her pain she returns to her quiet and peaceful inner-womb of the opioid state.[32]

The chemicals of the violence-prone couple – they fail to explain why it is that *women* are most often the targets of violence – are adrenalin and cortisone. The violent couple become locked into a relationship chemically induced by their own make-up: adrenalin for the violent male and cortisone for the passive female. The ultimate goal, state Pizzey and Shapiro, is death – the aim of the addiction to violence.

Some women return to violent men or become locked in violent relationships simply because there is no escape from male violence – outside or inside the home. Being with a man, however violent, seems to be better than being without a man. A world permeated by the male point of view, by self-esteem and power filtered through relationships with men, and by the ever-presence of male intimidation and violence toward women is a world which cannot expect all women to successfully avoid male violence or to regard it as anything but inevitable.

While there is a pattern, however, of conformity to the male point of view, there is strong resistance. Women leave jobs where they are devalued for their work but not their sexuality; they leave husbands who are violent to them; they avoid contact with men who are known to harass women. When the refuges and shelters grew up in both Britain and the United States, women flocked to them, filling them to capacity. Despite their powerlessness within a male-dominated world, women resist sexual objectification, refuse to be 'willing' partners to coercive sexuality, and reject stereotypes about how they are to conduct their lives as women.

Resistance to male intimidation and male violence is not without its stress. It is likely that women carry stress symptoms – paranoia, nightmares, mood swings, loss or gain of weight – with them for a long time. Some women, in their attempts to break out of women's roles or come to terms with experiences of male sexual or physical violence, seek therapy. Feminist therapy, that therapy which places women's individual reactions within an understanding of women's experiences, is most helpful. It discourages internalising a negative view of the women's reactions to very stressful situations. But psychotherapy is not without its male bias. Women's complaints about male behaviour, particularly aggressively violent behaviour, may be considered to be fantasy, exaggeration, or caused by the woman herself. These perceptions are incorporated into the practice of most of the helping professions; they too are enmeshed within a male world. As Phyllis Chesler has noted in her work on women and psychotherapy, 'despite individual differences among clinicians, most have been steeped, professionally and culturally, in both contemporary and traditional patriarchal ideologies. . . .'[33]

Interestingly enough, Chesler herself explores sexual abuse of female clients by male therapists. Her own findings bear striking resemblance to our discussion of male violence so far. Chesler interviewed women who had sex with their therapists. These women insisted that they were to blame, that they were the 'real' seducers. Most of these sexual contacts, moreover, take place between middle-aged male therapists and younger, female patients. The patients remained in therapy longer than any of Chesler's other studied group. Although many of these women describe being humiliated and frustrated by their therapists' emotional and sexual coldness or ineptitude, it was the therapist, more often than the patient, who ended the affair. In every case the woman was more hurt. Chesler herself makes the connection between this and other forms of typical male behaviour:

> 'Sex' between private female patients and their male
> psychotherapists is probably no more common – or uncommon
> – an occurrence than is 'sex' between a female secretary or
> housekeeper and her male employer. Both instances generally
> involve an older male figure and a young female figure. The male
> transmits 'unconscious' signals of power, 'love', wisdom and
> protection, signals to which the female has been conditioned to
> respond automatically. Such a transaction between patient and
> therapist, euphemistically termed 'seduction' or 'part of the
> treatment process', is legally a form of rape and psychologically
> a form of incest.[34]

Women's sexuality is therefore a likely target in many spheres within a male-dominated society. While feminists continue to wage the ideological battle and provide practical supports such as rape crisis centres or women's refuges, resistance most often occurs on an individual basis. Despite the social environment, as we have seen, which encourages women's silence about their sexual and/or physical abuse, women do break it. They call police to have their husbands/boyfriends/lovers arrested for battering and rape; they complain of rape and assault on the street; they complain to personnel and management departments about their bosses' and co-workers' sexually harassing behaviour.

How these complaints are handled by these institutional agencies is the focus of Part II. Women who have the courage to define typical male behaviour as unacceptable and harmful still confront institutional responses which view it as normal, or as that which has been precipitated, in fact, provoked by the women themselves. Not uncommonly, women's complaints about male behaviour are twisted around and are assumed to reflect the woman's behaviour, not the man's. Here, Sandra, quoted by Chesler, recalls the time she confronted her therapist for his sexual proposition, and the results:

> I decided, though, that I owe it to Mark [her husband] to go up with him and confront the group we're all in together [about her therapists's proposition]. So I go up and there's Dr X and his two assistants sitting there and I figure, well, the cards are stacked against me. . . . Dr X says, 'Well, well, tell us what happened.' So I tell the story again and then he proceeds to tell the group how I was provocative to him, how I wore a miniskirt – which I always wear. . . . He made it look as if I were coming up there to seduce him not to have a session. . . . Then he says I'm using this lie of a proposition to cop out of therapy. He reminded me that I didn't quit a job I once had just because my boss made a pass at me. . . . Then all of a sudden we're sitting there and he's starting to say things like: 'Sandra, you know how dishonest you are, how dishonest you are with Mark, there are things you haven't told him'. [He was referring to a brief affair she'd had], and I started crying, 'I'm getting out of here,' I mean it was like a kangaroo court . . . and when we left, Mark said to me, 'What haven't you *told me*, what did you do?' He forgot all about what Dr X did. . . . Everything got twisted.[35]

Met with suspicions similar to those women themselves harbour, women who complain about men's intimidating, threatening, or violent behaviour report that they feel twice assaulted. It is the police officer, the prosecutor, the judge, the defence attorney, the jury, the social worker, the personnel officer, or the union official, who acts as the second assailant. Those very stereotypes which contribute to women's own silence about men's behaviour are found in the reactions of those to whom women complain, externally imposing silence about the effects of men's behaviour on women's lives. Let us now turn to Part II which examines the features of this second assault.

Part II

The second assailant

On a warm night last August, I was raped in my sixth-floor apartment by a young man I had never seen before. He climbed through the window of my 'safe' apartment, which has a deadbolt lock on the door, stood before me as I lay in bed, and said: 'Don't scream or I'll kill you.' Seven months later, long after I had identified him to the police, a grand jury threw the case out.

It is no accident that my case took this long, and no accident that my assailant was not indicted. He had enough money to hire three lawyers, and as a white middle-class student he was able to persuade the district attorney's office to delay his case for months instead of bringing it to the grand jury within weeks, as usually happens in rape cases. He was also able to arrange for other nice middle-class people to testify for him. Since I was not permitted to read the grand jury transcripts I will never really know why he was not indicted, but I gather that his fraternity brothers told the jury he was with them in the fraternity house for at least part of the time during which I was raped.

I am 30 years old, white, middle-class and single. I live on a nice street on the Upper West Side, in a building with a doorman. I am, in short, what the detectives call a 'real person' – not the stereotypical welfare mother, lonely divorcee, teen-age girl or bored suburban housewife who society thinks, unfairly, are 'asking for it'.

In this past year I have learned some interesting lessons about rape and criminal justice in New York City. My case started auspiciously. When the police arrived, I calmly gave them a precise physical description of my assailant, down to the colors of his T-shirt, and a description of the jewelry he stole from my apartment. Less than one hour after the rape, while I was being examined at a hospital, the police picked up a man fitting my description – two blocks from my apartment. When I saw him sitting in the back of the police cruiser, a huge grin on his face, I identified him immediately. He turned out to be a student at the university where I teach. The police laboratory later discovered that he had semen in his underwear at the time of his arrest.

My identification, I was assured by the detectives, would be enough to get an indictment. Such was not to be the case. Though, to their credit, the police treated me with great sensitivity, they failed at something equally important: they did not gather evidence at the only time they could. They didn't, for example, obtain a warrant to search the suspect's apartment for my stolen jewelry and would not have taken the sheet from my bed for forensic analysis had I not reminded them to do so.

Perhaps police headquarters or city hall should take part of the blame for this well-meaning but inept performance; the police department's special rape unit had been disbanded, for budgetary reasons, in August. That month, I learned later, is the time of the year when rape is most frequent.

My frustrations were compounded when my case reached the Manhattan District Attorney's office. For three months nothing happened except that I was made to feel more like the accused than the victim. The prosecutor assigned to the case seemed more intent upon undermining my account of the incident than learning more about it; he never even asked me to tell my story in person. Only after another month of waiting and some pressure from an influential private attorney was another, more sympathetic, assistant district attorney assigned to my case.

I was soon to discover, however, that the new prosecutor was solicitous only as long as she thought she had a 'strong' case. Identifying your rapist and circumstantial evidence do not constitute a 'strong' case. One should leave a scar on your rapist's body or offer him a drink – taking care not to smudge the fingerprints on the glass. Also, when the accused is white and middle-class he is more likely to be believed than the usual rape suspect or victim. Had my assailant's name been 'Hector Lopez', the assistant district attorney later suggested to me, things might have turned out differently.

Evidence in rape cases is limited by the objective reality of rape; there are no witnesses and assailants rarely leave fingerprints. So, why is an impossible burden of proof placed on the victim? No one wants to convict innocent men, but why should a positive identification of the assailant and verified evidence of rape not be sufficient to bring an accused rapist to trial?

Throughout it all, I came to realize that being an inquisitive, insistent victim was more of a disadvantage than a benefit. Whenever I called to be apprised of the progress of my case, the authorities treated me as little more than an unwanted intruder.

Seven months after I was raped, the charges against the suspect were dropped. I still do not know why. But I suspect that the long delay and the palpable lack of enthusiasm from the prosecutor's office did not help. The Manhattan D.A.'s office is not interested in getting an indictment unless it is 99 per cent sure of a conviction.

The experience has left me feeling twice victimized; first by a sole assailant, second by the criminal-justice system. Having taught my students that the struggle for justice should be waged within the system, I wonder how much I should revise this year's lecture notes. Meanwhile, my assailant walks free – free not only to register for my classes but free to rape again.

Jane Doe, 1982[1]

Chapter 8

The rhetoric of protection

There was no doubt who killed her. All sides acknowledged Mary Bristow was killed by Peter Wood, who was described by defence as Mary's sometimes lover. Addressing the jury in Wood's trial for Mary's murder in Winchester, England, in June, 1982, Justice Bristow (no relation) explained the difference between murder and manslaughter: 'There is a difference between a villain shooting a policeman, and a husband or lover killing his wife or lover at a stage when they can no longer cope.'[1]

Mary Bristow, aged 36, was killed on 29 October 1981 in her own bedroom. Peter Wood first beat her with a meat tenderiser he took from Mary's kitchen, then smothered her with a pillow and strangled her with his hands. Wood was described by Mary's friends as a lodger in her house. According to her friends, Mary and Peter were never seen out together except, significantly, on Sunday, at a demonstration against nuclear weapons, just two days before Mary was killed. At the time it was thought really peculiar that they were together. Wood had been repeatedly kicked out of Mary's house; she even attempted at one point to request police assistance in having him removed from the house. Reported one of Mary's friends, '"Oh well," said a desk sergant at the local police station, "a big strong girl like you shouldn't have any trouble [getting Wood out]. Go and get some mates and chuck him out." '[2]

Patrick Back, QC for the defence, chose to portray the case as *Pygmalion* in reverse. Wood's defence was that he was Mary's lover and killed her in reaction to her supposed sexual infidelity. Wood contended that Mary did not want a monogamous relationship with him and was trying to kick him out of the house. No one asked Mary how she saw her relationship with Wood. Nor did anyone ask her friends (Mary had commented in letters to friends what a pest her lodger was).

The judge in his summation to the jury stated:

> Mary Bristow, with an IQ of 182, was a rebel from a middle-class background. [She was a single, self-supporting woman, employed as a local librarian who owned her own home.] She was unorthodox in her relationships [she was unmarried, without one 'steady' relationship], so proving that the cleverest of people aren't always wise. Those who engaged in sexual relationships should realise that sex is one of the deepest and most powerful of human emotions, and if you're playing with sex you're playing with fire [ironically, Wood set fire to Mary's house after he killed her so this imagery was highly charged]. And it might be . . . that the conventions which surround sex, [those of male control over female sexuality] which some people think are old hat, [read feminists] are there to prevent people if possible [from] burning themselves.[3]

Peter Wood successfully pleaded to manslaughter on the grounds of diminished responsibility and provocation. He received a sentence of six years with no requirement for psychiatric treatment.

In another 1983 English murder trial, a man, described by the judge as 'honest, loving and hardworking man of exemplary record', pleaded guilty to manslaughter of his wife and 1-year old daughter on the grounds of diminished responsibility. He first attempted to strangle his wife and finally stabbed her to death. He then strangled his daughter with a tie, having already stabbed her. The man was distraught, his defence attorney said, because he could not cope with the pressure of work. He received a sentence of probation for three years on the condition that he underwent medical treatment, with the judge stating, 'I am confident this is not a case for punishment.'[4]

In yet another 1983 English trial for murder, a man was given a suspended sentence for killing his wife of forty years. The woman, having suffered from arthritis for over ten years, leaving her 'house-bound and senile', was supposedly always 'nagging' her husband. Defending counsel stated, 'One morning, last October, she turned from her usual topic of attacking [her husband's] conduct to attacking other people. This caused her husband to snap and he throttled her.' The dead wife, not allowed to voice her stress and frustration for her enfeebled state, was killed by a man 'naturally' enraged by his 'nagging' wife. The newspaper headline read: 'Nagging drove a husband to kill.'[5] Strategies for establishing a defence to murder charges of men accused of killing women are commonly available: unfaithful or nagging women provoke men's emotions or some women are just in the way of the husband's stress and frustration.

In nine out of ten cases when women are killed, they are killed by men.[6] While the definitions of legally defined murder vary within Britain as well as within the United States, in general a charge of murder requires both intent and premeditation. Manslaughter charges, on the other hand, do not require the killer's premeditation. A defence attorney's typical strategy would be to argue that a defendant was not responsible for his/her actions (due to insanity or mental instability, thus undermining intent) or was provoked (due to the actions of the deceased, thus undermining premeditation). Most individuals charged with murder are likely, if convicted, to be convicted of manslaughter. (Convictions for manslaughter are likely to lead to a more lenient sentence, in some cases, sentences which do not require imprisonment.)[7] It is the possibility of establishing either diminished responsibility or provocation which is of interest, particularly in light of whether the killer be male and the killed female, or vice versa.

If a woman killed a man for sexual infidelity or nagging, would she also be successful in defending herself with the arguments of diminished responsibility and/or provocation? Jean Harris, who killed Dr Herman Tarnower, the 'Scarsdale Diet Doctor', in New York in 1980, was addicted to barbiturates and speed which Tarnower himself prescribed over a period of a decade. She was jealous of an affair Tarnower had with another, younger woman. She stated during the trial that she had really intended to kill herself when she shot Tarnower. On 24 February 1981, the jury found Harris guilty of murder in the second degree – the most serious charge under New York law (the State reserves murder in the first degree for killings of police officers and prison guards). Harris received a sentence of fifteen years to life in Bedford Hills Correctional Facility, the New York State prison for women.[8] Unlike Peter Wood, Jean Harris was not successful in establishing provocation or diminished responsibility in the killing of Tarnower, at least not on the basis of sexual jealousy.

No doubt, some women who do kill their husbands or lovers plead guilty to lesser charges. But the provocation is often characterised as different from that to which men respond. For example, in a 1983 trial for murder in England, a 'battered wife who killed her brutal husband' was given a suspended sentence after pleading to manslaughter on the ground of diminished responsibility and provoc- ation. The woman had taken refuge in a shelter for battered wives and had endured years of beatings and sexual abuse from her husband. Her actions were 'understandable' – particularly in the context of her life as filled with his violent action toward her.[9] Not all cases, though, in which women kill men in their own defence after years of beating are treated alike. Ann Jones found that many others are convicted of murder and are serving long sentences for killing their brutal husbands. In November 1980, for instance, in Atkinson County, Georgia, Elaine Mullins, a battered wife for thirteen years, was found guilty of murdering her husband. At the same time Connie Mullins was killed, he was in the process of battering his wife. She received a sentence of life imprisonment. One juror remarked after the trial, 'We couldn't let her go. It would have been open season on husbands in Atkinson County.' Similar comments were uttered by one man interviewed on the street after the Harris conviction: women should learn that they can't shoot men just because men cheat on them or else 'all men would get shot.'[10] Yet a fabricated relationship and allusions to sexual infidelity was 'self-evident' justification for Peter Wood to kill Mary Bristow.

Arguments used within trials for murder seem to parallel those found in our common sense. Defence strategies for men or women accused of murder follow socially based assumptions about men and women and their aggressive behaviour. Men who murder women for their irritating, humiliating or unfaithful behaviour are somehow understood; women's actions can lead men to lose control. Women, on the other hand, unless provoked beyond endurance – beaten and threatened over years – are expected to retain control. The process of inquiry within criminal trials integrates stereotypes about women which women already know only too well; these stereotypes already have an effect on how they respond to male intimidation and violence. At the same time, characterisation of men's behaviour – as typical or aberrant aggression – is embedded into the process as well. These characterisations of men's and women's behaviour are often contradic- tory, giving added flexibility, yet strength, to their use within the inquiry into women's experiences of male intimidation and violence.[11]

Marked by oak-filled chambers, robed judges, solemn proceedings (in Britain, judges and participating barristers wear wigs), and countless participants – from stenographers to clerks, from police officers to a motley crew of witnesses – the trial is indeed a formidable event within the legal fact-finding apparatus – the criminal justice system. Within the presumed objective forum for hearing the facts of a criminal event, the trial, bedrock of democratic society, is where attorneys present the state's case against the accused, and the accused's defence to those accusations. The trial procedure is supposed to sort out the nuances behind instances of criminal violence. After all, the trial procedure is the state's arena for ultimately assessing the legitimacy of any citizen's complaint and any defendant's guilt or innocence. All participants in the fact-finding process – the police, attorneys, judges and jurors – orient themselves to this task.

Judges and the members of a jury, the civilian assessors of guilt or innocence, listen to the evidence; prosecutors, for the state, and defence attorneys for the defendant, face each other as supposed adversaries debating the evidence and perception of the criminal event in question. This forum, many people believe, is a 'true' test of guilt or innocence of the defendant. The strength of 'fair justice' rests upon the belief that, at least in this instance (as many complainants hope), the 'truth' will be borne out during the trial. When someone is convicted, we are assured of his guilt; when he is acquitted, we are quick to insist on his innocence. Yet we still acknowledge that some people 'get off'. We implicitly know that sometimes guilt or innocence seems like such a fragile determination.

Despite the pageantry and the aura of objective fact-finding, the trial, its stage set for inquiry into 'what happened', takes its direction from contemporary thinking, which, of course, includes traditional views of women and male violence to them. Within the trial procedure, perhaps more publicly than elsewhere in the criminal justice system, prosecutors, defence attorneys and judicial officers tend to focus on the woman complainant in the few instances of male violence which come to their attention. (Many others, as we shall see in the next chapter, never reach the court; even fewer cases reach the trial stage.) The complainant's respectability, her credibility, her 'truthfulness', is put to the test. She is often the sole witness against her assailant; she is, as one police officer remarked, a 'living scene of a crime'.[12] So much of the strength of the state's case against the accused rests upon her word and how her word is believed by others. If the woman has been murdered, then how the woman is portrayed at trial is an important part of the case against the accused as well.

Yet the point of view from which a trial takes place, and from which to assess women's word, is a male point of view.[13] Its view of women's word takes additional cues from distinctions based on considerations of race and class status. The more credible one's social characteristics, the greater the likelihood that one's words will be taken seriously.[14] Being white and middle-class contribute to a woman's credibility. We know too that by and large defendants who are minority or lower-class have a greater chance of being arrested, charged, convicted and more severely sentenced than their white, middle- or upper-class counterparts. As the system is not blind to gender, so it is not blind to race and class. As one raped woman's mother commented, 'We had three strikes against us from the start. Who he [the defendant] was, a woman saying it was rape, and being black'.[15]

There are special ingredients available to assist attorneys, judges and jurors with their task of assessing credibility and truthfulness for women. [16] Quite expectedly, the ingredients are those women themselves use in maintaining silence about male intimidation and violence. One such ingredient, being 'nice', is a value for women, providing both a standard for others' judgments and a goal toward which women orient their behaviour. Niceness 'connotes chaste, gentle, gracious, ingenuous, good, clean, kind, virtuous, noncontroversial, and above suspicion and reproach.'[17] As a quality of a particular woman, niceness is not fixed, but can change depending on how the woman acts or is seen by others to act in various situations. 'Nice' girls, for example, don't accept rides from strangers, don't go into pubs alone, don't walk the streets at night, are 'chaste', in essence, are passive, compliant, sexually controlled within respectable boundaries. While women who do not avoid questionable situations risk being labelled 'not nice', they also risk being eliminated from the category of women who the judge or jury are supposed to believe. If some women can be characterised as solely at fault for whatever 'misfortune' befalls them, then any woman could potentially be similarly character-ised. Stereotypes are after all quite flexible. Hitchhiking women, for example, could easily be assumed to 'ask for' trouble and to have contributed to whatever happens to them. Women who have had multiple sexual relationships could easily be labelled as 'loose', and to have placed themselves in situations where they are likely to be sexually abused. Women, by stepping outside traditionally defined boundaries of niceness, reduce their chances of receiving sympathy from judges, lawyers, police, or jurors (many of whom are also likely to be men). 'Blaming the victim' fits well into people's belief in a just world (and in a criminal justice system which delivers justice); it is a world where individuals get what they deserve and deserve what they get. According to this type of thinking, if something happens (good or bad) to someone (here a woman), she is seen as deserving for one of two reasons: either she is an intrinsically good (or bad) person and her character merits the good or bad outcome; or she has behaved in a manner which brings about the good or bad occurrence.[18] The categories – good or bad – can arise at any point in time; success in retaining good/nice as indicative of a woman's character is unpredictable – there are so many ingredients which could contribute to either assessment.

Defence attorneys are particularly adept in searching the stereotypes about women for ways to portray a particular woman as deserving, provoking or contributing to men's actions. Knowledge about women's lifestyles, sexuality or occupations as respectable or unrespectable also connote innocence or provocativeness. A woman's behaviour is not, however, portrayed from a woman's point of view, but from an understanding of women's behaviour from a man's point of view. At any time, a woman can be portrayed as *provocateur* or even as a contributor to her 'misfortune'. Visiting a man's flat, accepting a ride home from a party, having dinner and a drink with a man: all are situations which could be construed as women's invitation for sexual relations. By surfacing the possibility of a woman's contribution to men's aggressive behaviour, defence attorneys fare a better chance in gaining acquittals or pleas of guilty to lesser charges. Harlots or virgins, women's sexuality is seen as underscoring women's relationships to men; any 'occasional' release of male aggression towards women and their sexuality can be portrayed as 'natural' behaviour.[19] Raising a 'reasonable' doubt about the criminal nature of men's actions is not difficult; the benefit of the doubt goes to men. Not surprisingly, these stereotypes about women and their contributory responsibility in sexual assault often arise during trial.[20] If a woman is badly beaten, or attacked by a stranger on the street, or threatened with a weapon in what has been termed a 'blitz' rape,[21] she is seen to be less responsible for the sexual attack. As we saw in Part I, she may still have to contend with questions concerning her dress, her resistance or her physical response. (And of course, generally if a man is giving advice to a woman about rape, he suggests that she 'submit' to the rape rather than endanger her life. 'Submission' however makes a lousy case for trial.) If the raped woman is a prostitute, for example, the assault may be considered to be merely an occupational hazard, her credibility as a witness the heart of the doubt. Unless she has sustained severe injuries accompanying the rape, she is likely to have difficulty combatting the powerful stereotype of the impure, vindictive prostitute seeking revenge for non-payment of services.

These stereotypes about women are so strong that even efforts (due to the concerted efforts of feminists) to exclude the woman complainant's prior sexual history within trial matter in rape cases are not totally successful. Despite the passage of the 1976 Sexual Offences Act in England and Wales, for example, the main provision of the act – to limit the admissibility of evidence about the raped woman's prior sexual history – does not protect women from the mudslinging tactics of defence attorneys. In over 60 per cent of the cases where the identity of the accused was not in question, according to a study by Zsuzsanna Adler, a formal application was submitted to introduce prior sexual history as relevant to the rape trial. Over three-quarters of these applications were partly or wholly successful. (Adler concludes, 'The inadequate implementation of the 1976 act largely reflects, and probably reinforces, precisely those assumptions and prejudices which the law was designed to eliminate.')[22]

The ordeal and outcome of the trial procedures in cases of male violence against women serves as an additional lesson to women. Similar to men's comments toward women on the street – the reminders to women of their vulnerability to men's threatening, intimidating or violent behaviour – strategies used at trials of men accused of criminal violence toward women, focusing on those same stereotypes, undermine women's confidence and credibility. In addition, these common strategies open up a weakness in the state's case against the accused and thus become an important consideration early on in criminal justice inquiry. Publicity surrounding trials regarding serious, violent crime against women contributes to women's feeling of vulnerability as well. As Carol Smart and Barry Smart have noted,

> The cumulative effect of press reports of rape [and of men's murder of women as well] is to remind women of their vulnerability, to create an atmosphere of fear and to suggest, as a solution, that women should withdraw to the traditional shelter of the domestic sphere and the protection of *their* men.[23]

But what if women's solution is to withdraw to the protection of men who are battering and sometimes murdering them?

Women's own experiences or the experiences of their friends or relatives in court and the surrounding messages they receive from press coverage in cases of violence against women contribute to their fear – 'fear' of crime, as found in the victimisation surveys, is perhaps women's own recognition that they cannot turn to men for protection, nor can they turn to the criminal justice system to protect them from men's threatening, violent and intimidating behaviour. That very intimidating behaviour is an integral part of the tactics defence attorneys use in trials concerning male violence against women. Women find therefore that their complaints about male violence – even in the courtroom setting – are continually being placed within a male understanding of men's sexual and/or physical violence toward them. Women's point of view is not the orientation of the process of inquiry into criminal violence.

Therefore, what judges do or say in their summations or sentencing reflects back upon women's feelings of vulnerability. Judge Bristow is not unique in commenting about women who act outside the traditional boundaries and therefore bring on men's aggressive behaviour. Women cannot avoid the possibility that their behaviour could be characterised as the cause of men's behaviour at any time during a trial. One Cambridge, England judge acquitted a man accused of rape and said that attention should be paid to the way in which a woman says 'no'.[24] In Ipswich, England a judge levied a fine of £2,000 against a man who pleaded guilty to rape. Rather than sentence the man to prison, the judge stated that the woman contributed to the rape because she was hitchhiking.[25] In another case, a judge in Massachusetts fined five young men for brutally gang raping a woman because she had willingly accompanied the men out of a bar: the fine, five dollars a week each for a year.[26] Even the infamous Glasgow case, where the woman was encouraged to pursue a private prosecution (due to the publicity surrounding the procurator fiscal's decision not to prosecute), two of the three convicted defendants were convicted not of rape, but indecent assault. The woman, the defence contended, had been drinking, the two defendants claimed she willingly accompanied them to a garbage pile where they assaulted her, and then collected two friends to do the same. The raped woman sustained injuries requiring over 150 stitches. The same woman has since been attacked again. She said that this time she would not press charges 'because I don't think I could face it all again'. The attack, on the street by a stranger, was, according to the woman, 'a nightmare – it brought all the old memories and fears flooding back.'[27] She did, however, press charges; the man was acquitted.

It is not surprising that women who complain about male intimidation or violence feel they are being placed on trial. They are. 'I feel like we were on trial. I felt like I was a criminal when I was up there [testifying]. Why should we have to defend ourselves?' stated one woman who was raped.[28]

In another example, a woman was driving back to a refuge for battered women. She was giving a lift home to three male friends, one of whom she had already dropped off. Her husband swerved his car, cutting the woman's car off, pulled her out of the car and began punching her about the head and face. Breaking away, the husband returned to his car and drove it toward her, narrowly missing her and driving through someone's garden instead. When she appeared in court the next day, her husband was sentenced to two weeks in prison. The judge, however, said to the woman, 'Running about in cars in the early hours of the morning with other men in the car is likely to attract the kind of response it did on this occasion.' He told the woman's lawyer to advise her not to behave like that again.[29] Could it be that the judge merely overlooked the fact that the woman had already fled from her husband to a shelter?

Even children are not immune to disparaging characterisations of their behaviour. In spring 1982, in Lancaster, Wisconsin, a Grant county circuit judge stated in sentencing a man to ninety days in a work release program for sexually assaulting the 5-year-old daughter of the woman with whom he lived:

> I am satisfied we have an unusually sexually promiscuous young lady [a 5-year-old child]. And he [the defendant] did not know enough to refuse. No way do I believe [the defendant] initiated sexual contact.[30]

Still, many contradictions exist in how women are treated by judges or juries. That the outcome of a trial cannot be predicted and that women anticipate their credibility to be of primary import in establishing men's intentions in a criminal act (when women themselves feel guilty that they should have anticipated the man's behaviour to be threatening or violent beforehand) significantly contributes to women's fear of the court and the trial process. The trial procedure is particularly upsetting because it is here that she confronts her assailant, endures cross-examination by a defence attorney, and experiences a publicly embarrassing and traumatic situation.[31] Frustrations caused by the slow-moving process, fed by the numerous delays in hearing court cases, merely add to the stress. Women's fear of court then takes its nourishment from the same ingredients as their fear of men's threatening, intimidating or violent behaviour on the street: women know that it is possible to have their account of their experience twisted around; the common strategies are all around them. When men are convicted of violence toward women, women are still not assured of their protection from male violence.

On 16 June 1983, a 42-year-old Oxford graduate lost his appeal against conviction of indecent assault. While holidaying on the Isle of Wight, England, he had made 'indecent or disgusting' advances to some young women on the beach. The judge remarked during the hearing, 'Pretty girls cannot go onto beaches and not expect to have advances made towards them. But they should not be violent or threatening advances.'[32] How did the judge make distinctions between 'expected' and 'violent' advances? We don't know. (If we were to rely on women's word, fewer men would probably be on the beach.)

One such place where distinction is made between 'expected' and 'violent' male behaviour is at rape trials. When men are convicted of rape at trial, often these rapists are portrayed as 'sexual maniacs'. The rapist – ski-masked, lustful, uncontrollable – is seen as a sexual deviant. (The fact that few of these rapists are ever considered to be 'sexually dangerous' within the prison system and thus sent to facilities for the sexually dangerous is always curious. Most convicted rapists who receive prison sentences serve time in regular prisons.)

The stereotype of the maniac allows the normal male to be separated from the abnormal male. For instance, on 19 May 1983, a judge in London sentenced a rapist to fourteen years in prison, telling him he represented a 'real danger to women'.

'There is no evidence of mental instability,' stated the judge. 'You were motivated by lust and desire, backed up by a determination to get your way. You represent a real danger to women. You will be kept off the streets until you are older and can control your lust.' The judge added: 'You stand convicted of four separate attacks on women, carried out by you without mercy and carried out at night at a time when you were armed with a knife and

acting as a nocturnal prowler looking for women to rape or rob.
You must have terrorised women in and around Mitcham and
Wandsworth.'[33]

The multiple attacks against strangers separate this rapist from normal
men; the rapist rapes strangers, not women he knows.

In another example, a convicted rapist's defence rested on the basis
that his idea to rape was fostered by 'sex horror videos'. These videos
suggested that if a woman was raped she was likely to fall in love
with her assailant during the ordeal – a typical male myth about the
conquering ability of male sexuality. (The same theme, by the way,
was incorporated into one of the most popular soap operas on
American TV.) The rapist was described by his defence counsel as

> emotionally immature and a glue sniffer. He feared he was
> unattractive to women. He had a history of burglary and when
> he broke into the housewife's home, his 'fantasies' were inflamed
> when he saw her emerge from having a bath wearing only a dressing
> gown.[34]

The judge made no comment about movies which portray such images
of women – only that this young man had not learned to control
himself in a world that, in effect, encourages otherwise. But this man
had a criminal record as additional 'proof' of his deviant status; he
also was in the process of burgling the raped woman's home. A
husband who rapes his wife, similarly 'inflamed' by a sex horror video,
would be able to carry on his 'normal' sexual aggression unheeded.
Diana Russell's US study of wife rape indicates that 21 per cent of
women who reported being raped by husbands also reported that their
husbands tried to do things to them that they had seen in pornographic
pictures, movies or books; one in ten of all women who responded to
Russell's survey answered that they were subjected to some form of
'upsetting' sexual experimentation prompted by pornography.[35]
Throughout Britain and in most US states, married men cannot be
held 'criminally' responsible for such behaviour to their wives.

Rapists who carry out a series of rapes against women unknown to
them are more likely to be considered 'real dangers' to women. They
are, however, still portrayed as acting out of natural sexual aggression
rather than out of anger toward or a hatred of women.[36] As one judge
said to a convicted man who, in the course of a burglary attempted
to rape and indecently assault a woman and her 14-year-old daughter,

'You must have the sex drive of a Don Juan.'[37] Abnormality, it seems, arises when men assault women unknown to them and are sexually uncontrolled. Though, of course, establishing women's provocation in the situation of stranger rape is not an improbability.

When 'truly dangerous' men are convicted of violence against women, the legal system is credited for the ability to protect women from such 'maniacs'. When, for example, Peter Sutcliffe, the 'Yorkshire Ripper', was convicted for murdering thirteen women and attempting to murder seven others, many reacted to his conviction by praising the legal system which 'brought to justice' this clearly dangerous man. Sutcliffe began his reign of terror in the summer of 1975, savagely beating a woman with a knife and hammer in Keighley, West Yorkshire. Another woman, attacked six weeks later, survived as well. Both these attacks were classified by the police to be Ripper attacks two years later. Six years later, another attack on a 14-year-old girl, which occurred immediately after the first attack, was reclassified as a Ripper attack. Sidetracked, the police believed the Yorkshire Ripper to only have a vendetta against prostitutes, his subsequent three murdered women. Adopting the approach that the Ripper only wanted to kill prostitutes, implying the 'understandable' nature of this hatred, police turned Sutcliffe into a modern-day Jack the Ripper. Thought by police to have made a 'mistake' at one point when he killed a woman police described as 'innocent, perfectly respectable', Sutcliffe's reign of terror began to erode the legal system's rhetoric of protection. All women, however, clearly knew they were at risk; after all, on the street at night, all women look alike.

Arrested in January 1981, Sutcliffe, interviewed by the police no less than nine times over six years, confessed to being the Yorkshire Ripper. The West Yorkshire police constable, anxious to re-establish the waning credibility of the ability of the legal system to protect women, held a press conference two days after Sutcliffe was arrested for a motor vehicle violation to announce that they were 'absolutely delighted' with the developments in the case.

Over the next five and a half months, the criminal justice apparatus moved to put to rest, once and for all, women's fear of attack which had developed throughout northern England. It did so with assumptions not dissimilar to those of the pursuant police, not unlike those found within the explanation of men's violent behaviour used throughout many of the examples reviewed thus far.

The twists in the adversarial approach to the Sutcliffe trial are also interesting. Acting on behalf of the prosecution, Sir Michael Havers, Attorney General for England and Wales – the highest law officer in the land – struck a pre-trial bargain with the defence. Sutcliffe would plead guilty to the seven attempted murders, and not guilty to the murder of the thirteen women. Instead, he would plead to manslaughter on the grounds of his diminished responsibility. Sutcliffe had stated that he was acting on a 'divine mission' to kill prostitutes. But the judge rejected the plea.

So began the trial, where the grounds for proving Sutcliffe's sanity, in large part, rested in demonstrating the 'understandable' motive of women's provocativeness. Spurned by one prostitute, 'given a rough time after his marriage', the underlying sexual component of his murders was argued by Sir Michael as indicating a possible motivating force behind Sutcliffe's desire to seek revenge against women. As Sutcliffe himself stated, 'I realise now I had an urge to kill any woman.' The trial, carefully monitored by members of the press around the world, exonerated the legal system from its responsibility for protecting women against Sutcliffe.[38] Equally important, it served as a mechanism for reinforcing a male point of view about men's violence toward women. 'Wanting to kill a woman' seems like such a natural response in a world which encourages the thinking that women are men's provocateurs.

So while the defence tried to prove Sutcliffe was insane – acting on behalf of a divine mission to attack unrespectable women – the prosecution tried to prove his sanity by showing how over his life he could understandably be provoked by women, women who rendered him powerless, frustrated, emasculated and therefore he could develop understandably, but not insanely, a wish to kill women. The sanity argument 'won'; ten to two, Sutcliffe was convicted by the jury of murdering the thirteen women. He is currently serving a sentence of life imprisonment. There have already been attempts to have him moved to a prison facility for the criminally insane.

It is unlikely that Sutcliffe's conviction removes women's fear about walking the streets after dark. As one writer reminds us, women coming forward with information to Yorkshire police were women turning in their husbands and brothers as possible suspects.[39]

Across the Atlantic, in the United States in July 1979, another man, Ted Bundy, was convicted of murdering two women and brutally assaulting and attempting to murder three others. He is suspected of murdering an additional thirty-three women across the country. A college graduate with some legal training, Bundy is a fast-talking charmer. All of the murdered women were young, one only 14; many were sexually assaulted, all were savagely beaten. He, like Sutcliffe, told detectives that he 'had the desire to do great bodily harm to females'. His trial, televised from Florida with Bundy himself assisting his own defence, focused solely on circumstantial evidence and the forensic evidence: a bite mark on the buttocks of one of the murdered women. In one evening, Bundy had attacked in no less than two locations, one a sorority house, bludgeoning five women in all, two of whom died and two of whom were sexually assaulted. The women, portrayed as innocent, helpless 'victims' (they all had been sleeping at the time), did not contribute to their fate; Bundy however was portrayed as a savage beast. But his façade was smooth; he did not appear to be a beast. Five years earlier, Bundy's name was submitted to police inquiries connected with similar murders in Washington State by at least two women who knew him, one his girlfriend. His ordinariness, his ability to create alibis left him to kill over those five years. When he was convicted, after only seven hours of jury deliberation, the focus turned to the forensic evidence – the bite mark – and the breakthrough in forensic science – matching the teeth marks on the murdered woman with those of Bundy. A book subsequently published by an acquaintance of Bundy describes the many murders and the bizarreness of their random nature. In it, the author dwells on the vulnerability of the murdered women: 'Something in the victims' lives had gone awry on the days they vanished, something that would tend to make them distracted, and therefore *easy* prey for a clever killer.'[40] A killer who can 'understandably' wish to murder women. Women who suspect that all male strangers might be killers are assumed to be paranoid.

Yet trials are rare occurrences in the criminal justice system. Typically, criminal cases are plea-bargained, and the bargaining takes place between prosecuting and defending attorneys. In situations of plea bargaining, the woman complainant generally would not have to give testimony. But this lack of control over decisions about how to handle the case means that the negotiation carried on is based on what is already known about the case and how other cases like it are handled.[41]

Not uncommonly, what is considered a serious life experience for the woman will merely be considered one of many cases handled by those in decision-making positions – police, attorneys, judges and so forth. As the state's witness, the woman testifying about male violence is essentially excluded from any determinations about the case. As outsiders to the criminal justice system, they are not likely to have much to do with their cases except to give testimony. Nor are they likely to be kept satisfactorily informed about their cases, or even the outcome, unless a sympathetic police officer informs them.

How a case is handled affects a woman's feelings about the whole criminal justice system.[42] Plea bargaining – standard practice within both American and British courts – effectively reduces the seriousness of a criminal offence upon the conviction of a defendant, in the eyes of the state and in the eyes of the complainant. One woman, infuriated when she found out that the American prosecutor agreed to drop the rape charge if the defendant pleaded guilty to a series of burglaries and robberies he had also committed, stated to the prosecutor:

> Are you telling me that after all I've gone through you're going to drop the charges? Do you know what an effect this has had on my life? Do you know what it's like to have two kids knowing that there are guys out there who do this, that there is a man out there who knows where I live? Do you know what it's like to walk down the street and want to break into a run when someone is behind you? You've lost something that can't be replaced. You've lost your freedom. They can return your property but they can't return your sense of security. I wake up at night scared. I can't enjoy myself. I used to love to go out. Now when the clock strikes 11 I get scared. All this has happened to me and now you're going to pretend it didn't happen – that he robbed a few people. It's a lie. He raped me and he should pay for it.[43]

In England, in 1983, one judge stated in sentencing a convicted rapist to eight years in prison, 'Within the space of a week you subjected two women to frightening experiences. The sentence would have been considerably longer had you not pleaded guilty.'[44] Would those two frightened women feel more protected knowing that their rapist received a lighter sentence because he pleaded guilty?

Many women who have gone through the entire ordeal of the criminal justice system say that they would report a crime to the police again – it's the only game in town. But not all women would.[45] If we are to take the evidence of women's non-reporting of physical and/or sexual assault – much of this assault potentially criminal in nature – we must seriously question the assumption that the legal system serves as any protection for women against male violence. A trial occurs after the violent event and then treats women's credibility as a major target for defence strategy. Any claim that the criminal justice system protects women from male violence and male intimidation is empty rhetoric; it is part of criminal justice inquiry.

Yet we've only concentrated here on cases which reach the trial or plea-bargaining stage. What happens before that? How are women's complaints about male intimidation and violence handled by police and prosecutors, the forerunners of the criminal justice system? The next chapters address the work of these two gatekeepers to the trial procedure.

Chapter 9

Male violence, criminal violence

Discretion is the range of choice available to a person in authority.[1] It can be very narrow, almost non-existent, when the written rules and the actual supervision governing, for instance, a police officer's or a prosecutor's official actions are minutely detailed, when there is no space for multiple interpretations. But for most people in official positions – certainly for most members of the British and American criminal justice systems – there is considerable room for discretion. Laws are vague, ambiguous, open to interpretation. That vagueness, deliberately created, leaves space for official discretion.

In level upon level of bureaucracy, level upon level of discretionary authority within the criminal justice system, women face obstacles posed by traditional interpretations of male violence to them. As we saw in the last chapter, male-female interaction can be characterised as intimate interaction, potentially sexualised and therefore potentially violent, regardless of whether the parties are, in fact, living together or even known to each other. So characterised, physical and/or sexual assaults to women are assumed to be a natural extension of men's and women's relationships and/or a natural part of family life. These characterisations, though not insurmountable – indeed, some crime to women is fully prosecuted – direct the type of inquiry necessary to sort out criminal from non-criminal and serious from not-so-serious behaviour.

Decisions to arrest or not to charge a suspect with a crime, decisions to charge a suspect with 'disorderly conduct' rather than assault, or decisions to refer 'incidents' of male violent behaviour to the social services instead of the criminal court all affect how men's threatening or violent behaviour comes to be defined as criminal or non-criminal behaviour. Not all physical and/or sexual assaults on women reported to the police are defined as criminal behaviour; many are filtered out of the criminal justice system through a standard, but crucial, process of decision-making. During this decision making process, police and prosecutors sort 'real' crime from the wide range of complaints they receive from citizens about potentially criminal behaviour.

Here, even before a woman's complaint reaches the court, real rape is separated from 'rough sex', assault from 'family quarrels'. As the front-running officials of the criminal justice process, then, police and prosecutors' actions mould what constitutes criminal behaviour. Questioning women's behaviour – a standard way of establishing the seriousness of men's criminal behaviour – is a routine aspect of police and prosecutorial inquiry in cases of male violence to women. It is also important: the probability of successfully gaining a conviction at trial would be reduced if the man's behaviour could be characterised as normal, not criminal or 'seriously' criminal. What jury, for example, would convict a man for participating in 'rough sex' or in a 'family quarrel'?

Police and prosecutors rely on their own common sense about men's behaviour toward women to assist them in their decision making.[2] They also learn from on-the-job experience what kinds of cases are likely to be successfully prosecuted. As they achieve competence as decision makers they arrive at choices of action 'without special attention or thought'.[3] Questioning women's behaviour, therefore, is essential to the task of determining which cases of male violence a jury would believe also involve criminal violence. Guiding police and prosecutor determinations is the trial. Albeit a rare occurrence, it is the standard against which the success or failure of prosecution decisions ultimately rests. With finite resources and overworked personnel, the chances are risky, time-consuming, and unrewarding.[4] Sure 'bets' counteract risk. One sure bet is to rely upon traditional thinking about women and men's behaviour toward them, a convenient assistant in the whittling down of the large number of complaints which come pouring into limited resources. A traditional (male) point of view about male violence provides information about a judge's and jury's reaction to a woman's complaint.[5] If, for example, women are assumed to be provoking or deserving of male violence, male defendants charged with these offences are less likely to be convicted than defendants charged with assaulting 'innocent' women. As complainants, then 'deserving' women are less likely to bring rewards to police or prosecutors' efforts than are innocent women. Whether police or prosecutors personally believe women deserve or provoke male violence is irrelevant (although far too many in fact do believe this); women's complaints – those which police or prosecutors feel are 'understandable' male behaviour – too easily fit unchallenged within traditional assumptions about male violence to women.

Discretionary decisions of police and prosecutors, then, embrace a traditional viewpoint about men's violence toward women. Regardless of law or criminal procedure in both the United States and in Britain, discretionary application of the law is just part of the job. The fifty-one different criminal penal codes in the US, the two different criminal processes in Britain (England and Wales, and Scotland) might lead one to believe that the process of criminal justice decision-making differs. (It differs even within one jurisdiction: the state of New York, for example, has sixty-two counties within it.) Most certainly, personalities and politics combine to create varying approaches to criminal justice processing. In both countries, police are empowered to arrest and control the first step in the criminal justice process. In the US and Scotland, all prosecutorial decisions, whether to prosecute a suspect for an offence after arrest, under what charge and in which court, are made by individuals independent of the police: district attorneys in the US and procurator fiscals in Scotland; they are trained lawyers. In England and Wales, only 'serious' cases are forwarded to the Director of Public Prosecutions for determination about the merits of prosecution; but there is already discussion about establishing a separate system of prosecution. In some English jurisdictions, for example, police now seek the advice of solicitors in their prosecution decisions.[6] Figure 9.1 illustrates some important decision-making junctions along the criminal justice process. From the time a woman picks up the telephone or walks into the police station to complain about male violence – which we know from Part I is contrary to encouraged practice, silence – up to the time of the trial proceeding itself, police and prosecutors focus on how a woman's complaint fits into the wider scheme of things.

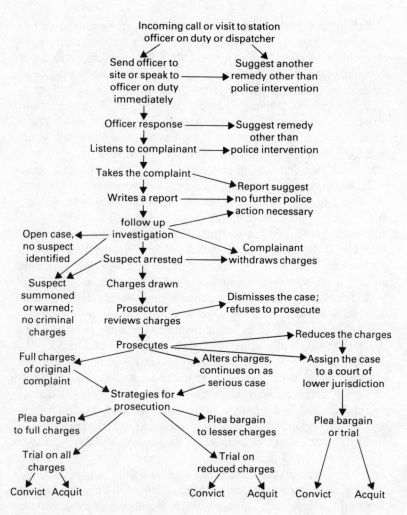

Figure 9.1: Key junctures of criminal justice decision-making

Policing male violence

As the front line in the operation of the criminal justice system, police have the greatest contact with crime, criminals, complainants and all citizens. As early as 1829 in England and 1840 in the United States, police, as part of a formal organisation, walked the streets. Originally concerned with 'keeping the peace', police work theoretically involved quelling disturbances, protecting property, and maintaining order; these tasks continue to be the primary duties of the police – they are tasks oriented to the problems of *public*, not domestic order.

Arresting 'criminals', thought by citizens to be the *most* important function of police, takes the *least* amount of time in today's police forces.[7] While citizens envision police as concentrating on the capture of criminals, they also expect individual police officers to respond to all kinds of disturbances, disputes, queries, and sundry calls for assistance. In just a single eight-hour tour of duty, a patrol officer might mediate a dispute between a landlord and tenant, assist a pregnant woman to the hospital, stop a car for running a red light, take a complaint about burglary, give directions to lost motorists, search a house for suspect prowlers, and take a lost dog to the pound. Much of what police do today is a result of citizens taking the initiative, phoning the police.

Police are, essentially, a twenty-four-hour response system.[8] Authority for intervention is backed by the readily available coercive power of arrest. Calling the police is to a large extent calling forth that authority. Whether a woman dials the emergency number, 999, or phones her local police station or stationhouse, she initiates a series of police assessments concerning the nature of her complaint. The 'dispatcher', who can be either a police officer or a civilian, male or female, takes the call and asks the woman why she is calling. Police dispatchers receive calls, decide what, if any, additional information to ask for, determine whether police assistance is required, and how and when an officer will be sent to the scene. Upon hearing a woman's reason for calling, a dispatcher searches his/her own categories of police responsibility and the type of response appropriate to each. This process by which dispatchers categorise incoming calls goes on twenty-four hours a day in little villages and large city police stations or stationhouses. It is a totally unremarkable process. Yet it is decisive in determining whether violence against women is taken seriously.

Imagine a woman calling the police to say there is a 'fight going on in the street'. The dispatcher might immediately send a police officer to the scene stating that there is an 'assault in progress on such-and-such street' or might report it as a 'disturbance' or a 'dispute' and assign an officer to the scene when one becomes available. These two descriptions will trigger quite different responses – in speed, mental attitude, numbers of officers sent to the scene and so forth. Various bits of information contribute to the way the dispatcher chooses to translate the information the caller provides into descriptions of circumstances which have meaning for the task of policing. The 'fight on the street', for instance, may happen in front of a pub notorious among local police for fights. On the contrary, the fight may occur on what local police and the dispatcher in particular imagines to be a 'respectable' street, where fights rarely, if ever, come to police attention. This additional information may come from the dispatcher's explicit questioning of the caller or it may come out of the mental cosmology police carry around in their heads, the product of job experience and familiarity with the local area.[9] It provides a context for the dispatcher and will in turn be passed on to the officer responding to the call.

'Dispatch information' is considered to be key information by the police officer. (There has in the past for instance been resistance on the part of the police when civilians took over the posts of dispatchers. The civilians, the police argued, did not know what it was like to be police and work the street and would be likely to give them faulty information when dispatching assignments to them.) Given a large range of possible circumstances for similar types of events – such as 'fights, 'disputes', or 'disturbances' – the police officer relies on the dispatcher to provide her/him with the necessary information to handle the call, safely and with appropriate haste. The type of call could require a speedy response, one accompanied by flashing lights and sirens, or could warrant being lined up in the queue awaiting police response when time allows. It depends on whether the dispatcher sees the call as either crucial or mundane.

Research indicates that dispatch information provides more than merely information on the type of circumstances to which the officer is responding. It also provides the police officer with the likely parameters of response. If the dispatcher describes the call as one in which the police officer is likely to discover 'criminal' behaviour, broadcasting an 'assault' rather than a 'disturbance' in progress, the officer is more likely to take the call as one requiring an immediate response, as well as a cue to a possible arrest resulting from that response. Moreover, describing a call as a possible criminal complaint brings forth the police's favourite self-image: that of the crime fighter. (The 'crime-fighting' stereotype is the one many of us know: police*men* are the pursuers of evil. To police, matters other than crime fighting are not considered 'real' police work, even though they tend to take up the bulk of the street patrol officers' time. The entire organisation of policing, moreover, is itself geared to fighting 'serious' crime. Efforts to launch 'war' on crime, 'crackdowns' on notorious burglars or robbers periodically receive publicity. The day-in and day-out complaints – those considered worthy enough to record as criminal events – are merely counted, compiled, and presented as representing the 'crime problem'. So too are arrest figures. Clear-up or clearance rates – the proportion of arrests to reported crime – supposedly measure the police effectiveness in the crime-fighting task. [In fact, these rates are generally quite low.] Police officers generally see 'arrests' as a measure of effective police performance and as the sort of action which earns them prestige, perhaps even promotions, within the police organisation. In the role of mediator, the police officer stereotype is changed to that of provider of service, not crime fighter, and is less likely to bring prestige and promotion than the work of the crime fighter.)

Not surprisingly in situations involving violence against women, there is no doubt that some special categories of dispatch information exist. The most notable is that of the 'domestic disturbance', a category which in the majority of cases means a woman being beaten by a man who is an intimate. This category is important dispatch information for police for two reasons: it alerts the responding officer to possible danger ('domestic disturbance' calls, police say, are particularly dangerous);[10] it orients the role of the attending police officer to that of 'mediator'. Neither of which police like. In my own observations in a police dispatch room, one dispatcher tried to talk a woman out of complaining; during another call, a woman was asked if she and her assailant were still living together and then the dispatcher suggested she speak to a lawyer. Dispatchers can, even before a woman hangs up the phone, begin the process of diverting battering – 'domestic disputes' – away from police intervention.[11] When these calls are passed on to street patrol, the patrol officer is likely to adopt a standard attitude toward 'domestic disputes': they are dangerous, thankless tasks that do no good anyway. (That is partially true. As we know from Part I, some battered women are trapped in battering situations for years. Police intervention is unlikely to reverse the other pressures on women to stay. Limited resources, unavailability of housing, emotional ties are all strong barriers to a woman's escape.) *None the less, in instances of acute violence, police intervention is crucial – a woman's life depends on it.* In the widely cited Kansas City study, researchers found that in instances of spouse homicide and aggravated assault (in most instances wife battering and murder), police had been to the address where the incident occurred for 'disturbance' calls in 85 per cent of the cases at least once and in 54 per cent of the cases five times or more.[12] What do police *do* when they get there?

Police officers have wide discretion in their handling of citizen calls: they decide whether there is a 'valid' complaint, whether to consider the matter minor or serious in nature, whether to write it up or report it, whether to investigate the matter and so forth. At any point a citizen's complaint could reach a point where the complaint goes no farther. On the other hand, the police could take the complaint as a serious one, and if a suspect could be identified and located, use their power of arrest. Once receiving an assignment from the dispatcher, a street patrol officer, the lowest-ranking officer in the police force, proceeds to a location – the home of the complainant, a street corner, a hospital – with some information about what to expect. Upon arriving, the officer knows he or she must assess the situation and determine what, if any, further involvement police will have in this particular incident.

In order to have a complaint defined as appropriate for police intervention, it must be defined by the officer as a criminal matter. All other matters, even situations with similar circumstances, are, for all intents and purposes, considered 'service-related' calls. It is important to note here the special dimension of police peer solidarity. The everyday working environment establishes a solidarity among police officers, often reinforcing typical patterns of responding to women's complaints. This solidarity emphasises mutual, male support, both on the job and off. What develops among police officers is a range of similar assessments about what constitutes 'legal' and 'illegal' behaviour, particularly men's behaviour toward women. These assessments are not the actual definitions of legal and illegal found written in the statutes, but informal procedures learned over time.[13] (Rookies, inexperienced police officers, for example, regard the written statute more closely than veteran officers.) As part of learning the job, police learn the informal way of responding to behaviour on the street, as well as in the situations to which they are summoned. And that response means learning the variety of ways so-called illegal events occur 'naturally', and are not regarded as ones requiring intervention of the police. So too many of the cultural meanings of police work itself are based on notions of masculinity and male behaviour. 'Crime fighting', as noted previously, reinforces the ideology of the masculine pursuit of 'serious' crime.[14] Male solidarity, then, presents yet another barrier to women complaining about male violence.

In the task of doing everyday police work, much of police activity revolves around finding simple categories for complex situations.[15] In responding to calls for assistance, strategies develop around these simple categories and their response strategy follows from there. Male violence to female intimates is one such complex category which is 'simply' slotted as a 'domestic dispute' or a 'family matter'. US research on police responses to 'domestic disputes' reveals a police strategy of quieting down any ongoing disturbance and avoiding arrests.[16]

Raymond Parnas's 1972 study identified four basic police strategies: 'talking out' the dispute, threatening all parties and then leaving, asking one of the parties to leave the premises, or (rarely) making an arrest. The reasons stated for using these non-arrest strategies are: the woman is unlikely to have her assailant arrested but wanted police intervention to stop acute violence or provide some authority to 'cool out' the situation; the woman needs the financial support of her assailant and therefore cannot afford to have him arrested; the woman feels her assailant's behaviour is her problem – a private matter – and it just got out of hand this time and scared her; the assailant may harm the woman more if he is arrested; the woman usually changes her mind later and drops the charges; the chances of the case actually being processed further are nil; if prosecuted, sentences are lenient; or family matters are not the realm of police work.[17] The sheer number of justifications for non-arrest strategies means that the likelihood that this type of complaint will advance to the next stage in the criminal justice process, the arrest stage, is quite low.

Even if police intervention in wife battering is sympathetic and helpful, few physical assaults are defined as criminal assaults. In both Britain and the United States, *all* research *clearly* indicates that police characterise wife battering as a non-criminal matter.[18] The 'helpful' mode of intervention follows what is termed a 'conciliatory' mode, essentially a cooling out of the situation. But even this 'conciliatory' invention is only available to certain segments of the population. Black and lower-class individuals (assailants and complainants) receive more coercive police treatment and less active conciliatory efforts than whites and middle-class persons.[19] This places women who are black or lower-class in even more untenable situations. In instances of acute violence – life-threatening situations – women of colour or of lower-class status might hesitate to involve police, fearing the response of the police as they fear the attacks of their assailants. One woman reported the following incident:

My cousin came in. He was in a real state about something. He had a knife. He grabbed me and the baby and held the knife to my throat. I was terrified. I didn't know what was going on with him. He's a lot bigger than me. Not that I'm small as you can see. My sister came in next. He started screaming at her. She was terrified and called the police hoping they'd come and make him see sense. Then my brother arrived. He started shouting at my cousin to give up the knife. Then the police arrived. Not the local one, but I think it was the riot police. They came barging in, about 12 of them and started smashing the place up. They did not ask what was going on or nothing. They arrested my cousin, my brother and my sister. They nearly arrested me as well. As if there'd be riots at 4.00 p.m. inside a house. That's what happens when we want the police to calm someone down, they send the riot squad. They're really stupid. The case is next week and we've got a solicitor. They really made a mess of the house. They really wrecked it. They had riot shields and everything. All we wanted was someone to calm him down. I know that it wouldn't have happened if we were white. We are all really angry about the police.[20]

If police do make an arrest in a domestic situation, it is most likely to be because their own authority was challenged, not because of the actions of the assailant toward his wife.[21] Arrest, however, is rarely used in the responses of police in both the United States and Britain. England's Women's Aid, the network of shelters for battered women, found in a study published in 1981 of the interviewed women who suffered severe assaults – life-threatening attacks such as attempted strangulation, drowning or an attack resulting in hospitalisation – that only one in five men had been arrested and charged.[22] Research indicates that American standards for injury in 'domestic' assaults require more severe injuries than assaults by so-called strangers.[23] The 'six-stitch' rule' (not arresting unless severe injury requires stitches) is also evident within 'victim compensation schemes', programmes in which those injured by criminal violence can be given monetary compensation. The scheme in England and Wales, for example, requires twice the minimum amount of injury (£500) for individuals injured by household members.[24] It is no wonder that when homicides and serious assaults occur, in the vast majority of cases they occur in households police have 'visited' before.

In Frances Wasoff's 1980 study in Edinburgh, one officer spoke to her about his impressions of 'domestic assaults'. His comments about the following case focus on the internal constraints of policing:

I think all she wanted was to get him out of the house. Because obviously she's quite frightened of him. I think I would say she's probably been assaulted by him in the past, and I attended there about a month ago, [it] was just identical. They'd had an argument as to who was to look after the child and he decided that he was going to take the child back to his mother's. She didn't want him to; she alleges that a lawyer's told her that he can't take the child because of its age but she's got nothing in writing regarding this. She says that she's waiting on it coming through the post. [Reply to query on the type of report on this to be submitted.] None whatsoever, so that's it. Probably [it will] come back to the station. If it had been a 999 call there would have been a half dozen words written on the treble nine book, probably say, 'man ejected' or something, 'man ejected from the house', 'matter resolved' or something. She alleges that she has been assaulted but there is no evidence at all to back it up. His conduct didn't amount to a breach of the peace, [at least] in front of us.

Most of these things really are quite unsatisfactory from the wife's point of view, because, I would say, you're 90 per cent certain that you know there has been an assault, but your hands are tied really, there's no evidence whatsoever. Well, as far as we're concerned that's a satisfactory end. Well, if we were to put everything on paper, all these things on paper we just wouldn't have time. We just haven't got time. We haven't got time to attend to the calls let alone write things about them.

It's only as a last resort [arrest]. It's quite unsatisfactory, but I
would say really it's a marriage guidance counsellor they want
rather than the police in most of these cases.[25]

Not surprisingly, stereotypes about women – that they are masochistic,
'asking for' or 'deserving' their battering – also surface during police
intervention. Studies in both the US and Britain confirm that even
when confronted with severe violence, police still produce these stereotypes. In 1976, the New York City Police Department was sued for
its policy in handling domestic disputes by seventy-one battered
women who had been 'repeatedly and violently threatened, harassed,
assaulted, beaten, and brutalized by their husbands, in clear and
absolute violation of the laws of [New York] state.' 'Throughout their
marriage,' the legal brief in Bruno v. Codd stated, 'these women have
been slapped, punched and kicked by their husbands, in the head and
all over their bodies. . . . They have been struck and beaten with fists,
chairs, pots, ropes, bats, hammers, wrenches and iron bars.' One
woman claimed that when a police officer responded to her call for
help, he said to her assailant, 'Well, maybe if I slap my wife around
a couple of times she might behave too.' The lawsuit, settled out of
court on the agreement that police would intervene in domestic crisis
situations, still leaves the decisions on how to handle situations firmly
to the discretion of street patrol officers. Across the states in Oakland,
California, a similar suit was filed. Scott v. Hart (1976) challenged
the no-arrest procedures of the Oakland Police Department. As of
1982, police are distributing information to battered women when they
respond to domestic disturbance calls and have made a commitment to
treat domestic assault like other offences. However, the on-the-job
pressures remain similar to those which existed in 1976.[26]

Is there any evidence of 'effective' police intervention? Only tent-
ative results from a 1982 US Police Foundation study indicate that
arrest might be a deterrent to future violence. Preliminary findings,
the research team concludes, point to 'all other things being equal,
police should arrest suspects for simple domestic assault rather than
sending them out of the residence, or even (perhaps) advising the
couple.' 'Arresting most suspects of domestic assault may reduce the
likelihood of the suspect repeating that violence,'[27] the report added.
But as masters of discretionary decision making, police are unwilling
to be told when to use the power to arrest. Other aspects of policing
– that of the self-image of the crime fighter, the masculine peer

solidarity, and the shared stereotypes about women – encourage police to avoid using arrests in domestic violence situations. In addition, if police predict the outcome of an arrest, they predict a 'no complaint'. Police often assume that women, once her assailant has been arrested, will have second thoughts and drop the charges. Research evidence contradicts this assumption. In a 1983 US study, only 7.1 per cent of women refused to initiate criminal proceedings at the stage of police intervention; over 60 per cent eventually signed formal complaints at police stations later.[28] But predicting that all women will drop charges excludes women's complaints from the system. In Scotland, of the 933 cases examined by the Dobashs, only 6 per cent of women dropped the charges.[29] But the mythology lives on.

Day after day on the job, fed by traditional attitudes about male violence, coupled with constraints of time and resources, police are unlikely to gain any sympathetic understanding of men's violence to female intimates. Their own job safety, relationships with their fellow officers, frustration caused by the inability to prevent violence, and cynicism from the reactions of courts to the cases they forward for consideration for prosecution discourage creative approaches to inter-vention. All these factors together serve to create a great barrier for women who need access to police intervention in situations of *acute* violence. Not surprisingly, the number of police reports filed on male violence are only a minority of the reported incidents. Indeed, police officers are much more likely to make reports on property complaints (burglary or purse snatching) than on complaints of interpersonal violence. One US study showed that only 41 per cent of cases involving family members were filed as 'crimes', compared to 84 per cent filed in cases involving strangers[30] *Much of violence to women (incest, indecent assault, rape, battering) however, involves attacks, often repeated attacks, by men known to them.* Overall, in situations of violence among intimates – including instances of sexual violence, police presume an arrest will not 'solve' the problem of 'family dynamics', or problems in male-female intimacy. The result: few, if any, cases involving woman battering ever proceed to be considered for prosecution. One examina-tion of the processing of 'spousal assaults' found less than 10 per cent of incidents in which police intervened were ever forwarded for prosecution.[31]

While we have estimates of how many crimes are recorded by police, police and researchers alike assume that the most serious crimes about which citizens complain are verified as 'true' crimes:

they are recorded crimes.[32] Women's experiences of male violence question this assumption.[33]

If a record is taken by police of a woman's complaint or her assailant is arrested, then the criminal justice process begins to address the matter. For 'serious' crimes, the next stage in the decision-making process is the follow-up investigation conducted by detectives. Research on detective investigation indicates that few cases ever receive detailed, thorough investigation.[34] Like their uniformed colleagues on the street, detectives create strategies of handling typical incoming cases. Decisions about which cases to investigate often relate to practical considerations of clearing their caseloads. Certainly if a suspect can be identified, detective work is more straightforward. So too detectives apply their common sense to the priority of cases. In more 'serious' cases and cases involving complainants of 'special status' (famous people, beautiful women, a friend of a government official), detectives are likely to investigate straightaway.

There is no guarantee that, once recorded, a woman's complaint about male violence will proceed through the criminal justice system. Once investigated, detectives do eliminate complaints, ostensibly for 'police' reasons, but commonly for practical reasons. 'Unfounding' or 'no-criming' figures represent the complaints which detectives, upon investigation of patrol officers' reports, determine are not in fact 'criminal events'. These figures, in overall proportion to all reported crime, are generally quite low, usually less than 10 per cent.[35] However, for rape, the proportion is at least twice that.[36] For police, unfounding a woman's complaint is couched within presumptions that her allegations are false, indeed malicious. It seems from an important 1977 Canadian study by Loreen Clark and Debra Lewis that the unfounding of rape complaints reflects more an orientation toward internal, policing criteria for the kinds of cases police know result in successful convictions.[37] The founded cases – only 36.2 per cent of the total complaints of rape – display one or more of the following features:

1 The raped woman is a 'credible' witness; that is she is likely to be believed by a jury because she conforms to established norms of 'respectable', 'acceptable' female behaviour.
2 The facts of the case are so strong that a founded classification is unavoidable, e.g. when the woman was severely beaten.
3 The police are in a position to pursue the investigation actively

because the woman can name her attacker, or provide information about his whereabouts, place of residence or employment. (There are of course disadvantages here because of assumptions about male-female familiarity also including sexual familiarity.)

4 The police perceive a strong similarity between this particular case and others currently under investigation.

Clark and Lewis, after examining the unfounded complaints, suggest that only 10 per cent of the 63.8 per cent of the cases that police determined to be unfounded cases could be considered false allegations: the remaining 53.8 per cent of the cases were eliminated because of 'problems' in predicting outcome at trial. In England, of 384 cases of rape over a five-year period details of which were made available to Richard Wright, 92 or 23.9 per cent were determined by police to be unfounded. Wright could not determine how these decisions were made by police. In one case, for instance,

police officers discovered an immigrant woman and an Englishman having intercourse in a car park. The woman immediately complained to them of rape. The police classified this incident as 'No Crime' pointing out in their report that the woman probably alleged rape because she was embarrassed at being discovered in such compromising circumstances. What they did not mention (though the information was contained in the police records) was that the man and woman were found lying on a bed of broken glass and, according to the police surgeon's report, both had received several cuts.[38]

In Texas in 1982 Vicki McNickle Rose and Susan Carol Randall note that police decision making about sexual assault is rooted in guaranteeing successful convictions.[39] The most important feature in that guarantee is the raped woman. While investigators may not doubt whether an offence took place, the authors suggest, their suspicions of the woman's 'moral character', her complicity in the offence, her reasons for reporting the offence, or the likelihood that she will co-operate in the investigation and prosecution of the case' reduces the chances that a woman's complaint will be fully prosecuted. Factors such as the woman's age, occupation, marital status, race or ethnicity, and class also contribute to an assessment of a woman's overall credibility. Circumstances surrounding the rape and/or sexual assault –

the woman's relationship with the assailant, circumstances surrounding the rape incident, physical force and her resistance mould a composite of the woman's 'consent'.

Clearly, both these features fit firmly within characterisation of women in general, as provocative and deserving or innocent, chaste or unchaste. Not surprisingly, police use what has been termed the 'respectability' criteria to assess the legitimacy of a complaint and use their assessment to decide upon what follow-up actions seem appropriate.

> A respectable woman was brought to the detective office along with her roommate. The roommate had apparently encouraged the woman to report a 'rape' incident, but the woman seemed reluctant to do so. The detectives spent five hours trying to talk the woman into following through with her complaint and giving a written statement on it. The evidence was judged problematic by the detectives because the woman said she had willingly gone to the suspect's apartment, delayed reporting the matter, and taken two baths before a physical examination. The detectives decided to apprehend and charge the suspect, and willingly worked a continuous 16 hour period on this case, on behalf of a woman they characterized as 'naïve' and 'respectable' and in need of police assistance to develop and sustain the case.[40]

Those suspected of being 'unrespectable', who are seen as dishonest or, as some police say, are 'in need of attention', are treated much differently.

> They said I would have to take a lie detector test and that I had to have a doctor's examination and semen had to be found in me before they could swear out a warrant to go and look for the man. That's what the cop told me at the beginning of his interview of me when he didn't like me. Then at the end, when I was acting more friendly, more like a sweet little girl who had recently been raped and needed protection, he said, 'Well, we don't need a doctor's examination. We can go out and get this man.' I said, 'But I thought you said legally you had to have that as evidence?' and he said, 'Well, not necessarily. You see, this man could confess, and then we would have him.' Then I said, 'I'll take the lie detector test as soon as possible because you say that you can't go out looking for the man until the test has been

taken. When is the soonest time that you can schedule it?' He said, 'A week from today.'[41]

While many police would say that the above incident 'just wouldn't ever happen here like that', sexually assaulted women receive all sorts of treatment from police ranging from polite to abusive treatment. Police treatment, like male behaviour, is unpredictable.

Not uncommonly, police direct their anger toward women who they believe easily lodge false complaints about sexual assault – those unchaste women. Inevitably, in any discussions of sexual assault or rape, police mention examples of false complaints they have handled in the course of their police careers. Those complaints, while they require filtering out of the system, are often held up as the way all women are likely to behave: that is, 'hysterical' women tend to imagine attacks; 'vindictive' women maliciously fabricate attacks; 'cheating' women report rape rather than admit to having affairs; 'young' women cry rape out of fear of spoiling their reputations. A few women do allege rape when rape did not occur; I would be wrong to state that there are never false allegations. Yet false allegations of rape are referred to by many British and American police as common occurrences. The 1983 study by Gerry Chambers and Ann Millar of sexual assault investigation in Scotland attributes the overall attitude of 'police scepticism' to their feelings about false complaints. (In this study, 22 per cent of sexual assault complaints were said to be unfounded by police.) Said one detective inspector, 'About 1 in 20 complaints are "real rapes" and all the rest are wee girls in a gang bang.' Another detective remarked:

> Yes, it's [false complaints] really common. I've only dealt with *one like that myself where it came to a court case.* The woman was done for wasting police time, she accused someone when in fact it hadn't happened; but it's fairly common especially these days; you get married women and they go out with blokes, they go back and tell their man the story: they're almost obliged to go and say they've been raped. That sort of thing happens.[42]

The contempt expressed by police toward the woman who 'falsely' complains about rape spills over into their questioning of all rape complainants. Given that few rape cases ever get to court, it seems this hostility is more rooted in the stereotypes of women who 'easily' make complaints of rape: women somehow have the power to put any innocent man behind bars. As part of stereotypes about women, then, any women could potentially lie about rape. As research in the US, Canada, Scotland, and England indicates, police use their own category of 'unfounded' to mean 'false complaint'. To the contrary, the 'unfounded' category reflects police use of 'respectability' recipes (ingredients: stereotypes about women) for predicting successful trial outcomes, effectively undermining a significant proportion of women's accounts of their experiences about rape and sexual assault, and creating an atmosphere of scepticism about all women's complaints about rape and sexual assault.

Intentionally or unintentionally, police act as a second assailant to women. The Chambers and Millar study in Scotland reports women's feelings about police treatment. While 40 per cent of the complainants thought police had done a 'good job' of the investigation, 81 per cent of the women replied that they had found one or more of the investigations stressful.[43] Clearly the police felt it was their duty to 'grill' a woman about her story:

> Don't get me wrong. I don't try and dissuade girls from making such a complaint but I think it's only fair to point out to them what's liable to be thrown at them in the witness box. In fact, it's going to be alleged that she was more than willing and only because he got his way was she screaming rape in case she got pregnant or something like this.[44]

When the woman is badly beaten, bruised or otherwise sustains additional physical injuries than 'just' rape, police are much more likely to believe her story.[45] So too police have assumptions about how raped women should respond: they should be hysterical, tearful, and show signs of resistance. Without resistance, the woman's account is suspect. Women themselves assess the police response according to how they feel police respond to them. In two following examples, we can see that police response to reports of indecent exposure are treated differently by the same police force:

> I was much comforted and calmed by their [the police] behaviour. I was not made to feel it was a trivial incident or a waste of their time. The seriousness with which it was handled was most important.

> They were not bothered, very disinterested. They took a statement and they followed it up two months later with a visit from the

vice squad. They wanted a better description. They asked if he had a beard.[46]

But women, even if treated politely by the police, do not know whether their complaints will be taken seriously by the police, that is, whether they will be investigated.

> There were three linked occurrences of indecent exposure/indecent assault that had occurred over several weeks in the elevators of an apartment complex. The same offender was believed to be responsible for all occurrences, but four months had elapsed since the first occurrence without any apprehension of a suspect. Following initial interviews with the women, detectives did nothing in relation to these occurrences until a 'rape' incident was reported in a private area of an apartment residence located two blocks from the one where the indecent exposures/indecent assaults had repeatedly occurred.[47]

We already know that women are not likely to inform police about male violence. And when police are informed, many of their complaints go no further than their own doorsteps. Complaints of rape, unfounded, never find their way into official statistics (one questionnaire distributed to police surgeons in Britain suggests that roughly three to five times more rape complaints are seen by them as end up in the annual statistics).[48] Complaints of incest, as the literature describes, are more likely to be referred to social service agencies; battered women, if they are lucky, are referred by police to the few women's agencies addressing their needs. But on the whole, just as women's complaints of employment discrimination or educational discrimination have not resulted in major upheaval of the system that maintains gender distinctions, too many of women's complaints about male violence never find themselves considered among the ranks of 'real' crime. Those few who are forwarded to the next stage, the decision to prosecute, meet another set of critics – the prosecutors.

Prosecuting male violence

After the police have decided to arrest a suspect, the next stage in the criminal justice process involves decisions about prosecution. In separating the prosecution function from the police function, the decision to charge provides an additional independent assessment of the 'usefulness' of bringing a particular suspect before the court. Whether a suspect will be charged, what the nature of the charge will be, which court will see the suspect, and which prosecution strategy will prevail within the assumed adversarial process are all prosecutorial concerns.[49]

Just as police determinations affect the tenor of the criminal justice process, so too do these prosecutorial decisions. Prosecutors are under no obligation to fully prosecute any particular case; they focus on the supposed 'legalities' of the case, orienting the process of inquiry into a criminal incident away from what-happened-at-the-scene to what-will-happen-in-court.[50] Efficiency – the administrative goal of prosecutors – is enhanced by early decision-making about cases coming across their desks. Having a wide range of choices, ranging from dismissing the case to full prosecution, prosecutors orchestrate courtroom activity, selecting only the most 'serious' of cases for the higher court and disposing of other cases through the lower courts or, alternatively, diverting them elsewhere, to social services for instance.

In sifting through the evidence, prosecutors search for potentially weak spots in the state's case. Eliminating 'weak' cases or those inappropriate for processing in the criminal justice system – for instance, those cases involving individuals with long histories of mental illness which might be, prosecutors state, best dealt with through social services – allows the prosecutors to concentrate on supposedly 'serious' matters while taking care not to overload the system with unnecessary work. Thus administrative concerns, along with concerns for the 'needs' of the 'community', are other functions prosecutors perform. Scrutiny into the legal basis for prosecution – is there sufficient evidence? was the evidence correctly obtained? – fits together with the prosecutor's measures for competence – will the case be successful in court and result in the conviction of the defendant? – and with the role of the prosecutor in determining the 'community's' needs for protection against particular types of criminal behaviour.

Theoretically, prosecutors are strapped with two sets of directives in addition to their task as legal advisors. First, as the state's representatives in legal decision-making about criminal events, prosecutors must be aware of the 'need of the community' to be protected from various types of criminal behaviour. In their capacity as community protector, moreover, prosecutors have an obligation to protect the rights of both the complainant and the suspect, no minor juggling act.

Yet all these textbook considerations take place within the rather routine context of prosecution. Often mundane, the context of the 'community' is generally a taken-for-granted one, one which the prosecutor, with the common knowledge gleaned from living in the community, rarely considers.

It is the bureaucratic, administrative function, the second directive, which, as many studies have documented, often dictates the form of decisions prosecutors make.[51] There is an overwhelming need to keep cases moving through a system which is already known for its laboriously slow manner. Saving time, increasing efficiency, eliminating unnecessary tasks, in effect 'streamlining justice', have become a major, if not a number one priority for today's prosecutors. Cases which have at least a 50 per cent chance of being successfully prosecuted are more likely to be kept amongst the ranks of the most 'serious' cases than cases with less predicted probability of success.

Merging the goal of efficiency with the legal goal of protecting the community gives a unique twist to prosecutorial decisions. More precisely, it welds the rhetoric of protection to the measure of success. Prosecutors publicly claim that their goals of efficiency link directly to efforts to get the most dangerous criminals removed from the streets. 'Tough on crime' read posters for some of the campaigns of American prosecutors, who, unlike their British counterparts, are elected to office. Both American and British prosecutors rely on successful conviction records to underscore their role as a community protectorate; the very credibility of the system rests on their ability to achieve success. And as any organisation does in order to assure that what they produce demonstrates success, prosecutors pick and choose cases which are most likely to bring them success.

Commonly known as 'screening' in the US and 'marking' in Scotland, initial prosecutorial determinations, similar to police decisions to report a complaint, play an important role in the processing of a case, and for that matter, in limiting the later workload for the prosecutors themselves. 'If you put the wrong charge or draft it badly, you usually suffer at the end of the day for it,' said one Scottish procurator fiscal. 'It's the substance of our courtwork and if it isn't given the consideration it should be you are undermining your own responsibility,' said another.[52]

There is a veritable 'laundry list' of considerations prosecutors use in reviewing cases: how serious a crime is, the strength of the evidence, the defendant's characteristics, including whether the defendant has ever previously been arrested or convicted, and the complainant's characteristics are all important. Each bit of information assists the prosecutor in piecing together a reading on how well the case will fare in trial. While some factors may weigh more heavily than others, the overall decision reflects all of these factors. It is this overall decision, moreover, which represents the prosecutor's *legal* opinion, even though at times s/he may be basing the decision on other-than-legal-grounds; not believing a woman, in other words, is a legal, not a social, assessment.[53] Thus, because of their role within the overall bureaucracy of criminal justice, prosecutors regard each incoming case as a problem for the court rather than as a problem of justice. In general, then, problematic cases do not end up in the 'solid case' category – those serious crimes to be tried by the court of higher jurisdiction – but are left for the lower courts or magistrates to sort out or dismiss altogether.[54]

The prosecutor's witness – the raped or battered woman – is a key element in establishing the seriousness of a criminal event. Guaranteeing successful convictions is closely linked with the assurance that the witness is, as prosecutors used to tell me, a 'stand-up' witness – one who can withstand any cross-examination and have her version of the criminal event believed by judge and jury. The version thus becomes a version of a 'serious' crime. In commenting about one such 'good case', one prosecutor said to me, 'Any case that has a stand-up complainant should be indicted [and tried in higher court]. You put her [the complainant] on the stand [and] the judge loves her, the jury loves her!'[55] Certain *types* of women in certain *types* of circumstances of physical and sexual assault are more likely to be considered 'stand-up' witnesses, and their complaints worthy of public prosecution (e.g. those women assaulted by total strangers) than women who can be portrayed as 'provocative' or 'deserving'.

Two essential features of convictable cases rest on the witness: the complainant's credibility and the complainant's willingness to prosecute. Women complaining of male violence who have 'survived' police screening must again face scrutiny. Credibility is, after all, a fragile reality. Prosecutors review the legal issues around 'consent' and 'provocation' in anticipation of defence attorney strategies.

'You see,' [as one U.S.Massachusetts district attorney stated] 'the whole case will really rest on her [the complainant's] credibility and her ability to tell her story and convince the jury. Her demeanour and sincerity will lend itself to her credibility as far as the jury is concerned. She seems to be sincere and if she comes across this way at the trial, it will go well.'[56]

Prosecutors know that unless a woman presents herself well, chances for successfully convicting a woman's assailant are significantly reduced. For instance, in one case described to me by a detective, a young woman of about 16 was testifying during the trial of her assailant accused of rape. She and her girlfriend, the story goes, had been to a pub, and both drank soft drinks. A young man offered them both a lift home; they both accepted. (Her girlfriend testified to these facts.) After her girlfriend was dropped at her home, the man drove the complainant to a nearby park and raped her. In her struggle to escape, the complainant broke her ankle. During her testimony, however, the complainant was so nervous she giggled occasionally on the stand. The judge, outraged by behaviour unbecoming of a 'truly' raped woman, immediately stopped the trial, reduced the charge to a simple assault, to which the defendant pleaded. The nervous giggling, perfectly understandable for someone intimidated by the formidable setting of the Old Bailey, undermined the young woman's credibility to the judge.[57]

A woman's credibility, particularly in cases of sexual assault, is also undermined by cross-examination about women's prior sexual history (there are very few cases of physical asault against women reaching the higher courts – generally the 'serious' cases are of murder and manslaughter). So damaging was this information that eventually England and Wales and Scotland, as well as many US states, passed legislation preventing testimony relating to prior sexual history being heard – unless there is a prior sexual relationship between the complainant and her assailant. Yet there are many ways to allude to 'loose', disreputable character during the complainant's questioning. Questionable lifestyles, current sexual relationships outside monogamous marriage ('oh, you say you are living with your boyfriend now'), questionable occupations and so forth, which may apply to women's life experiences and situations, drag up additional stereotypes threatening a woman's credibility.[58] Prosecutors themselves know these stereotypes. As one prosecutor stated to the complainant, 'Any girl that hitchhikes is asking for it.'[59] (This woman was raped while hitchhiking.) Potentially, prosecutors, too, are women's second assailants. (And recall Chapter 8; judges and juries too are potential assailants.)

The highly publicised Glasgow rape case (mentioned in the previous chapter) illustrates the point that procurator fiscals focus on the prediction of success at trial.[60] As part of her assault, the raped woman was repeatedly slashed with a razor, requiring over 150 stitches. Her reactions to being raped were not unlike other women's: excessive fear and anxiety. The rape had also shattered her confidence and thrown her into a deep depression. She had, according to a psychiatrist's report, attempted suicide. Despite all the evidence, including that of one young man who had been present during the assault testifying for the Crown, confessions by the three involved admitting they were present during all or part of the attack, immediate reporting to the police and the presence of medical evidence, the final decision of the Scottish Lord Advocate's Office, from whom the procurator fiscal had sought advice (in particularly serious or 'sticky' cases they do so), was to decline prosecution. It was, said the Lord Advocate's Office, in the best interests of the raped woman to decline prosecution. Could it be however that the case was dropped for other reasons as well? Moreover, despite the woman's ordeal, she was never consulted in the matter, never informed of the decision to drop the case (if the Lord Advocate's Office was so concerned for the woman, it might make sense that he would see to it that her mind would be 'set at ease' knowing she did not have to give testimony).[61] The woman maintains she would have given testimony. Could they not have also doubted the woman's credibility and her 'stand-up' status? (The 1983 Chambers and Millar report on sexual assaults in Scotland indicates that the proportion of sexual assault cases not prosecuted is three and a half times greater than the average proportion of cases not prosecuted: 30 per cent as opposed to 8 per cent!)[62]

A row soon stormed over Glasgow, and the whole of Britain, when the newspapers learned of the decision. The Lord Advocate's Office came under attack, and the solicitor general of Scotland, Nicholas Fairbairn, resigned in the heat of the controversy. Because the 'Crown had spoken', they could not initiate criminal proceedings against the three young men. The only way out was to provide a mechanism for private prosecution (more, I believe, in the interests of the credibility of the criminal jurisdiction than in the interests of the raped woman). The raped woman was encouraged to initiate her own proceedings against her assailants. But private prosecution is not quite the equitable access to the court that one might believe. First of all, the person initiating the prosecution must pay for it. The woman was fortunate in finding legal assistance free of charge. (If the case hadn't become so notorious, it is unlikely she would have found low-cost or no-cost legal assistance. She was also hounded by sections of the British press which revel in salacious stories of individual tragedy, particularly if they involve sex and violence.) *Five* lawyers argued in favour of private prosecution for four days in front of the three highest judges in Scotland – with the defendant's lawyers arguing as well – in order to receive permission to conduct a private prosecution. The last private prosecution in Scotland was conducted in 1909 – it is hardly something a 'private' citizen would be able and qualified to do. Of course, the woman was granted permission to bring her assailants to court.

Even the furore over the prosecution didn't protect her from cross-examination concerning her character and her demeanour on the evening of the assault. Alleging the woman was drunk and incapable of giving consent, the defence strategy revolved around her physical condition. In charging the jury, Lord Ross, presiding justice, charged the jury as follows:

> Now ladies and gentlemen, the issue of drink arises in this case and there are several things I want to say to you about that in relation to rape. If a woman voluntarily consumes alcohol to such an extent as to be virtually insensible, it is not rape to have intercourse with such a woman, just as it is not rape to have intercourse with a sleeping woman. It might, of course, be indecent assault, but it would not be rape. That is the situation if the woman were virtually insensible as a result of the voluntary consumption of alcohol ... where a woman is not insensible but is drunk, that is to say, under the influence of alcohol, the matter of course is different and in such a situation what you must determine is whether intercourse took place forcibly and against her will. The fact that a woman is drunk may mean that a lesser degree of violence is necessary to overcome her resistance than in the case of a sober woman. On the other hand, if a woman is drunk it may mean that she is less inclined to withhold consent, and of course if she was capable of withholding consent and did not in fact withhold consent, there is no rape.[63]

As noted in chapter 8, two of the three young men were convicted of indecent assault, not rape. Only one young man was convicted of rape;

he was also convicted of slashing the woman with a razor. The woman's testimony that she had been hit on the head and dragged into the garbage pile was ignored; the jury chose to believe the young men themselves who alleged she 'willingly' accompanied them to the garbage pile, too drunk to 'consent'. The case, subject of a recent book which sheds some light on the bureaucratic decisions involved, is portrayed as restoring one's faith in a legal system which eventually sees to it that 'justice' is done. But the woman was not so easily convinced. In August 1983, she declined to report a subsequent assault. (Police found her 'cowering with fear' in bushes on a darkened wasteground near Gallowgate, Glasgow, and she refused to make a complaint or to be medically examined.)[64] A detective later convinced the woman to file yet another complaint of assault with intent to rape. The man was acquitted this time.

Credibility, then, is tied to notions of appropriate femaleness; it is a flexible notion as well. None the less, within the interstices of bureaucratic decision-making, prosecutors do present and successfully prosecute cases of rape and assault against women who might be portrayed unfavourably. Every prosecutor speaks of the cases s/he has tried involving women who are prostitutes, single parents, strippers, alcoholics, students – women whose credibility might be open to attack. Quite likely, many of these offences involve greater bodily injury to the woman, or are part of a series of attacks perpetrated by the same assailant. In many more cases, prosecutors reduce the charges or plea bargain to reduced charges.[65] These contradictions allow the rhetoric of protection to carry on uncriticised.

In addition to credibility, research on prosecutorial decision-making indicates that 'victim non-co-operation' is another major obstacle to full or even partial prosecution.[66] The little US research available indicates that some complainants do not appear at the initial stages of prosecution – the arraignment or the preliminary hearing. Non-co-operation is given as the most common reason for case attrition at this point. Perception of non-co-operation, however, also strongly relates to prosecutors' attitudes. In the following example, a prosecutor speculates about a woman's co-operation in a case involving a man's assault upon her:

An off-duty corrections officer was arrested and charged with assault in the first degree (causing grievous bodily harm). The report from the police indicated that he had visited his girlfriend, an argument ensued, and the woman was shot in the head. The defendant stated that the gun discharged unintentionally. The woman could not be interviewed, for she was in surgery with a bullet lodged in her head. The prosecutor who reviewed the case summarized its chances in stating: 'If she dies, we have manslaughter. If she recovers, and remains a vegetable, we have an assault one [first degree]. If she recovers with minor complications, we barely have a case. If she fully recovers, she will probably drop the charges.'[67]

The assailant's actions – shooting the woman in the head – are a constant. Other variables – the woman's chances of recovery and her motivation to continue pressing charges – are the prosecutor's speculations.

Prosecutors in the United States often suggest that the only motivation for non-co-operation – dropping the charges – is a reconciliation between the man and the woman. Other considerations – fear of retaliation, long, frustrating delays in court processing, misconceptions about the criminal justice system – are deterrents to complainants, particularly to women complainants who are more likely to be in emotional and financial entanglements with their assailants, or whose involvement with the criminal justice system is a continuous source of humiliation.[68] (One California district attorney observed that half the complainants who came to her office to drop charges were accompanied by their assailants, who had threatened them with further abuse unless they dropped the charges!)[69]

Not surprisingly, wife assault as a category, then, fits neatly into the types of cases eliminated for the sake of efficiency. As one prosecutor stated,

> There is no way in hell we can try 6,000 cases a year with our staff, so which ones should we try? Take a felonious assault case involving a domestic quarrel. Does this deserve to be tried by a 12-man jury? No. We are much better off if they kiss and make up rather than if we put them in jail.[70]

Time and resource constraints are also mentioned in the following letter a woman received from the procurator fiscal's office in Edinburgh:

> Because of the current difficulties due to the strike in Edinburgh Sheriff Court decisions have had to be taken in this office to

reduce the workload in the Court and, clearly, only the most serious of cases can be proceeded with in these difficulties. Decisions, therefore, were taken that no further proceedings were to be instituted against the above named in respect of 2 separate assaults upon you. Further the outstanding cases against him in respect of dishonesty will still proceed to trial in the future.[71]

The institutional mythology 'the woman drops the charges' is very strong. It also reminds prosecutors that this type of 'crime' is not the sort of successful prosecution which brings additional kudos. Scottish procurator fiscals, during interviews about their work as 'public' prosecutors, comment about 'domestic violence' – which they themselves interpret as violence against women:

> Wife assault is always a bit difficult because what happens with a lot of them is that initially the complaint is made and later the wife wants to withdraw it.[72]

Dobash and Dobash found only 6 per cent of women withdraw complaints.[73]

> We regularly interview wives, exercise discretion and decide whether or not to drop the charges. We consider what effect a prosecution would have on that marriage ... if you've a wife coming along saying 'everything is solved, we're back together again' we might consider dropping it.[74]

> There have been cases where I felt the husband acted in a way you would expect a normal person to react ... perhaps finding his wife with another man, provided he did not go beyond reasonable assault.[75]

Some fiscals do treat wife assault seriously, allowing for the contradictory application of legal intervention.

> 'Every wife beater,' [one fiscal remarked] 'in my view, is a potential murderer ... one has to think of one's self protection [the repercussions on the fiscal where a history of unprosecuted wife assaults culminates in fatal attacks].'[76]

While individual prosecutors no doubt treat cases of wife assault differently, the prosecutorial perspective often excludes wife battering as 'crime' which deserves full prosecution, as that which represents a threat to society as a whole, and as that which is not likely to be followed through by the woman herself.

Administering jurisdiction of women's complaints, another task of the prosecutor's function of monitoring court workload, has an effect on how 'serious' wife beating is considered. In all three jurisdictions she studied, Frances Wasoff found that 'domestic violence' (of which 70 to 80 per cent were cases of wife beating) tended to be allocated to District (lower) courts rather than Sheriff (higher) courts.[77] Allocating wife assault to the lower court limits the range of possible sanctions that can be used against an assailant. In my own observations in New York, few cases of woman assault (perhaps one in twenty) were forwarded to the higher court as 'serious' crime. As one prosecutor commented, 'The people in Supreme Court don't like prior relationship cases.'[78] Indeed, the lawsuit filed in tandem with Bruno v. Codd (1976) against the New York district attorney's office cited the policy of automatically assigning cases of violence against wives to family court,[79] where 'family quarrels' are sorted out.

What proceeds to criminal court as a 'serious' crime, then, is a small proportion of men's violence to women which comes to the attention of police. Once in court, the negotiation of the case falls into the hands of the lawyers and administrative priorities take precedence. Plea bargaining, the preferred method for settling cases, results in many of the original charges being reduced. Even social scientists, in an attempt to account for the low conviction rates in crime against women, fail to see the problem as one fostered by the process of criminal justice inquiry – a process which rests so heavily upon assumptions about women and men's violence to them. One explanation follows for the low rate of conviction in rape cases:

> Perhaps the crucial difference between sexual assault and other crimes is that sexual activity can, under the right circumstances, be desired by most individuals, male or female. In contrast, nobody wants to be assaulted, burglarized, or robbed. Of course, nobody wants to be raped either, but a prosecutor, judge or jury must decide whether the particular sexual crime at issue was a traumatic, hostile assault, or whether it was a consensual encounter.[80]

But women do not control the definition of 'consensual' in sexual assault or physical assault. Women are the 'legitimate victims' in the criminal justice system[81] – their complaints about male violence are too often assumed to be 'no complaints' at all. Above all, the process of inquiry – from police to prosecutors to judges – is assaultive to women.

Chapter 10

'Typical' men's behaviour: working women's grievances

Working women today face a dilemma. Survey after survey indicates that most women have experienced sexual harassment during their working lives. How do women complain about men's behaviour toward them while they are at work? Should they complain about men's typical behaviour – behaviour women know will be considered to be harmless by those to whom they complain? However threatening, intimidating or coercive the sexual advances, how does sexual harassment affect a woman's working life? If a woman is not actually fired from her job, how can she characterise sexual harassment as harmful? Using women's perceptions of the potentially coercive nature of sexuality, sexual harassment is a form of men's threatening, intimidating or coercive sexual behaviour and is a form of discriminatory treatment at work. Looks, comments, pats, pinches, propositions – actions that men say are 'appreciative' of women as women in the workplace (as opposed to an appreciation of women as workers) – are experienced by women as harassing, as abhorrent, and as an abusive working condition. Yet silence is still the rule; few women complain.

Complaining as an employee about conditions of employment – men's sexual advances – involves complaining about behaviour which is generally not considered a part of the workplace.[1] It is a point of view women already know so well: sexual advances are 'private' matters; women who receive them encourage them; women can adopt a 'cool and businesslike' attitude and avoid sexual advances. Those to whom women complain – the personnel manager or union official – commonly hold such assumptions;[2] in questioning women's behaviour, these administrative decision makers focus on whether a particular man's behaviour is typical or aberrant in light of women's behaviour.

133

Just as raped, battered or incestually assaulted women found their experiences being distorted by the criminal justice process, so too do sexually harassed women when facing an employee grievance process. Once inside the process of inquiry, a male point of view emerges. Filing a grievance about sexual harassment then is like calling the police: women are unable to predict how their complaint will be handled, and if they are to predict, they are likely to predict that it will not be taken seriously.

In the United States, women started complaining about sexual harassment in different public forums before British women. Contemporary women's magazines (the first survey about harassment was conducted by *Redbook* in 1976), the press, annual academic meetings, even a committee of the United States Congress, reported details of sexual harassment from working women in many different worksites and educational institutions.[3] The typical characterisation of sexual harassment – that of the male boss chasing the female secretary around the office – indeed exists, but alongside are similar situations experienced by female police officers, coal miners, university professors, domestic workers, lawyers, civil service workers, file clerks and students, to name but a few. These women too experience forms of uninvited and unwelcomed sexual attention at their place of work or learning. Indeed, men's sexualised behaviour, assumed to be a form of flattery, can terrorise women.

Accompanying public debates, the US civil courts, which in the US have the function of raising private troubles to problems of public policy (in this case, defining sexual harassment as a form of sex discrimination rather than as a private problem between two parties), became another locus for women's complaints. Having gained the right to work, women demanded the right to work in settings which were not oppressive, hostile, or which served to drive women away from worksites, into which they had fought so hard to gain entry. Under Title VII of the 1964 Civil Rights Act, a few women filed lawsuits against their employers for failing to mediate their complaints about working situations in which their compliance to sexual advances was an expected condition of their employment.[4] Legal arguments focused on illustrating the coercive element of imposed sexuality which served as a form of sexual discrimination in the daily working situations of many women.

As could be expected, the initial lawsuits failed. Rather than recognising the wider implication of unwelcomed sexualised interaction in the workplace, the judicial decisions characterised women's complaints about behaviour as isolated misconduct or behaviour due to a 'personal proclivity, peculiarity or mannerism'.[5] Only one man's behaviour has gone awry. Today, however, some of those lawsuits have been successful, establishing legal precedence which defines harassment not as an individual problem (an argument which shows striking resemblance to characterisations about wife battering and rape as problems of individual women), but as a condition of employment which makes sexual compliance a 'job retention condition'. These legal decisions recognise that sexual advances can be coercive and can have economic consequences: either go along in a friendly manner with the sexual suggestions, laugh at sexual jokes or innuendoes, or lose a chance for a job, a promotion, be fired or quit. (It remains interesting that an issue so important to workers rights is only seen as a women's issue.)

Yet women's experiences of sexual harassment – and thus their complaints – continue to be overshadowed by complex but often misunderstood issues about contemporary sexuality. This is because these issues are viewed from a perspective moulded from a male point of view, a view which assumes that sexualised behaviour between men and women is 'typical', 'natural' and 'welcomed', in all places, at all times. In any discussions of sexual harassment, at least three assertions about male-female sexualised interaction crop up: sexual advances are (1) a sign of a 'true' romance; (2) just a sexual (but unthreatening) game; or (3) a conscious manipulation on the part of a *woman* to gain benefits. All three assertions ignore the issue of men's power over women and women's sexuality; all three incorporate traditional stereotypes of men and women; all typically arise during women's attempts to complain about sexual harassment. Accordingly, women are valued for their sexuality, wooed, cajoled, either for 'romance' or 'sport'. On the other hand, women, it is assumed, promote their sexuality for personal gain using the aura of the temptress to men's ultimate weakness, sexual gratification.

The office romance: Man meets woman and sparks of romantic interest fly; sexual advances represent a natural acting out of physical attraction. While some people do form deep friendships and loving relationships within the working sphere, the problems of unequal power between men and women, supervisor and supervisee, must always be kept in mind. Indeed, we all know couples who met at work and formed ongoing, intimate relationships. We also know others who are pestered by suggestions of 'romance' when they are not at all interested. To overlay the stereotype of romance on to all sexual advances, however, is surely a mistake, one that obscures all other examples of power and violence disguised in the name of desired and welcomed sexuality.

The sexual game: A second assertion impinging upon perceptions of sexual harassment is that sexual advances or comment are merely sexual game playing and thus 'innocent' sexual teasing. Sexual jokes and innuendoes can and do become powerful, intimidating tools for trivialising a woman's contribution to the worksite. Furthermore, a woman's sexuality, in effect, becomes a public commodity, for all to use, just as women's bodies are used as commodities in advertising, TV or film. It is this sexual game playing, moreover, that can change the work atmosphere to a hostile environment for a woman who daily faces men's view of her sexuality, one that is embarrassing, irritating, even frightening. Men don't seem to realise that what they do to their female colleagues can be unacceptable, for they treat those colleagues as they would women with whom they are intimate (for whom it might also be unacceptable!). In one company, for example, a personnel manager was told by a man defending his behaviour – grabbing a woman's breast – as 'something my wife or girlfriend likes, and I was just teasing'.[6]

The office temptress: Inevitably, in discussion of sexual harassment, the third assertion – that of the seductress seeking job promotions – arises. This suggests that all women *use* their sexuality for personal gain, and that an instance of office sexuality is just another instance of a woman sleeping her way to the top (the top of what I am not sure). Aside from the tandem stereotype of the gullible male, so controlled by his crotch that he submits to women's wiles, and so overwhelmed by the sexual experience, who rewards her with promotions, this stereotype promotes the corollary that women's true work is only done on their backs.[7] It also belittles working women's contributions to the workplace. The 1982 Alfred Marks survey conducted in Britain for instance asked a question about people in the office 'unduly' benefitting from sexual favours. Some 29 per cent of employees and 19 per cent of managers stated they know of cases where 'an employee of lesser ability was promoted' or achieved benefits from sexual favours.[8] To automatically place the blame on the woman, and not the man giving the job benefits, is just another form of woman blaming.

The publicity surrounding Mary Cunningham in the United States is perhaps one of the best illustrations of how many images about women and sexuality become enmeshed.[9] Mary Cunningham was 28 years old when she was promoted to be vice president of Bendix Corporation in 1980. A Harvard University graduate, Mary was an up-and-coming executive, at least until eyebrows raised when she was promoted to vice-president. Her boss, thinking he was setting rumour to rest, announced, 'While it is true that Mary Cunningham is a close friend of mine and my family, that has nothing to do with the way I or others in this company evaluate her.'[10] Immediately the media caught wind of the situation (due, some think, to jealous colleagues) and all eyes focused on Mary, who soon resigned her position because she could no longer effectively manage. Mary herself confronted the over-whelming power of the stereotype of women who gain promotions because of their relationships with their bosses. As Mary herself reflects,

'What I was subjected to was sexual harassment, pure and simple. All the rumors, all the gossip, all the innuendoes, that's what it came down to. There is no other word for it. In business settings it is common. . . . It is a weapon used against successful women to undermine their credibility, and it undermined mine.'[11]

She was soon hired by another major corporation as a vice president, but still carries the scars: 'I felt like a rape victim. I was afraid of the perpetrators, whether they would continue to attack and hurt me,' said Mary.[12]

Treating complaints about sexual harassment seriously necessitates throwing off the above assertions and conceptualising sexual harassment as a form of sexual coercion. *Unwelcomed* sexual advances, particularly those day-in and day-out encounters (many sexually harassed women work daily with their harassers), begin to take the form of 'little rapes', with the growing fear for women about what possibly will come next. Will the 'touching up' become more aggressive? Will it escalate to rape? Will it affect my job?

Sexual harassment, like men's threatening or violent behaviour else-where, raises women's concern in two areas: concern for physical safety and concern for employment or economic safety. Both concerns revolve around the ambiguous nature of harassment, and the woman's inability to predict what the outcome might be. Particularly within the wider sphere of men's threatening, intimidating or violent behaviour towards women, sexual harassment itself must be viewed within the framework used for an understanding of rape, incest, or battering. No longer an innocent sexual game playing, it is one more example of how men's power over women operates in women's everyday lives.

Women who become targets of sexual harassment, like, for example, women who experience 'flashing' or receive obscene phone calls, find that they are often viewed by others as complaining about 'trivial' behaviour. As the supervisor of Carmita Wood, an American woman who left her job because of harassment, stated about Carmita's original complaints, 'I don't remember [the behaviour Carmita complained about] specifically, but it was my impression [that] it was mentioned among a lot of things that I considered trivia.'[13] In another US case, a woman informed a high university official about her own complaint about sexual harassment which was to be filed alongside the complaint of a woman in her own department. The official remarked that he 'hoped it wasn't as trivial as the other one'.[14]

A woman employed in a comprehensive school in England gave this account of her experience of complaining to her supervisor.

> I was sexually assaulted in my first year of teaching by four boys.
> It was so bad that I've had to block it out of my mind, just to
> cope. A group of boys were always asking me about my sex life
> and had left porn on my desk on one occasion. I remember going
> into those lessons shaking. One day I got fed up and told them I
> wasn't going to answer any of their questions. One said, 'We
> frighten you, don't we Miss? You know we could knife you,' and
> another said, 'We can get her now.' The whole group came at
> me, grabbed my breasts and shoved me against the wall. I ran out
> and locked myself in a stock cupboard. I reluctantly reported it
> to my Head of Department, who was very suggestive to me,
> himself. He asked me if I'd considered ways of making my
> lessons more interesting! I don't report things like that any more.[15]

Questioning women's behaviour is a typical response of supervisors or personnel officers to whom women complain. Clothing, demeanour, working habits all become the focus for determining whether the harassed woman somehow encourages her harasser's behaviour. The pervasive assumption is that 'good women' are not harassed, only the ones who deserve it. Phyllis Schlafly, one of the leading proponents of the myth of the 'good woman' and anti-ERA campaigner in the United States, testified before a US Senate committee:

> Sexual harassment on the job is not a problem for virtuous women, except in the rarest of cases. Men hardly ever ask sexual favours from women from whom the certain answer is no. Virtuous women are seldom accosted.[16]

In both the United States and in Britain, some women have been successful in bringing sexual harassment cases to the US courts and British tribunals.[17] In reviewing the facts of the cases, many of the stories sound familiar. Women fired for refusing to have affairs with supervisors, fired for refusing sexual advances, fired for complaining about men's threatening, intimidating, coercive or sexual behaviour. Despite the existence of sex discrimination legislation in both the US and in Britain, women are not being protected from sexual harassment. Training programs launched in the US which were initiated because of the fear of dealing with costly lawsuits are still met with resistance: 'Hey, we're going to see a film on sex. This is going to be a fun way to spend a morning,' joked one executive who was to attend a management training session.[18] British trade unions, too, are trying to grapple with issues of sexual harassment.[19] Published in August, 1983, new guidelines were characterised as 'a laugh' or worse, 'The sex commandments of the TUC'.[20] Commented one newspaper, 'I reckon they'll have a hard time legislating against human nature'[21] – or did the commentator mean 'typical' male behaviour? The power of sexual harassment, be it directed through assertions about women as temptresses, as in the Mary Cunningham case, or directed through comments about women's behaviour, has the effect of dismissing women's experiences of men's threatening, intimidating, or violent behaviour within the workplace.

To look at the process of inquiry more closely is to see the male point of view emerging. The following is one English woman's struggle to complain about sexual harassment; it is not much different from struggles of American women. Elaine's situation is particularly interesting.[22] The harassment began after she began to lodge complaints about equal pay. Her situation is useful, for it seems that the harassment was launched as a deliberate act to terrorise Elaine, undermine her credibility and confidence, and jeopardise her claim for a proper salary. The tactic worked; Elaine ended up leaving her job.

Elaine had been employed with a major chemical company in London for seven years. Some time around November 1980, Elaine complained about her job rank and salary. One of the men she had worked with retired, and Elaine began supervising others. At times, she acted as the deputy to her head of section. She knew others in the company were receiving higher salaries for work with lesser responsibilities and duties. She wished to be treated more equitably, and be compensated for her work. She began the standard company procedure for filing pay grievances.

Some time around February 1981, her boss's behaviour toward her began to change.

Well he started following me around, particularly if I went from my room to another lab. Occasionally I would go down [to the main lab] to do some odd bits of work. They had some calculators down there. I might go and use those. There were quite a few people in this large lab, men, and obviously they chat to you. He'd come down and sort of walk up and down.

He had a 'flexiclock' in his main lab. He'd come down and pretend he was looking at his clock. He'd watch me and what I was doing and he'd stomp back to my own lab, that sort of thing. Then he said that I couldn't have any outside telephone calls. This was around February, March, something like that. I'd noticed that he was getting upset when I had phone calls, regardless of who it was from. A couple of people commented on it. So they'd obviously noticed.

[So other people in the office were noticing his change of behaviour?]

Yeah, he was very changeable – he'd come in one day and be really stroppy and not talk. Then he could come in a few days later and he'd be quite normal. It was as if it had all blown over and everything was ok. So really I didn't know from one week to the next how it was going to go. He might come in and decide that this week he wasn't talking to me at all. So he'd start leaving me notes of what to do. He wouldn't actually speak to me, he'd write notes and leave them on my desk. He often went out, disappeared – he used to go swimming and go home, things like that, which was probably just as well, because if he was around – when he was at work he was in awful moods, he used to just write in his diary. I reckon now that he did about two hours at work a week, but he might write in his diary for four hours (all day) which seems a very long time that he'd be writing, you know, it would be very excessive. It was difficult because the other people in the lab worked outside of the lab, so if he was around there was just the two of us. It could be really very uncomfortable, and also it meant if he was ever a bit funny to me, there wasn't anyone around to hear it. We'd have some awful arguments, but there wouldn't be anyone there.

[So this kept going on and on. So how did you figure out that he was starting to write things about you and this obsession with you and 'other men'?]

Well I knew something was going on. I hadn't seen the diary I don't think then, but then he refused to sign my time slip once and I eventually asked him why. He said, 'I'm not signing for you to go and meet your boy friend.' Well I got really angry with him and we had an argument, eventually we sort of resolved the problem. Later on I found that he'd written in the diary – 'I'm not signing for her screwing time.' Throughout he had this fixation that I was meeting somebody. Another time he'd written I'd come in dressed up and perfumed. He'd also written this 'boy friend' of mine must have worked in the shop or something and had Wednesday or Wednesday afternoons off because I always met this 'boy friend' on a Wednesday. I used to go home early Wednesday, which I usually did because I could do my shopping on Wednesday and [my husband] picked me up.

One day he said I was obviously meeting my 'boy friend'. He'd put [in the diary] that I'd been hanging around waiting for a phone call and that I'd come in dressed up for my lunch break. He wrote 'for a wog lunch.'[23] I probably have got quite a few black friends and I think that probably he didn't really like that very much – there's no particular reason for that, it was just one of the things; I think he actually thought that it was a black person taking me out. I came upon the diary accidentally. I think it must have been around March.

He used to leave his diary open, on his desk. He'd be writing in it and he'd go and come back, this is how it'd go on, and because he was out a long time from the lab if his phone was ringing, I always answered it.

If you're sitting there and the diary's there you just can't help but see it. So I actually found something written about me purely by accident. And then after that I looked in it a few times. Then I started to get too upset and stopped looking. So I didn't look for sort of months, but I still knew that he was writing about me because he'd look at me as though he were; he'd look really angry and he'd be writing furiously in his diary. He'd always get it out if I had a telephone call or if I went to lunch and I was a long time. Then he started taking the diary home with him at night.

I think he thought that I was going to tell someone about this diary towards the end because he didn't leave it around just, at all – he always took it home. In fact it went for about a week at a time. At one stage I thought that I wouldn't see the diary again. It completely went, the only times that it came back was when I upset him by going for a long lunch time – sometimes I did things which would trigger it off so I could show it to my union representative. He'd need the diary and would have to bring it in. So I would trigger it off and I started to know that I could trigger his behaviour off.

The other girl in the section (he didn't actually say anything to her) noticed he was behaving very oddly and she was getting very upset. I showed her some of the things in the diary. One day I was trying to see what had been written, she watched to make sure he didn't come back in the lab, and she got very upset. She told her husband, and he said, 'I don't want you going in there, he doesn't sound normal.' Her husband was also concerned that if my boss moved me or if I left or whatever, she'd be left there on her own with him. So, she went to personnel and complained and said that she wasn't going to stay there, and she wasn't going to come in to work and work in that unit because she was afraid. It sounds odd now after, but we were both frightened. We both thought that he might do something to us. She was terrified that he might come in and catch us looking at the diary, and what he would have done I just don't know. We both made sure we weren't left there late or something on our own. Neither of us fancied that.

[Because you didn't know what he was going to do? You didn't know how he was going to act next?]

Yeah, because he was behaving so irrational. He'd be in these awful tempers, I mean, if I had phone calls he'd be throwing things around the room, or he'd storm out, or he'd storm in.

[Did you start complaining to others before they started telling you that they noticed something strange was going on?]

Well, I tended not to say too much – I commented he'd been using bad language, something like that, to the other members of the lab on my section. They certainly noticed that he was giving me some funny looks but I mentioned it to the girl who was the secretary on the section and she used to pass on some of the phone calls. Sometimes I used to go and use her phone because by that time he'd told me I couldn't use the phone to dial out.
  She knew what was going on. I tended not to say anything really, but I did tell a man who was my chief technician. I didn't go into a lot of details. I just said that there was something wrong with him. The problem is that I don't think anybody ever did take it seriously. I did go to my departmental head. I stayed after work till everyone had gone and I said I thought my boss had a 'mental problem' and I was very worried about him. And the departmental head said, 'Well he's always been like that. I mean he's always been that kind of a character. He's always had a vicious streak in him, so, what you're describing is what I've known for years.' So he didn't really see it as being anything to worry about, but as far as he was concerned it was his normal personality.
  The departmental head knew that there was a breakdown between us and he said that he was worried about us and considered taking us over to the bar and trying to get us to talk over a drink. I told him I didn't see that was going to help anything, because I thought there's something really wrong. I think he just thought we'd had a falling out or something and it was just going on and on. But he did not appreciate how serious it was. I think he probably was trying to be helpful but then he

actually told my boss that I'd said something about him. I'd found an entry in his diary saying that he'd had this discussion with the departmental head. What he'd put in his diary was that I'd said some very disturbing things about him. So I think what I said had actually gotten back to him. So of course, it was then that he'd been forewarned at about what I might say in any complaint to my divisional head. So prior to this he thought perhaps I wouldn't say too much. The divisional head phoned him up one day just to give him a lecture about his management of the staff because I was complaining [about him to my departmental head]. I found in his diary again that he told the divisional head about my schizophrenic, paranoid obsessive behaviour. This was before I actually went to the divisional head in person, and while those same people evaluated my grievance about my rank and salary. It was in August that I mentioned the sexual harassment to my union rep [representative]. It was when I told my union rep about the diary. She first of all told me to take it – and I didn't want to do that because I knew that from the way he behaved, I knew that if I took it and he found it missing, he would have known I'd taken it. I thought he'd just go over the top. I just didn't feel safe at all. I said that I was too frightened and she said she'd come across and she'd take it, or help me take it. I showed it to her one lunch time when he was at lunch. She said I must tell my personnel officer. She came with me and I told the personnel officer. She phoned him and he said to get me to bring the diary over. I said no way, so I just took some photocopies and that was awful, because I just didn't know when my boss was going to call back in. I just took, oh I don't know, about five pages, something like that. I didn't take very many pages because I was just so worried that he'd walk back in and catch me and just really really go over the top. Because it obviously was very important to him, I mean, he was so obsessive about it. He'd just sit there for hours writing and looking up and looking at me – you could see the sort of hate in his eyes. I thought that I didn't particularly want to look at the entries in his diary but I wanted to show my divisional head that – I really wanted to illustrate the man's mental attitude. It was all part and parcel of what I was complaining about in my equal pay grievance: he wasn't doing the work, he was putting so much work on me, but it was more than just saying that he was lazy, it was more than

just laziness, it was something actually wrong. It wasn't that I
wanted him to get the sack, I just wanted to show what was
going on in the man's mind. It wasn't enough to say well he
stopped me having phone calls, and he's not working. I thought
if he'd seen the entries and the way he'd written – it just, it didn't
look like the writings of a normal person. [Elaine's boss was
writing obscene descriptions of Elaine's supposed sexual liaisons.]

[When you xeroxed the pages and you took them into this
personnel person, what did he say about them?]

I think he looked pretty shocked, I think he just said something
like – oh, charming, and I don't think he said anything else. He
said that when I went to see my divisional head I would have to
show it to him. I hadn't wanted to all along, I kept saying that
to my union rep. I didn't really want to (show the diary). It's
embarrassing. I still was afraid that if I showed them to somebody
and my boss got to find out something would happen. I just didn't
feel safe. It's as simple as that – it was OK them saying to me get
the diary, do this, do that, but they didn't have to go out in the
dark or work with him. They didn't have him throwing one of
them around. It's OK to tell someone to do it but if anything had
happened to me. . . . So you can imagine, you're in an emotional
state anyway and perhaps you overreact, but at that time I was
scared. My husband started taking me to work and picking me
up every evening so that I didn't have to even walk to the car park
on my own. So he knew, you know, just how agitated I was, and
he was concerned too. You see, my boss was also following me
around the worksite. I felt so uncomfortable, always being
followed, always being asked about my 'boy friends'. [At this point,
Elaine had not intended to mention her sexual harassment – her
boss's obsession with Elaine's fantasy lovers. She was quite
confused and embarrassed by it all. She continued to feel strongly
about her equal pay claim, but did not know how to fit this new
behaviour toward her by her boss into an employee's grievance.]

[What happened in your meeting with the divisional head?]

At the first meeting, I tried to show him the diary entries. He was
a bit abrupt even at that first meeting because he'd already had

a big telephone conversation which my boss had said that I was a bit crazy, I said that he [her boss] was never there. He said, 'but oh, you're never there, you're always away sick.' So he had an answer. [Elaine had some physical problems for which she had been to hospital for a series of tests.]

At one stage, I don't remember if it was at that meeting or the next one but he insinuated to me that because I had been away sick my absence had put stress on my boss and made *his* job more difficult to do.

I tried to show him the copies of the diary and he wouldn't look at them. I sort of put them under his nose there and he just wouldn't look. I said, 'well would you like me to read them to you?' So I read just one page – I think it was the one about not signing for my 'screwing time', just one paragraph. He just sort of tutted like that, 'I don't want to hear it. I don't want to hear this man's private diary – that's enough,' and he wouldn't read any more for himself. I walked away from that meeting and thought, well perhaps it's understandable, he'd probably not come across this before and I thought he was shocked. Perhaps he was so abrupt to me because he was embarrassed? Then when I went back for the next meeting he was nasty. I realised that it wasn't that at all.

[What did this divisional head do?]

The divisional head sent me home for a week, so that he could investigate it – and I didn't want to go home, but he insisted. He said, 'oh, it will be much easier', which I didn't see but in the end I said I'd go.

He then called me in to start work in another area. It was a different time, a completely different area, everything. [For this job Elaine was to be placed in another part of the worksite, in a room by herself.] I said well no, but I'll come in and discuss this with you. When I went in he was really aggressive, and so nasty. It was just unbelievable. He handed me a formal letter about my sickness, I had some time off when I was going to hospital. He handed me a letter saying that if I didn't improve I wouldn't come into a raise next year. He just said that I just had to start work in this other section and that was that. I said that I didn't want to work in this other section. He was really nasty, thoroughly

aggressive and tried to intimidate me. I mean he asked me
questions like: 'was *I* having an affair? had I been having an affair
with my boss?' Going through all that (in the diary) which in a
way wasn't really relevant. It resulted in me ending up in tears
and just storming out and saying I was going home.

That was it – I just stormed out. So, the attitude was that if I
hadn't been there it wouldn't have happened, which I think it is
true that it wouldn't have happened at that time. But I think no
one could possibly say that it's not going to happen again. Maybe
I tripped it off that time but there's no saying that it's not going
to happen again. It wasn't just a question that he was shocked
and embarrassed, because if he had been he could have at least
said 'this is really awful, I don't know what to say but I don't
think you should work with him at the moment, we'll try to find
you something else more suitable,' if he'd been like that, just a little
bit compassionate as it were let's find you something else, I think
I probably would have well said, 'OK I don't want to leave but you
know under the circumstances.' That's probably what would have
happened. But because he was so antagonistic towards me it
really put my back up, and that was the reason why I took it to
the tribunal. *It wasn't just the fact that my boss had tried to harass
me it was the response that I got from the people when I took it further.*
And if they'd just been a bit more human about it and said, 'well
look there's nothing they can, we can do, really, we agree to move
you and then we'll sort it out', I think I would probably have just
said, 'OK I'll work somewhere else.' But it was this attitude of
you haven't got any choice, and he actually said to me – 'you do
as I say, you will go and work in this other area as from now.'
And when I said well I need to go back, I've left belongings, he
said, 'you can never go back there again.' I often think that he did
believe me and think it was a case of victimisation. But if he
admitted to it, it would look bad on him as a manager: he hadn't
supervised the staff well. After my boss there was the
departmental head, and there was the divisional head.

Elaine spoke to a variety of people; including staff of other unions,
the Equal Opportunity Commission, the National Council for Civil
Liberties, even women law professors. All the original paperwork for
the tribunal Elaine sent in herself. She was still interested in pursuing
her equal pay claim and added a complaint of sexual harassment to

it. Her union did not feel she had a 'good case', and consequently they did not support her. In January 1982 she was assisted by the NCCL in finding herself a lawyer to represent her. Elaine felt very isolated, but was determined to carry on. Besides the assistance of the NCCL, Elaine turned to the Rape Crisis Centre for support.

> I phoned the Rape Crisis Centre on several occasions and they were really supportive, particularly around the 1981 Christmas period, and I was very depressed with what happened. I was also worried about seeing my boss in case he just went a bit crazy. At times I just felt I needed somebody to talk to about things, so I found that they were really very good and supportive. The first time I phoned, I was really worried about phoning because I thought, 'God! have I got the right to take up their time over this petty thing when this could be a woman raped.' That was the only thing. I can remember picking up the phone and dialling it about three times and said no I mustn't call. I got through once, it was one evening I was here on my own. They said dial this other number. I can remember dialling it and the woman was so nice and helpful. There wasn't any hint of, 'what the hell are you doing phoning for such a trivial thing', and so I probably phoned them about perhaps three or four times throughout, just really to have a chat with somebody who wasn't saying, 'Don't be ridiculous. Why do you feel like that?' That was the only thing that I felt that maybe I was over reacting and that I shouldn't be wasting their time but they certainly didn't make me feel like that.

Elaine started work in her solitary office in mid-March. The tribunal did not occur until October – almost two years after Elaine initially began her grievance for equal pay. She also had to pay £300 for a barrister to assist her at the tribunal.

> I didn't mind paying the money but I feel that it was wrong because it's putting people into a position where financially there's absolutely no way they can do it then they just have to drop it. The other thing is you're sort of thinking you're spending that money and is it worth it? You're going through that all the time – is there really any point? When I submitted papers to the tribunal, I put in two claims, one was on a sex discrimination claim, and the other one was on an equal pay claim. When I

went to see the barrister on the Friday before, we were chatting and he thought for various reasons I could lose the equal pay claim quite easily, which could jeopardise the sex discrimination claim. Now, although they were both important I felt that the sex discrimination claim was more important so I agreed to drop the equal pay claim. So the barrister telephoned my company's solicitors and said we're not going ahead on that particular claim. When I got back home on the Friday afternoon I had a phone call from the NCCL. They'd phoned up and said that they weren't prepared to fight the case on just the sex discrimination claim so they were dropping out. Would we go along on the Monday morning to discuss some sort of agreement?

[Does that mean the company would just concede the case?]

That's right – so really on the Friday it was, it was cut and dried. The company had admitted guilt and were dropping out of fighting it. They weren't going to fight it at all. So it was all very straightforward. But when we got there it wasn't so straightforward. Well here it's a bit confusing because at times it was a bit beyond me. More or less what happened was when we got there the only person that turned up from my company was the solicitor, no one else. Which I thought was bad to begin with, because there was no one to discuss what we could agree to. I asked for a personnel officer to come and tell me about any jobs that were available. The barrister went up to the people sitting on the tribunal, which was a chairman, another man, and a woman, and said that we were going to come to an agreement outside of it. There was some argy bargy in the first place, some argument about whether I actually had a case within the three-month time limit because what the company had said was I actually stopped working in that lab on 26 November and my claim got into the tribunal on about 2 or 3 March. So they were saying it was outside of the time limit, but the point about it was that I wasn't claiming that discrimination occurred on that day but actually a week later when my divisional head said you cannot return to that job.
  Eventually that was accepted and that was all agreed and they said yes you have got a case. Then they said well if you're not going to have it heard because you're going to come to an

agreement we want a statement of what the agreement is. So then, my barrister had to write out this lengthy statement of the sort of things that had gone on and try and include the important things, and reach an agreement. And this took a long time. It took us up to about lunch time to try and get this right.

My company said in the morning, you know, that they were withdrawing, that they weren't going to fight. My barrister said too that under the circumstances they'd admitted guilt – then my company's solicitor said, 'Oh we're not admitting guilt, we're not prepared to pay the expenses for this case.' OK, so they kind of wanted their cake and eat it – they were saying – we're not prepared to fight it but we're not admitting guilt. Anyway eventually this statement went up to these people that were sitting on the tribunal – for some reason they all had a copy to read. The chairman said, 'We want you to read it out.' I had to go and read out the statement. There was a part of it saying what the diary had said, so some of it wasn't particularly pleasant reading. I don't think I really showed my feelings. I don't know whether that was right or wrong from their point of view. I mean it may have come across that I was being very cold, but you had to get a bit like that over the months because you can't keep reading it and being upset by it. Anyway, the gist of it was that although the company were saying, almost admitting guilt, the people, the chairman of the tribunal was insinuating that they didn't necessarily agree that they were guilty because they didn't necessarily agree that I had a real sex discrimination claim. You know perhaps it was a clash of personality, they said. But more than that it was very cleverly worded, the whole thing, and they said that we had either to agree on this statement and have an end of it that day or have the case heard or we could take it to a Court of Appeal.

By this time my barrister was saying things aren't going well. In the morning it was all smiles, we're doing so well, by the afternoon it had changed. It was clever, the way it was worded. My company knew that if the case had gone on then I wasn't going to win because the people on the tribunal had indicated that they weren't accepting that I had a case. So whereas in the morning my company had said we're not going to fight it, we're going to pay, in the afternoon when the barrister asked them they said we're going to fight it. Because they knew that they can win. So, really it was the politics of the tribunal.

My barrister said, well if you go ahead it's going to be really awful. . . . 'You won't win here, not with these people. If you go to this Court of Appeal that could be months and months to wait and you're still not going to sort out your job problem, so, probably the best thing you can do is agree this statement'. And by this time we'd made this statement which couldn't be altered. It would have been what went to this Court of Appeal, we couldn't add any more or something. There was something there that it would be difficult to have other witnesses – that what we had given was our evidence. Anyway, so they thought it would probably be best if I agreed to this statement. But in the end, we weren't in any bargaining position. I think my barrister kind of had had enough by this time. It had been going so nicely in the morning, then by the afternoon it was awful. We just weren't in a position to say, 'well this isn't good enough; we'll have this or we'll have that'. We just had nothing. They knew that they would win.

So in the end it, really they were offering me nothing. Well, they awarded me £500 compensation which they said if I left and took severance, which I don't know if I can do anyway, that would be taken out of it. The legal fees came to just under £300 – plus I probably spent not far short of that because I did a lot of phoning and travelling around. I wasn't out of pocket but I wasn't in pocket.

They said they'd offer me a job within twenty-eight days. The job they offered me was the job they'd already offered me six months before – it was an awful job. I'd asked for an apology and you know, something to be given to me to clear my name so people would know, and they said no. And they said they'd put something up on the notice board saying it had been settled between me and the company. By that stage, as I said, what good was that? I didn't have any bargaining power and I didn't particularly want this thing written on the board. I couldn't get what I wanted. I felt well what can I do – if I've got sort of people like a barrister who knows what's happening I just have to take their advice. It was an awful day and I certainly didn't feel that I won.

And then, I don't remember the exact wording of it but the barrister wanted it to be worded somehow that the company had sort of withdrawn so it made it look like we'd kind of won, we'd certainly in theory, and the Chairman wouldn't even let that happen. He wouldn't even allow it and he said that he didn't want to know anything about the settlement. He didn't want to know about the compensation, or anything. He wasn't interested and as far as he was concerned, the application had been dismissed. My barrister said, 'well, it's not dismissed because you haven't heard the case, so how can it be?' And there was a lot of arguing going on about it. Something I didn't understand, but he just wouldn't even let us win on a piece of paper. So, if anyone read about it later, it didn't look as if I'd won at all. It didn't look as if the company had said, 'yes, we accept that there's something wrong here and we're guilty in that respect'. So I didn't even have that satisfaction. It was awful because I still had to go in to work. I had hoped that even if I'd gone through the three days tribunal, even if people had heard the whole sordid details, even if my boss had been there and been saying, 'she was doing this and she was doing that', I would have been glad because people would then have known what I had been putting up with from him. The kind of accusations that he'd been making, I wanted all that to come out. I still felt that I was going back on to the site and bumping into people who still didn't know why I had been removed from my job. To me it just seemed that I was the person who was moved over to another job. I can't even return to the building. People are going to think that I have done something awful. You know, if somebody is guilty or something, then, you treat them like that – you don't do it to an innocent person. So there must be people that think I really have done something awful. I can understand that. I think I'd probably be thinking the same. I'd been isolated from the people that I know, my friends and the people that I'd worked with for seven years. I'd been put the other side of the site. It's a huge site and I'm away from anybody I knew who might have had any understanding of what had gone on. Then I found myself not even wanting to go out to the canteen. I never went to the canteen. In the time that I went back to work in March to the tribunal in October I never went to the canteen to eat anything, never, because I couldn't face seeing people. Because every time I'd see them, either they'd blank me because 'there goes that terrible girl who did this awful thing that we don't know what it is', or they might come up and say some very cruel things. They might sort of say, 'oh, you'll have to leave because you're a trouble maker.' This kind of thing. So I found that I was isolated. It seemed that because I wasn't with anyone I knew I would have to go to the canteen on my own and I couldn't face seeing people in case they would start probing and saying a lot of things. I'd get so I'd dread seeing people in case they did say anything that would upset me.

I had a letter from one of the personnel officers saying would I like them to visit me. So I think that it's suddenly dawned on them that they were stroppy about me having sick leave which was very genuine. I spoke to one of the nurses recently and said that I really resented the fact that the doctor hadn't backed me up. I had genuine problems and I wasn't getting any support. In fact I'd been intimidated which is really awful when you're not feeling 100 per cent fit anyway. She asked me if I thought that the job had actually made my physical problems worse. I know it's made it worse. The doctor at the hospital said it was making it worse. So I think possibly they are realising what's the point in not helping me because if I'm just going to stay off sick, it's not helping me, but it's not helping them. I'm not doing anyone any good, so maybe they will try and help. What worries me is, you know, just the thought of actually going back there and people still not knowing what went on. I just don't know if I can face it. You know I want to go in and wear sort of a T-shirt with written on, 'I was sexually harassed this, this, this happened to me, then this happened', that's what I want everyone to know – and this all OK, you know this can happen to you. I'd like people to know, if people knew, I would feel easier in my mind. It doesn't matter if they say, 'well why was he writing these things about her – perhaps it was true'. I'd rather they knew the whole story than just be picking up bits and pieces and you know, coming to the wrong conclusion. But I reckon that it must definitely be happening in my company to other people. It may only be a handful but it can so easily be happening right now. The point is if my union had published just some of what had happened – because there were some points that were relevant – I think someone would have come forward.

In fact the Divisional Officer wrote and said that it could be actually bad for other women if you go ahead with this case. But I don't see that. The more women that go ahead, whether they've got good cases or bad cases, the more it's going to encourage other people. If for instance the results of my case had been published, somebody else on the site who did have a problem could speak to me about it. It can't do anything other than help. But at the moment that won't happen. But some day, somewhere, somebody is going to win. It might be ten years, but it could be two months. If you just take my company where there are, I'm not really sure, about 1500 people or something like that, if you just take it that there's say five women who are having problems, and by talking to somebody who's going to offer some support, say somebody in the union or whatever, all five of them decided to take it to a tribunal. If that was just from my company, and then it went on to other places, the more people that go to the tribunal, eventually someone's going to have to change.

By the time she was transferred from her worksite, where she had been for over seven years, Elaine's complaints had succeeded in isolating her from her fellow employees, her reward for saying out loud what the company was not willing to hear. Only through her tenacious efforts did Elaine even manage to have the case taken to tribunal. Her reception there, however, was less than a welcoming one, with the ultimate dismissal ruling representing the decision of record. From her union representative to the tribunal, Elaine faced discouragement, indeed denial that her complaints were anything other than a 'personal' dispute (the tribunal ruling bears a striking resemblance to the early decisions that came from American judges about sexual harassment cases there).

Elaine has since quit her job. Her anger over her treatment had led her to seek employment with a woman's agency. While she does miss the work she grew to love in her old job, she now sees more clearly how women can so easily be dismissed.

Elaine's experience typifies many of the experiences of sexually harassed women – regardless of the form of harassment – who struggle through the maze of grievance personnel in search of a remedy. Similar to the treatment of women who complain of criminal victimisation, Elaine found her credibility questioned and her confidence undermined during the grievance process. Like women who are physically or sexually assaulted in their own homes, Elaine's everyday environment became an environment filled with terror. So did the process of complaining.

For women, the promise of contemporary democratic society is the promise of protection – from violence, from discrimination, from oppression. Taken together, women's experiences of men's threatening, intimidating, coercive or violent behaviour and their attempts to complain about that behaviour challenge any notion of protection. Bound tightly to an inquiry process which too often denies, trivialises or ignores women's experiences of male violence, women's complaints are commonly seen as unfounded, indeed, as no complaint at all. Explained as conscious or unconscious, intended or unintended, typical or aberrant, men's behaviour – as behaviour of the dominant gender – is not questioned or challenged. It is time to question both men's behaviour and the process of inquiry surrounding women's complaints about men's behaviour. Indeed, women have lots of complaints.

Chapter 11

Lots of complaints: strategies for survival

To live in an illusion, not to know the truth is the most dangerous of all things for a human being, woman or man, because it deprives people of their most important weapon in the struggle for freedom, emancipation and control of their own lives and future. To be conscious that you are still living under oppression is the first step on the road to emancipation.

Nawal El Saadawi

Vision of a society that does not enslave women involves first the pain of recognizing the worst of women's oppression. But with hope there is the opportunity to create a new political structure and social order. To have this vision means demanding and finding a world that will be free of sexual terrorism. Knowing the worst frees us to hope and strive for the best.

Kathleen Barry

Kathleen Barry, in her book *Female Sexual Slavery*, reminds us that women who have been physically and/or sexually assaulted are survivors. They have endured sexual terrorism and they are now on the 'other side of being a victim'.[1] Women who have been raped make significant changes in their lives – they change jobs, husbands or lovers, move house, muster personal strength and skills they never thought they had.[2] Sexually harassed women, their experience often similar to that of their raped sisters, change jobs, even if it means economic disadvantage; emotional survival is more important than daily working conditions of humiliation and degradation.[3] Battered women, fearing their lives more than the judgments of others, flee from their batterers.[4]

156

Surviving entails creativity; its form is affected by variables such as personality, financial resources, ethnicity, race, social context, stamina and so forth. We must not expect all attacked women to physically defend themselves adeptly by immediately remembering the one or two self-defence techniques they were taught in a night course. Some women may, and escape attack; others, for many reasons (physical impairment, terror or whatever) may not. Women must do what they can do in particular situations of male violence for survival. When for instance Patti Hearst argued that she 'joined' the Symbionese Liberation Army for her own survival, the fact that she was first kidnapped, then locked in a dark closet for fifty-seven days and raped by her captors was ignored. (Hearst received the maximum sentence for her participation in a bank robbery – seven years in a federal prison.)[5] When Linda Lovelace revealed her abuse over years, she too was ignored; she is still considered a 'willing' participant in the pornographic films in which she played.[6]

To understand women's experiences of male violence and their strategies for survival is to put oneself in their place. All women have some experience of male violation – be it from actual physical and/or sexual attack, from sexual harassment on the street or in the workplace, or from those daily invasions of privacy which occur in most public settings. To be told to smile while walking on the street by a stranger is to be told how we are to 'appropriately' display our femininity. *To walk the streets warily at night is how we actually feel our femininity.*

Women know the anger, the humiliation, the shame of being considered a target for men's comments, men's frustrations, or men's needs to reinforce their masculinity. Yet many fail to use their own experiences to understand their sisters' experiences of male violence. Instead, an 'objective' assessment, derived from a male perspective, is used to judge women's survival techniques.

Objectively assessing women's survival techniques separates women from each other: those who experience male violence and those who do not. By saying, 'Well, if someone attacked me I would ...' or, 'I certainly would never allow my husband to beat me ...' or 'I mean if you had been raped or indeed an assault was carried out on you I think the first thing you would do is you would go and tell somebody about it.'[7] Police officer, prosecutor, next-door neighbour, co-worker – male or female – often characterise women's reactions to male violence as inadequate, insufficient, a sign that the woman 'willingly' participated or desired the abuse.

It is easier to characterise raped, battered, or incestually assaulted women's behaviour from a male point of view than from women's point of view. All of the supporting assumptions already exist. Just as it is easier for white people to dismiss racism, non-Jews to dismiss anti-semitism, middle-class people to dismiss classism, assessments based on a male point of view dismiss women's experiences and descriptions of male violence. They do so simply by calling forth 'common sense' – and that 'common sense' has roots in so many other sectors of society. Given the current structure of women's employment, it is also not a coincidence that it is most likely to be men making decisions about women's complaints of male violence. As we saw in Part II, they are likely to use assumptions about women in their assessments of women's complaints and train incoming personnel to do the same. As we saw in Part I, women too assess their own experiences of male violence from a male perspective. Some women, whom Andrea Dworkin describes as 'right-wing women', even act as the voice of the male point of view by encouraging women to live under the illusion that they will be protected from male violence if they are 'virtuous', good housewives, and good mothers.[8] The ever-presence of male violence seems so overwhelming sometimes that it is easier for women to hope they will be protected by men, by law, by *something* rather than to confront the illusion of protection or proclaim its false promises. Stripping women of the illusion that they are protected exposes all women's vulnerability and challenges the perpetuation of expectations which can never be met under current social conditions. Leaving one's physical and sexual wellbeing to 'male' protection, either through law or individual men, merely reproduces many instances of male violence towards women. Many women and a small number of men now recognise that this position continues to get women killed. It leaves the solution to male violence to the very conditions which are responsible for the problem in the first place.

Male violence against women is still defined as a problem for *women*; men have yet to define their own behaviour as problematic. Diana Russell, in her outstanding work on rape in marriage, points to this contradiction:

> If 90 per cent of the crimes of violence were perpetuated by a particular minority or social class, that minority or social class would be viewed as a distinct problem and treated accordingly. But when 90 per cent of the ruling gender is responsible for

such crimes, the fact of this collective responsibility is totally ignored.[9]

USA 1983: Two men in Big Dan's bar in New Bedford, Massachusetts watched, *even cheered*, as four men grabbed a 21-year-old woman, stripped her, hoisted her on to a pool table, raped, buggered, and beat her. She had entered the bar to buy a pack of cigarettes. Asked why no one called the police, the men shrugged off the question by asking where the crime was being committed. The woman immediately informed the police, who arrested her physical assailants whilst still drinking at the bar. And the other by-standers? Were they not also participants in the woman's physical abuse?[10]

Britain 1982: two members of England's football team are accused by a Swedish woman of rape. Immediately an outcry in Britain claiming that the 'lads' are good lads, one about to be married. The woman's prior sexual history was used as a perfectly reasonable explanation for dismissing her accusation of rape: no 'innocent' woman could be raped by such nice lads, she must have been a 'willing' participant, so the thinking goes.[11]

A 1982 series televised in Britain called 'Jury' explored the worlds of the members of a jury. The case they were hearing was a rape case. The verdict? Not guilty. It was decided that the woman, known only to the rapist as a fellow passenger on a train, 'invited' the man into her home and was a 'willing' participant to forced intercourse. This program was discussed by my friend's 14-year-old son in school. While he protested, the class came to a consensus opinion that the woman 'led the rapist on' and that the verdict was a fair one. Again and again, all around us, the male point of view dominates the perspective about men's violence toward women.

There is a tendency today to believe women have achieved 'liberation' in the Western world, particularly in the US and to some extent in Britain. No doubt, women's status has changed since the struggles of the late nineteenth-century feminists for legal recognition as 'persons' in Britain and 'citizens' in the US.[12] We now wear different clothes from our nineteenth-century sisters, but many of the struggles for autonomy and power are frighteningly similar. A 1983 survey in New Jersey, for example, examined sex 'discrimination' in the state court system. Of the female attorneys interviewed, 86 per cent reported hostile or demeaning remarks to them from male peers; two-thirds reported hostile and demeaning remarks or jokes from judges.

The study also found that housewives received lower personal injury damage awards because juries 'fail to recognise' the economic value of their work, that divorced women frequently received inadequate awards of child support and that sanctions against non-payment were weak, and that judges were failing to enforce the Domestic Violence Act passed last year and aimed at wife beating.[13] A 1983 article in the *Wall Street Journal* reports 'proliferating' numbers of complaints of sexual harassment and male violence to women on US university campuses.[14] A British justice in December 1983 stated to a man given a suspended sentence for attempted rape, 'Anything can happen when you put your arms around a woman's neck.'[15] *In this golden era of women's liberation, women are afraid to walk the streets after dark even in their own neighbourhoods for fear of attack.*

With respect to *all* indicators of social status, women occupy secondary positions to men. Women are treated differently in employment, education, law, medicine, and by every major institution which exists. Women are still the primary childcarers, and are responsible for the household. Women's social worth in many respects still depends upon their relationships with men – as wives, mistresses, girlfriends, mothers. Heterosexual coupledom, whether it be a marital relationship or not, is still likely to be an expectation for most members of society – both men and women.

What people point to when espousing so-called women's liberation is sexual 'liberation', presumably co-equally desired and shared sexuality. Readily available birth control provides the 'liberated' woman with greater control over her reproductivity. (The fact that much of this birth control is deterimental to women's health remains an interesting contradiction.) We have also been inundated with sex therapists who tell us that sexual pleasure is achieved with a little practice or with the right positions. This laissez-faire sexuality brings with it the notion that sexuality is an equal negotiation between two consenting adults. Labelling all sexuality as a co-equal exchange however fails to account for inequality based in gender inequality. As such, women's experiences of being sexually harassed or abused by their teachers, doctors, fathers, uncles, bosses, therapists, or their husbands are obscured by the presumption of co-equal exchange.

Within what is assumed to be our achieved 'liberation' are the strongholds of our oppression. Our liberation exists within a world controlled in large part by men and dominated by a male point of view. It is the very foundation for our 'common sense'. This common sense continues to gloss over women's experiences of male violence. As long as this common sense is perpetuated in everyday life, in films, in pornography, in advertisements, on TV, in popular songs, as long as men by gender status are in positions of power (regardless of how many token women achieve positions of individual status), the point of view from which violence against women is understood will remain ultimately a male point of view. This view automatically prevents what Kathleen Barry recommends – placing oneself in women's place. For it is in women's place that women are subjected to the perpetual reminders about their status as women.

The figures tabulating women's experiences of male violence are a cause for alarm. Yet opposition to male violence is dismissed as a 'feminine' plot to undermine men as men. Why is it still a political statement to refer to *male* violence against women rather than to 'private' violence? Clearly, women understand the nature of the violence against them or they wouldn't be so wary on the street and so ready to speak up when you begin to talk about your own experiences of male violence.

The struggle against male violence is the struggle against women's oppression. It is the struggle against a gender status which includes systematic physical and/or sexual assault as a part of our normal, routine daily existence. It is a struggle that demands that women are no longer at risk physically and sexually at the hands of men who promise protection. That is why the struggle against male violence should be a *woman-defined* struggle, with strategies aimed at intervention on every level in society where women find themselves. And these struggles are already taking place, on individual, institutional and societal levels. To acquaint you with them, as well as solicit your participation in them, I will briefly address each of them.

Individual struggles: support for survivors

Each person – whether you be friend, sister, mother, co-worker, counsellor, teacher and so forth – can play a role in individual women's survival from male violence. It is the support or the lack of support women receive from those around them which contributes to the maintenance of silence or encourages the breaking of it. A process of recovery from incestuous assault, sexual assault, or physical assault takes a long time, sometimes a lifetime. Some women's scars are more visible than others; the memory is deep and can be brought to the surface by a smell, a visual image, or a string of words. Through mutual support, women who have experienced male violence can regain a sense of dignity; their struggle is all women's struggle.

It was the contemporary feminist movement which took the initiative to set up today's systems of support for raped and battered women in both the United States and Britain. Establishing rape crisis centres and refuges for battered women was an early response to unmasking the daily experiences of male violence. (Most of these support networks are less than fifteen years old.) Through these woman-defined support networks, women recognise the unique contribution their womanhood lends to other women's survival. Twenty-four hours a day women have immediate access to another sympathetic ear, one that does not question women's point of view. Day or night, in times of acute crisis and in total anonymity, women seek the support of other women. So much so that even feminists continue to be surprised by the numbers of women seeking assistance and support. At the same time, women's personal experiences are, to women staffing support networks, the symbol of women's overall status within Western society. The personal is indeed the political substance of women's lives.

Self-help and fostering women's personal autonomy are the aims of women-run survival centres. Incest survivor groups, battered women support groups, sexually assaulted women's groups, composed of women of all ages, classes, ethnic and racial groups, work together to confront the scars of their experiences of male violence. Sharing strategies for survival as well as sharing the many setbacks, depressions, anxieties or anger give women strength. Throughout the US and Britain, many such groups meet regularly.

As individuals assisting in women's survival, by far the most important and perhaps the most difficult task is for us to learn the art of listening, and listening from *women's* experiential base. For many, listening to tales of abuse, violence and terror are very difficult. These tales unlock our own fears, remind us of our own potentially violent or violent experiences, and at times make us feel as vulnerable as the woman herself. Becoming a good listener means that we too must not block out what has happened to us. It means being empathetic, putting oneself in women's place as *women*. For many of us that also means seeing our own experiences in a different light. We are more acutely aware of women's vulnerability, aware that the gender status 'woman' significantly affects our own lives and the lives of our children. Supporting women's survival also demands that we rid ourselves of our own prejudices and assumptions that women provoke or ask for the violence against them. No doubt some women's lives or lifestyles are exposed to greater potential for violence. In today's complex world, not all individual situations involving male violence will be totally understandable to us; all are not easily categorised, there are many contradictions. But relying upon traditional male notions – notions which all too easily blame women for any violence which befalls them, merely re-establishes grounds for victim blaming. Just as each person is capable of assisting in individual women's survival, each person is also capable of reproducing a male point of view which prevents woman-defined experiences of male violence emerging and being understood. In examining our own 'common sense', we can monitor how it might foster or maintain a male point of view. This often means that we lose much of socially acceptable senses of humour or that we are less tolerant (or even intolerant) of sexist comments. (We are also likely to lose friends this way.) Questioning explanations for male violence that turn to women's provocation or men's uncontrollable lust or anger is yet another way to stop reproducing dominant explanations for male violence. It is far too easy to overlook the power of gender inequality rather than question that which is so 'commonsensical'. At the same time, personal strategies for women surviving male violence feed into the need to find strategies to challenge institutional processes which serve to foster, to maintain and to reproduce male violence against women.

Struggles on institutional levels

Armed with a woman-defined orientation toward male violence, feminist intervention on institutional levels and into institutional thinking and practice has taken two approaches. The first is directed at the wider structural obstacles found in legislation. The second entails feminist efforts in face-to-face challenges of those in decision-making capacities, such as monitoring police behaviour or participating in the training of police or court personnel. Through both strategies, women hope to alter the practice of discretionary decision-making which is, as we saw in Part II, heavily entrenched in a male point of view. Not surprisingly, institutional intervention becomes a much more difficult and much more complex task.

On the legislative level, intervention opens up the *structural* possibilities of changing the obstacles everyday decision makers face. For example, removing a defence attorney's four aces, that of testimony concerning the prior sexual history of the complainant in rape trials, also structurally removes the excuses used by some in decisions to forward a prosecution for rape because of the woman's so-called 'credibility' problems. However, there are still many ways in practice that defence attorneys can allude to women's sexual character. Clearly, legislative efforts are only the first step. Efforts now surrounding the struggle to remove marital exemption from the rape statutes are ongoing. (On the other hand, some states have rewritten statute to include exemption for cohabitees.)[16] The issues concerning the assumptions behind prior sexual history or marital exemption and their relationship to women's experiences and women's right to say 'no' are at least being raised publicly – even if, as in the debate over marital rape in the California legislature, comments such as those of one senator are spoken aloud: 'But if you can't rape your wife, who can you rape?'[17] (At least we clearly see the male point of view!) In addition, revision of sexual assault statutes in some of the US states have included changing the definition of rape from vaginal penetration by the penis (the current definition in England and Wales and in Scotland) to forcible penetration of any orifice by penis or other 'foreign' objects. This definition widens the definition of *sexual* violation to experiences of forced oral or anal intercourse or sexual mutilation by other objects. In this way the focus about rape concentrates on experiential basis of forced sexuality regardless of form and away from traditional notions of 'consensual' intercourse. Legislative changes and the discussions surrounding them involve the unmasking of the images about sexual assault that remain sedentary until the waters are stirred.

By the same token, legislation concerning wife beating (termed, of course, 'domestic violence' for many of the legislative debates) has been effected in Britain and in almost every US state. For the most part, this legislation opens up hithertofore unavailable civil and criminal remedies for women to take against violent men. In Massachusetts, for instance, women now have access to a judge twenty-four hours a day in order to obtain a restraining order (or order of protection) against their husband or cohabiting boyfriend's abuse. (Abuse here also included forced sexual relations.) In addition, this statute gives police the power to arrest without a warrant on the grounds that a man's violence or threat of violence violates the court order. There are also provisions within the legislation for transporting an injured woman to a hospital or shelter and supposedly remaining on site until the woman feels safe. (In practice, this last bit of legislation is seldom done.) What is interesting about this statute is that it tries to intervene into the typical police practice of non-arrest. Some US state statute changes mandate the reporting of 'domestic disputes' to other agencies for statistical purposes or for providing social services. The most important part of any legislation is how decision makers put the provisions of the statutes into practice. Unfortunately, once legislation is passed, it is mistakenly credited with solving the problem. One Massachusetts official, for example, remarked in a meeting that now that the state had a special domestic violence statute, shelters would no longer be needed! (The official was in charge of allocating funds for shelters.)[18]

Following on the footsteps of efforts surrounding sexual and physical assault against women, legislation concerning sexual harassment emerged in the US. The 1980 guidelines issued by the US EEOC recognised sexual harassment as a form of sexual discrimination. As a result, all government institutions and all private institutions receiving federal funds were mandated to establish grievance procedures for complaints about sexual harassment. A number of private lawsuits addressed the issues; enough have been successful to inform institutions that they must at least have grievance procedures available to complaining employees. In Britain, the work against sexual harassment has grown up within the unions. In September 1983 the first industrial tribunal case filed on the grounds of sexual harassment was successful. Policy statements are now at least being adopted by many unions; training programs have begun.

Legislative efforts are important ideologically, but are not a solution to women's unequal status. We must keep in mind that neither the US nor Britain has passed an equal rights declaration! Despite the groundbreaking work of legislative change, many of women's complaints about male violence are not being heard. Therefore, a second strategy accompanying any legislative changes involves the monitoring of institutional practice and policy concerning the daily decision-making of those in authority to hear women's grievances. What this means is that on all levels, decision makers too must be exposed to a different way of viewing women's grievances – through training and through changes in the internal reward or promotion structure. In order to stop the 'commonsensical' approach to organisational decision-making – that common sense which reflects a male point of view – decision makers as well as the organisations themselves have got to be willing to take risks, and lose.

It is an art to argue and defend women-defined experiences of male violence and the flaws in existing complaints procedures in order to actually implement existing legislation – legislation that on its face is innovative. It is yet another art to translate this legislation into a form meaningful to the everyday practitioner or personnel officer who ultimately makes decisions about women's complaints. These decisions are made easier if the social climate in which these decisions are made also reflects women-defined needs in areas such as financial autonomy, occupational choice, reproductive choice, and so forth. Clearly, many women's efforts are needed in these areas as well.

Social climate of gender inequality

Today, research in both Britain and America contains volumes of information on women's position in society. While there continues to be disagreement as to the root of this inequality (is it due to the economic structure, gender structure, or a combination thereof?), the fact of the inequality bears out under the most rigid of tests. It is this inequality that sets the social climate within which male violence to women is viewed; it is one which also fosters the reaction of women themselves to men's threatening, intimidating, coercive or violent behaviour.

The struggle against the perpetuation of gender inequality is a struggle against male violence. As we saw in Part I, women's survival strategies often rest upon their resources. Employment possibilities are affected by occupational choice, which is affected by education, which in turn is affected by social factors such as class, race and gender. As girls grow up, they learn about women's vulnerability to men. At the same time, women's world is often distinct from and separate from men's world. The private sector – domestic life – remains rooted in family and domestic responsibilities. This sexual division of labour has profound effects on women's participation in public life. Women's status will be lowest in conditions of sharp separation of domestic life, 'the private', and the life outside the home, 'the public', proposed anthropologist Michelle Z. Rosaldo.[19]

Even if women work outside the home, their identity is still tied to the 'domestic' self – in image and reality. 'Public' (men's) world versus 'private' (women's) world seeps into the understanding of male violence to women. If most violence to women takes place within the confines of a woman's own home (and most data indicate this to be the case – in contrast to the fear women have of open, outside spaces) then a society which segregates public and private for purposes of legitimacy, status and so forth will be unlikely to elevate crime against women which occurs in this 'private' sector to that of serious 'crime'; a threat to society is a threat to the public sector. Crime to women outside the home can also be characterised as a 'private' matter and thus given secondary importance. Certainly there is evidence to support the statement that in any crime of personal violence inside and outside the home between men-as-assailants and women-as-complainants, the violence is likely to be treated as a 'private' dispute. Just as often, instances of sexual harassment tend to be treated as 'personality conflicts' or 'personal attractions' rather than features reflecting the general treatment of women elsewhere.

Struggles for women's autonomy outside the confines of domestic life and without the restriction of sexual objectification is essential to combating male violence against women. Overturning stereotypes about women within, for example, the education or employment spheres has an impact upon the traditional stereotypes of women in other sectors as well. Women still earn from three-fifths to two-thirds of what men earn; are likely to occupy part-time or marginal employment positions; and are most likely to be employed doing 'women's' work in both the United States and Britain. The educational system reproduces the female labour market; educational systems prepare women more for their traditional domestic roles as wives and mothers than for more 'public' roles in the workforce.[20] A struggle against traditional stereotypes in employment or educational systems is another strategy to remove the foundation for the conditions which contribute to male violence against women.

Above all, our institutional systems – legal, educational, employment and so forth – are integrally linked to the economic structure. Today we are seeing a turning away from government spending on essential services for all citizens. Public expenditure budgets are so constrained that policies of screening out criminal complaints, for example, are sometimes also related to budgetary constraints. Cuts in government spending have a profound impact upon women, who are the largest recipients of subsistence benefits in both the US and Britain. Women with children and elderly women alike depend upon government subsidy for basic subsistence. Fluctuations in the labour market, affected by decisions in economic policy, are likely to hit women hardest, with part-time and recently employed workers the first to be laid off in times of economic recession. Both the US and Britain look to world markets outside of their own countries; their defence budgets alone are crippling their economies. A struggle against male violence is also a struggle against an economic system which does not put people first. We also know that male violence is likely to exist at a higher rate under militarism and war-induced violence; at present, both the US and Britain participate in war actions all over the world. Both the US and Britain pride themselves on their prowess as protectors of democracy; that prowess merely serves to perpetuate conditions which encourage violence against women within their own boundaries.

The next time you walk home and find that you are taking precautionary measures – holding your keys in your hands, crossing the streets when you see a man on the same side – remember that you are not alone. All over the country, on both sides of the Atlantic, on many streets, women are doing the same thing. Don't you think it is time we started complaining?

Notes

Chapter 1

1 William J. Goode, 'Why men resist', in Barrie Thorne with Marilyn Yalom, *Rethinking the Family: Some Feminist Questions*, New York, Longman, 1982, pp.131–50.
2 See for example Kathleen Barry, *Female Sexual Slavery*, New York, Avon Books, 1979, pp.14–38; Judith R. Walkowitz, *Prostitution and Victorian Society*, Cambridge, Cambridge University Press, 1980; Jeffrey Weeks, *Sex, Politics and Society*, London, Longman, 1981.
3 Judith R. Walkowitz, 'Jack the Ripper and the myth of male violence', *Feminist Studies*, vol.8, no.3, 1982, p.560.
4 Walkowitz (1982), op. cit., p.561.
5 Walkowitz (1982), op. cit., p.562.
6 Elizabeth Pleck, 'Feminist responses to "crimes against women", 1868–1896', *Signs*, vol.8, no. 3, Spring 1983, p.466.
7 See for example Clarice Feinman, *Women in the Criminal Justice System*, New York, Praeger, 1980, pp.39–52, 65–68; Weeks, op. cit., p.215.

Part 1

1 Anja Meulenbelt, *The Shame is Over*, London, The Women's Press, 1980, pp.192–3.

Chapter 2

1 Jalna Hanmer and Sheila Saunders, 'Blowing the cover of the protective male: a community study of violence to women', in Eva Gamarnikow,

David Morgan, June Purvis and Daphne Taylorson (eds), *The Public and The Private*, London, Heinemann, 1983, pp.28–46. For information about the methodology and a practical 'how to' guide for conducting studies of women's experiences of male violence, see Jalna Hanmer and Sheila Saunders, *Well Founded Fear: A Community Study of Violence to Women*, London, Hutchinson, 1984.

2 Hanmer and Saunders (1983), op. cit., p.30.

3 See for example, Mike Hough and Pat Mayhew, *The British Crime Survey; First Report*, London, HMSO, no.76, 1983. Data released to me by the Home Office indicate that over 50 per cent of women as opposed to 14 per cent of men reported they felt a 'bit' to 'very' unsafe on their neighbourhood streets alone after dark. The United States Department of Justice, Law Enforcement Assistance Administration, *Criminal Victimization in the United States* (many volumes), summary findings on fear reporting differences in men's and women's fear in the *LEEA Newsletter*, March 1974, p.15, 6 out of 10 women, versus 2 out of 10 men, report fear about walking on the street within a mile of their homes.

4 See Margaret T. Gordon, Stephanie Riger, Robert K. LeBailly and Linda Heath, 'Crime, women, and the quality of urban life', in Catharine R. Stimpson, Elsa Dixler, Martha J. Nelson and Kathryn B. Yatrakis (eds), *Women and the American City*, Chicago, University of Chicago Press, pp.141–57.

5 C. A. MacKinnon, 'Feminism, marxism, method, and the state: an agenda for theory', *Signs*, vol.7, no.3, 1982, p.530.

6 MacKinnon, op. cit., p.539.

7 Mike McGuire, *Burglary in a Dwelling*, Cambridge Studies in Criminology, XLIX, London, Heinemann, 1982.

8 For a discussion of the 'wise', see Erving Goffman, *Stigma*, Englewood Cliffs, New Jersey, Prentice-Hall, 1963. See also Florence Rush, 'Freud and the sexual abuse of children', *Chrysalis*, no.1, 1977, pp.31–45, for an interesting analysis of how Freud's theorising set women up for the blame for abuses to their own sexuality.

9 See for example, Hans von Hentig, *The Criminal and His Victim*, New Haven, Connecticut, Yale University Press, 1948; Israel Drapkin and Emilio Viano (eds), *Victimology: A New Focus*, Lexington, Massachusetts, D. C. Heath & Co., 1975 (five volumes); Stephen Schafer, *The Victim and His Criminal*, New York, Random House, 1968.

10 For a feminist critique of victimology, see Loreene Clark and Debra Lewis, *Rape; The Price of Coercive Sexuality*, Toronto, Canada, The Women's Press, 1977, pp.147–158; Nicole H. Rafter and Elizabeth A. Stanko, 'Introduction', in N. H. Rafter and E. A. Stanko (eds), *Judge, Lawyer, Victim, Thief: Women, Gender Roles and Criminal Justice*, Boston,

Massachusetts, Northeastern University Press, 1982, pp.1–28; and Kurt Weis and Sandra S. Borges, 'Victimology and rape: the case of the legitimate victim', *Issues in Criminology*, vol.8, Fall 1973, pp.71–115.

11 Beniamin Mendelsohn, 'The origin of the doctrine of victimology', *Excerpta Criminologica*, vol. 3, May-June 1963, pp.239–344.

12 Von Hentig, op. cit., pp.404–38, for his categories of victims.

13 Stephen Schafer, 'The beginning of victimology,' in Burt Galaway and Joe Hudson (eds), *Perspectives on Crime Victims*, St. Louis, Missouri, C. V. Mosby Company, 1981, my emphasis.

14 Kathleen Barry, *Female Sexual Slavery*, New York, Avon Books, 1979, pp.40–2.

15 Barry, op. cit., p.42.

16 Barry, op. cit., pp.43–6.

17 MacKinnon states, 'Sexuality, if noticed at all, is like "everyday life", analysed in gender-neutral terms, as if its social meaning can be presumed the same, or coequal, or complementary, for men and women', op. cit., p.526. For an enlightening discussion of the male point of view with regard to male violence, see Catharine A. MacKinnon, 'Feminism, marxism, method, and the state: toward feminist jurisprudence', *Signs*, vol.8, no.4, 1983, pp.635–58.

18 MacKinnon (1982), op. cit., p.532.

19 See, for example, Carol Gilligan, *In a Different Voice*, Cambridge, Massachusetts, Harvard University Press, 1982; and Jessie Barnard, *The Female World*, New York, Free Press, 1981.

20 Susan Brownmiller, *Against Our Will*, New York, Bantam Books, 1975, p.5, states that rape is 'nothing more or less than a conscious process of intimidation by which *all men* keep *all women* in a state of fear' (emphasis in original). I disagree. Not all men consciously threaten women with rape. But men, by virtue of their membership in the category 'men', are potentially threatening to women because of women's knowledge about and fear of rape. Men, however, do acknowledge women's fear of rape. See Timothy Beneke, *Men on Rape*, New York, St. Martin's Press, 1982.

21 Susan Griffin, *Rape: The Power of Consciousness*, San Francisco, Harper & Row, 1979, p.24.

Chapter 3

1 Jessie Bernard, *The Female World*, New York, Free Press, 1981, pp.133–4.

2 Raphaela Best, cited in Bernard, op. cit., p.133.

3 Elizabeth quoted in Jean Renvoize, *Incest: A Family Pattern*, London, Routledge & Kegan Paul, 1982, pp.110–11.

4 Jenny quoted in Louise Armstrong, *Kiss Daddy Goodnight*, New York, Pocket Books, 1978, p.22–3.

5 Sigmund Freud himself was confused by women's accounts of childhood sexual encounters. He even went so far as to say that childhood sexual trauma was the origin of women's hysteria. However, he soon grew uncomfortable with this analysis, attributing accounts of his patients to their fantasies, thus denying women's own experiences of sexual abuse. See Sigmund Freud, 'The aetiology of hysteria', *The Complete Psychological Works of Sigmund Freud*, trans. James Strachey, Standard Edition, London, Hogarth Press, 1962, vol.III, pp.191–221. See also Florence Rush, 'Freud and the sexual abuse of children', *Chrysalis*, vol.1, 1977, pp.31–45 for an analysis of Freud's backpeddling and Judith Lewis Herman, *Father-Daughter Incest*, Cambridge, Massachusetts, Harvard University Press, 1981, pp.9–11, for an understanding of Freud's work in the silencing of women's incest experiences. I highly recommend Herman's book for its detailed, insightful feminist analysis of incest and her commitment to understanding incest from the woman's perspective with a clear understanding of how that perspective has been distorted within male-dominated thinking, psychoanalytic theorising and practice.

6 Sandra Butler, *The Conspiracy of Silence*, New York, Bantam Books, 1979, p.2.

7 These five surveys are: Carney Landis, *Sex in Development*, New York, Harper & Brothers, 1940; Alfred C. Kinsey, Wardell B. Pomeroy, Clyde E. Martin and Paul H. Gebhard, *Sexual Behaviour in the Human Female*, Philadelphia, Saunders, 1953; Judson Landis, 'Experiences of 500 children with adult sexual deviance', *Psychiatric Quarterly Supplement*, vol.30, 1956, pp.91–109; John Gagnon, 'Female child victims of sex offenses', *Social Problems*, vol.13, 1956, pp.176–92; and David Finkelhor, *Sexually Victimized Children*, New York, Free Press, 1979. Herman's summary and analysis of these surveys is particularly useful and enlightening. See Herman, op. cit., pp.12–15. For a discussion of incidence in Britain, see Renvoize, op. cit., pp.44–9.

8 Butler, op. cit., p.13. Similar incidences of childhood sexual abuse are reported by Florence Rush, 'The sexual abuse of children: a feminist point of view', in Noreen Connell and Cassandra Wilson (eds), *Rape: The First Sourcebook for Women*, New York, New American Library, 1974, pp.65–75.

9 David Finkelhor, cited by Renvoize, op. cit., p.51, as personal communication in 1980.

10 Researchers finding incestually assaulted women's reactions as 'frightening' or 'upset' are J. Landis, op cit., J. Gagnon, op. cit., Finkelhor, op. cit.; as 'unpleasant' experiences, C. Landis, op. cit.; and

'unpleasant' and 'negative', Herman, op. cit., p.28, citing work by Warren Farrell and Jean Nelson, who were initially looking for 'positive' incest experiences, and found overwhelming negative experience.

11 Wini Breines and Linda Gordon, 'The new scholarship on family violence', *Signs*, vol.8, no.3, 1983, pp.490–531, raise some interesting points concerning generational and gender inequality in cases of incestuous assault. Herman, op. cit., discusses the 'seductive daughter' assumption, pp.36–42.

12 Judith Herman and Lisa Hirschman, 'Father-daughter incest, *Signs*, vol.2, no.4, Summer 1977, p.743.

13 Woman quoted in Renvoize, op. cit., p.18.

14 Herman and Hirschman, op. cit., p.748.

15 Carol Gilligan, *In a Different Voice: Psychological Theory and Women's Development*, Cambridge, Massachusetts, Harvard University Press, 1982, p.38.

16 Barbara Myers quoted in Renvoize, op. cit., p.65.

17 Evelyn quoted in Butler, op. cit., p.51.

18 Ibid., pp.51–2.

19 Mavis Tsai and Nathaniel Wagner, 'Therapy groups for women sexually molested as children', *Archives of Sexual Behaviour*, vol.7, 1978, pp.417–29; Jill Miller, Deborah Moeller, Arthur Kaufman, Peter Di Vasto, Dorothy Pathak, and Joan Christy, 'Recidivism among sex assault victims', *American Journal of Psychiatry*, vol.135, 1978, pp.1103–4; Renvoize, op. cit., pp.157–60; Herman, op. cit., pp.29–30.

20 Jennifer James, 'The prostitute as victim', in Jane Roberts Chapman and Margaret Gates (eds), *The Victimization of Women*, Beverly Hills, California, Sage Publications, 1978, pp.196–7.

21 Maggie quoted in Armstrong, op. cit., pp.105–6.

22 Erving Goffman, *Stigma*, Englewood Cliffs, New Jersey, Prentice-Hall, 1963.

23 Carmen quoted in Butler, op. cit., pp.18–19.

24 See Renvoize, op. cit., for a presentation of the gender-neutral explanation of incest. She focuses on the concept of family dysfunction for her explanations of incest.

25 Evelyn quoted in Butler, op. cit., pp.32–53.

Chapter 4

1 Letter to the Editor, *The Village Voice*, 4 October 1979, p.4.

2 For an illuminating discussion of this issue, see Catharine A. MacKinnon, 'Feminism, marxism, method, and the state: toward feminist jurisprudence', *Signs*, vol.8, no.4, 1983, pp.635–58.

3 Susan Brownmiller, *Against Our Will: Men, Women and Rape*, New York, Bantam Books, 1975.

4 Carol Smart, *Women, Crime and Criminology*, London, Routledge & Kegan Paul, 1976, pp.95–107; Julia Schwendiger and Herman Schwendiger, 'Rape myths: in legal, theoretical and everyday practice', *Crime and Social Justice*, vol,13, 1974, pp.18–26; Kurt Weis and Sandra S. Borges, 'Victimology and rape: the case of the legitimate victim', *Issues in Criminology*, vol.8, no.2, 1973, pp.71–115.

5 The Uniform Crime Reports provide yearly statistics on the number of crimes reported to police in the United States. In Britain, the Home Office Criminal Statistics for England and Wales, and Scotland publish yearly data on reported crime.

6 Even the FBI Uniform Crime Reports note that reported rape is only a proportion of committed rapes. The estimate, that 50 per cent of all rapes are reported, is much higher than the proportion of unreported rapes which come to the attention of Rape Crisis Centres.

7 M. Jean McDermott, *Rape Victimization in 26 American Cities*, US Department of Justice, Government Printing Office, 1979, pp.2–4.

8 Mike Hough and Pat Mayhew, *The British Crime Survey*, London, Her Majesty's Stationery Office, 1983, p.21.

9 Loreene Clark and Debra Lewis, *Rape: The Price of Coercive Sexuality*, Toronto, Canada, The Women's Press, 1977, pp.61–2.

10 McDermott, op. cit. and *Forcible Rape: Final Project Report*, US Department of Justice, Government Printing Office, 1978.

11 Diana E. H. Russell, *Rape in Marriage*, New York, Macmillan, 1982.

12 Allan Griswold Johnson, 'On the prevalence of rape in the United States', *Signs*, vol.6, no.1, 1980, p.145. See also Diana E. H. Russell and Nancy Howell, 'The prevalence of rape in the United States Revisited', *Signs*, vol.8, no.4, 1983, pp.688–95.

13 MacKinnon, op. cit., p.651.

14 Susan Griffin, 'Rape: the all-American crime', *Ramparts*, 10, September 1971, pp.26–35.

15 See Brownmiller, op. cit., pp.424–5; Russell (1982), op. cit., pp.42–53.

16 'The meaning of rape', *The Sunday Times* (London), 10 January 1982.

17 Kathryn Quina, 'Long-term Psychological Consequences of Sexual Assault,' unpublished manuscript, University of Rhode Island, Kingston, RI, 1979, p.2.

18 Ann Burgess and Lynda Lytle Holmstrom, 'Rape trauma syndrome', *American Journal of Psychiatry*, vol.131, 1974(a), pp.981–6; and Ann Burgess and Lynda Lytle Holmstrom, *Rape: Victims of Crisis*, Bowie, Maryland, Brady, 1974(b).

19 *The Sunday Times*, op. cit.

20 Burgess and Holmstrom (1974a), op. cit., p.983.

21 Lynda Lytle Holmstrom and Ann Wolbert Burgess, 'Rape; the husband's and boyfriend's initial reactions', *The Family Coordinator*, July 1979, p.323.

22 Cathaleen Jones and Elliot Aronson, 'Attribution of fault to a rape victim as a function of responsibility', in Deanna R. Mass (ed.), *The Rape Victim*, Dubuque, Iowa, Kendall/Hunt, 1977, pp.27–34, and Lawrence G. Calhoun, James W. Selby and Louise J. Warring, 'Social perception of the victim's causal role in rape: an exploratory examination of four factors', *Human Relations*, vol.29, no.6, 1976, pp.517–26.

23 Russell (1973), op. cit., p.43.

24 Jalna Hanmer and Sheila Saunders, 'Blowing the cover of the protective male: a community study of violence to women', in Eva Garmanikow, David Morgan, June Purvis and Daphne Taylorson, *The Public and The Private*, London, Heinemann, 1983, p.37.

25 Lee H. Bowker, 'Women as victims: an examination of the results of L.E.A.A.'s National Crime Survey Program', in Lee H. Bowker (ed.), *Women and Crime in America*, New York, Macmillan, 1981, p.173.

26 Lynda Lytle Holmstrom and Ann Wolbert Burgess, 'Rapists' talk: linguistic strategies to control the victim', *Deviant Behaviour*, vol. 1, 1979, p.105–6.

27 Hanmer and Saunders, op. cit.

28 Diana E. H. Russell, *Rape in Marriage*, New York, Macmillan, 1982, p.153.

29 Marilyn French, *The Women's Room*, London, André Deutsch, 1978, pp.557–9.

30 Russell (1982), op. cit.

31 Burgess and Holmstrom (1974a; 1974b), op. cit.; Noreen Connell and Cassandra Wilson, *Rape: The First Sourcebook for Women*, New York, Plume, 1974; Russell (1975), op. cit.

32 Joanna Shapland, J. Willmore and P. Duff, 'The victim in the criminal justice system', Final Report to the Home Office, October 1981.

33 MacKinnon (1983), op. cit., p.646, n.23; Ann Wolbert Burgess and Lynda Lytle Holmstrom, 'Rape: sexual description and recovery', *American Journal Orthopsychiat*, vol.49, no.4, October 1979, pp.648–57.

Chapter 5

1 Del Martin, *Battered Wives*, New York, Pocket Books, 1976, pp.4–5.

2 Both the US and the UK held hearings about the 'problem' of domestic violence. See *Battered Women: Issues of Public Policy*, Washington, DC, US Commission on Civil Rights, 1978, for testimony presented in the US. The House of Commons appointed a Select Committee on Violence in Marriage in 1974 and proceedings from these hearings are published.

3 For a history of the battered women's movement in the US, see Susan Schechter, *Women and Male Violence*, Boston, Massachusetts, South End Press, 1982; in Britain, see Val Binney, Gina Harkell and Judy Nixon, *Leaving Violent Men*, London, Women's Aid Federation, England, 1981 and Anna Coote and Beatrix Campbell, *Sweet Freedom*, London, Picador, 1982, pp.40–2. It is important to remember that the sheltering movement arose from the feminist movement.

4 Dorie Klein, 'The dark side of marriage: battered wives and the domination of women', in Nicole H. Rafter and Elizabeth A. Stanko (eds), *Judge, Lawyer, Victim, Thief: Women, Gender Roles and Criminal Justice*, Boston, Northeastern University Press, pp.83–107. For a comprehensive examination of wife battering in Scotland, see R. Emerson Dobash and Russell Dobash, *Violence Against Wives*, New York, Free Press, 1979.

5 Suzanne Steinmetz, *The Cycle of Violence: Assertive, Aggressive, and Abusive Family Interaction*, New York, Praeger Publishers, 1977.

6 Dobash and Dobash, op. cit., pp.19–20.

7 Diana E. H. Russell, *Rape in Marriage*, New York, Macmillan, 1982.

8 Murray Straus, Richard J. Gelles and Suzanne Steinmetz, *Behind Closed Doors*, New York, Doubleday, 1980.

9 Russell, op. cit., p.99: Dobash and Dobash support this criticism, op. cit., p.19.

10 Dobash and Dobash, op. cit., p.20, pp.97–123. See also R. Emerson Dobash and Russell P. Dobash, 'The antecedents and nature of violent episodes', paper presented at the Annual Meetings of the American Sociological Association, San Francisco, August 1982.

11 Russell, op. cit., pp.87–101; Irene Henason Frieze, 'Investigating the causes and consequences of marital rape', *Signs*, vol.8, no.3, 1983, pp.532–53.

12 Evidence before the House of Commons Select Committee on Violence in Marriage, 12 March 1975, question 73, pp.21–1.

13 Pat Carlen, *Women's Imprisonment: A Study in Social Control*, London, Routledge & Kegan Paul, 1983, pp.39–44.

14 Dobash and Dobash, op. cit., p.111: Table 8 in the Appendix specifies the extent of women's injuries, p.238.

15 Evan Stark, Ann Flitcraft and William Frazier, 'Medicine and patriarchal violence: the social construction of a "private" event', *International Journal of Health Sciences*, vol.9, no.3, 1979, p.466; and Binney, Harkell and Nixon, op. cit., pp.21–1.

16 Linda Lovelace, *Ordeal*, New York, Berkley Books, 1981, pp.80–1. I highly recommend this book for insight into the process of sexual terrorism and the sexual enslavement of Linda for many years.

17 Letter to the Editor, *Spare Rib*, no.122, p.32.

18 Dobash and Dobash, op. cit., p.125.
19 Dobash and Dobash, op. cit., p.125.
20 Personal communication, May 1983.
21 Phyllis Chesler, *Women and Madness*, London, Allen Lane, 1972, p.42.
22 Carol Gilligan, *In a Different Voice*, Cambridge, Massachusetts, Harvard University Press, p.67.
23 Russell, op. cit., p.221.
24 Adrienne Rich, 'Compulsory heterosexuality and lesbian existence', in Catharine R. Stimpson and Ethel Spector Person (eds), *Women: sex and sexuality*, Chicago, University of Chicago Press, 1980, pp.62–91, (esp. 78), discusses the power of heterosexuality in women's lives. Far deeper than keeping male/female relationships together – despite violence – compulsory heterosexuality also impinges on our expected interaction with men on the street, at work or in the home.
25 Binney, Harkell and Nixon, op. cit., p.8.
26 Dobash and Dobash, op. cit., p.145.

Chapter 6

1 Donna J. Benson and Gregg Thompson, 'Sexual harassment on a university campus: the confluence of authority relations, sexual interest and gender stratification', *Social Problems*, vol.29, no.3, 1982, p.242.
2 Benson and Thompson, op. cit., p.245.
3 Dierdre Silverman, 'Sexual harassment: working women's dilemma', *Quest*, vol.III, no.3, Winter 1976–7, pp.18–19; also cited in Catharine A. MacKinnon, *Sexual Harassment of Working Women*, New Haven, Connecticut, Yale University Press, 1979, p.47.
4 See, for example, Phyllis L. Crocker, 'An analysis of university definition of sexual harassment', *Signs*, vol.8, no.4, 1983, pp.696–707; MacKinnon, op. cit., pp.25–55; Nathalie Hadjifotiou, *Women and Harassment at Work*, London, Pluto Press, 1983, pp.7–26; Sue Read, *Sexual Harassment at Work*, Feltham, Middlesex, Hamlyn Paperbacks, 1982, pp.9–29.
5 Read, op. cit., pp.70–1.
6 Ximena Bunster, personal communication.
7 For an analysis of this survey, see Susan E. Martin, 'Sexual harassment in the workplace: from occupational hazard to sex discrimination', paper delivered at Law and Society annual meeting, Amherst, Massachusetts, 1981.
8 E. G. C. Collins and T. B. Blodgett, 'Sexual harassment – some see it – some won't', *Harvard Business Review*, vol.59, no.2, 1981, pp.76–95.
9 Ann Sedley and Melissa Benn, *Sexual Harassment at Work*, London, NCCL Rights of Women Unit, 1982, p.11 for the Liverpool survey

results; Hadjifotiou, op. cit., p.10 cites the results of the Alfred Marks Survey; Carey Cooper and Marilyn Davidson, *High Pressure: Working Lives of Women Managers*, London, Fontana, p.100.

10 Lin Farley, *Sexual Shakedown: the Sexual Harassment of Women on the Job*, New York, McGraw Hill, 1978, pp.83–4.

11 Read, op. cit., pp.69–70.

12 Lynn Wehrli cited in MacKinnon, op. cit., p.48.

13 Farley, op. cit., pp.81–2.

14 Farley, op. cit., p.74.

15 Farley, op. cit., p.85.

16. Benson and Thompson, op. cit., p.246.

17 Silverman, op. cit., p.18.

18 Ximena Bunster personal communication. See Ann Field, 'Harassment on campus: sex in a tenured position?', *MS*, September, 1981, pp.64–73 and Fairness Committee, 'The politics of sexual harassment', *Off Our Backs*, May 1982, for an analysis of the Clark University case.

19 Read, op. cit., p.57.

Chapter 7

1 Catharine A. MacKinnon, 'Feminism, marxism, method, and the state: toward feminist jurisprudence', *Signs*, vol.8, no.4, p.651 makes this point more eloquently than I do. Her work addresses the locus of the difficulty in understanding women's experiences of male violence: distinguishing so-called aberrant male behaviour from what is considered to be typical male behaviour. Many of her ideas will be found throughout this book.

2 The position of women as experienced by them relates to the social and cultural process in which they live. While I am generally speaking about American and British societies, and Western society in general, much of what I say relates to women in other societies as well. For a discussion of these processes, see Sherry B. Ortner and Harriet Whitehead, 'Introduction', in Ortner and Whitehead (eds), *Sexual Meanings: The Cultural Construction of Gender and Sexuality*, London, Cambridge University Press, 1981, pp.1–27. In a revealing study of similar silencing processes among Arab women, see Nawal El Saadawi, *The Hidden Face of Eve*, London, Zed Press, 1980.

3 There are volumes of information on girls' socialisation, acquisition of gendered identities, and the construction and meanings of women's world. Jessie Bernard, *The Female World*, New York, The Free Press, 1982, and Ann Oakley, *Sex, Gender and Society*, New York, Harper & Row, 1972 are useful in their approaches to women's world. See also Sherry B. Ortner and Harriet Whitehead, 'Accounting for sexual

meanings', in Sherry B. Ortner and Harriet Whitehead (eds), *Sexual Meanings: The Cultural Construction of Gender and Sexuality*, London, Cambridge University Press, 1981, pp.1–29.

4 Carol Gilligan, *In a Different Voice*, Cambridge, Massachusetts, Harvard University Press, 1982, particularly p.24–63, addresses the psychological development of boys and girls in relation to their image of relationships.

5 Catharine A. MacKinnon, 'Feminism, marxism, method and the state: an agenda for theory', *Signs*, vol.7, no.3, p.515. MacKinnon discusses women's sexuality as that which is primarily objectified by men. This objectification then becomes 'the primary process of the subjection of women' (p.541). The ideas presented in this article are crucial to my discussion.

6 MacKinnon (1983), op. cit., p.646, note 23: Lynda Lytle Holmstrom and Ann Wolbert Burgess, 'Rape: the husband's and boyfriend's initial reactions', *The Family Coordinator*, July 1979, pp.321–30.

7 MacKinnon (1983), op. cit., p.646.

8 Holmstrom and Burgess, op. cit., p.328.

9 Dierdre Silverman, 'Sexual harassment: working women's dilemma', *Quest*, vol.III, no.3, Winter, 1976–7, p.18.

10 Anonymous, personal communication, November 1983.

11 Sandra Butler, *Conspiracy of Silence*, New York, Bantam Books, 1979, p.52.

12 Ann Wolbert Burgess and Lynda Lytle Holmstrom, 'Rape trauma syndrome', *American Journal of Psychiatry*, 131, 1974, p.983.

13 R. Emerson Dobash and Russell Dobash, *Violence Against Wives*, Shepton Mallet, England, Open Books, 1980, p.111.

14 Lin Farley, *Sexual Shakedown*, New York, McGraw-Hill, 1978, pp.102–3.

15 Louise Armstrong, *Kiss Daddy Goodnight*, New York, Pocket Books, 1978, p.23.

16 Russell (1973), op. cit., p.43.

17 Farley, op. cit., p.82.

18 Jean Renvoize, *Incest: A Family Patttern*, London, Routledge & Kegan Paul, 1982, p.65.

19 Letter to the Editor, *Spare Rib*, no.122, p.32.

20 Russell (1973), op. cit., p.59.

21 Sue Read, *Sexual Harassment at Work*, Feltham, Middlesex, Hamlyn Paperbacks, 1982, p.70.

22 Renvoize, op. cit., p.65.

23 Holmstrom and Burgess (1979), op. cit., p.323.

24 Dobash and Dobash, op. cit., p.125.

25 Read, op. cit., p.70.

26 Renvoize, op. cit., p.18.
27 Dobash and Dobash, op. cit., p.125.
28 Read, op. cit., p.70.
29 Jalna Hanmer and Sheila Saunders, 'Blowing the cover of the protective male: a community study of violence to women', in Eva Gamarnikow, David Morgan, June Purvis and Daphne Taylorson, *The Public and The Private*, London, Heinemann, 1983, p.37.
30 Del Martin, *Battered Wives*, New York, Pocket Books, 1976, p.85.
31 Erin Pizzey and Jeff Shapiro, *Prone to Violence*, Feltham, Middlesex, Hamlyn Paperbacks, 1982.
32 Ibid., p.170.
33 Phyllis Chesler, *Women and Madness*, London, Allen Lane, 1974, p.62.
34 Chesler, op. cit., p.131.
35 Chesler, op. cit., p.143.

Part II

1 Jane Doe, 'Two Rapes', *The New York Times*, 28 August 1982.

Chapter 8

1 Ian Walker, 'The double killing of Mary Bristow', *Observer*, 19 June 1983, p.20.
2 Walker, op. cit., p.23.
3 Judith Mullard, 'Death of a Librarian', *New Statesman*, 9 July 1982, p.3. I have also gained insight from my discussions with two of Mary's friends.
4 'Mercy for a husband who killed twice', *The Standard* (London), 6 June 1983, p.5.
5 'Nagging drove a husband to kill', *The Standard* (London), 12 September 1983, p.5.
6 For figures on murder of women in the United States, see William Wilbanks, 'Murdered women and women who murder: a critique of the literature', in Nicole Hahn Rafter and Elizabeth Anne Stanko, *Judge, Lawyer, Victim, Thief: Women, Gender Roles and Criminal Justice*, Boston, Northeastern University Press, 1982, pp.151–80.
7 For a clear discussion of this distinction, see Wilbanks, op. cit., and Jill Radford, 'Womanslaughter: a licence to kill? The killing of Jane Asher', in Paul Gordon and Phil Scraton (eds), *Causes for Concern: Cases in Criminal Justice*, London, Penguin, 1984. I do not address the process of sentencing here. Determining whether a sentence is lenient or severe

must take into account many factors. My point in this book is that the reason stated for lenient or harsh sentences given to convicted men or women are entwined within our readily available, commonsense knowledge about why someone would kill. For a discussion of issues of gender and sentencing, see Nicolette Parisi, 'Are females treated differently?' in Nicole Hahn Rafter and Elizabeth A. Stanko (eds), *Judge, Lawyer, Victim, Thief: Women, Gender Roles and Criminal Justice*, Boston, Northeastern University Press, 1982, pp.205–20. See also Jill Box-Grainger, *Sentencing Rapists*, London Radical Alternatives to Prison, 1982 and Roy Walmsley and Karen White, 'Supplementary information on sexual offences and sentencing', Research Unit Paper 2, Home Office (London) 1980 for discussions of differential sentencing of rapists. Remaining a complex issue, stereotypes used in characterising rape and murder of women are often cited by judges in justification of sentences given to men convicted of these crimes.

8 Ann Jones, *Women Who Kill*, New York, Fawcett Columbine Books, 1981, pp.322–33.

9 'Wife who shot husband is freed', *The Standard* (London), 31 October 1983, p.5.

10 Jones, op. cit., pp.324–331.

11 The strength of stereotypes about women in the reproduction of women's secondary status within both British and American societies cannot be underestimated. The strength of these stereotypes lies in the flexibility and in the ability to capture widespread cultural understanding. That stereotypes are in fact commonsensical means that they then have power over point of view, which is, in a gendered society, a male point of view. For a useful discussion of stereotypes, see J. E. Perkins, 'Rethinking stereotypes', in Michèle Barrett, Philip Corrigan, Annette Kuhn and Janet Wolff (eds), *Ideology and Cultural Production*, London, Croom Helm, 1979, pp.135–59.

12 Comment to me from a police officer, London, November 1983.

13 See Catharine A. MacKinnon, 'Feminism, marxism, method and the state: toward feminist jurisprudence', *Signs*, vol.8, no.4, 1983, pp.635–58. See also Albie Sachs and Joan Hoff Wilson, *Sexism and the Law*, Oxford, Martin Robertson, 1978.

14 See, for example, Martha A. Myers and John Hagan, 'Private and public trouble: prosecutors and the allocation of court resources', *Social Problems*, vol.26, 1979, pp.440–1; Elizabeth A. Stanko, 'These are the cases that try themselves', unpublished PhD dissertation, City University of New York, 1977; Erving Goffman, *Stigma*, Englewood Cliffs, New Jersey, Prentice Hall, 1963; Kirsten M. Williams, 'The effects of victim characteristics on the disposition of violent crimes', in

William F. MacDonald (ed.), *Criminal Justice and the Victim*, Beverly Hills, California, Sage Publications, 1976.

15 Lynda Lytle Holmstrom and Ann Wolbert Burgess, *The Victim of Rape: Institutional Reactions*, New York, John Wiley & Sons, 1978, p.255.

16 See, for example, Elizabeth Anne Stanko, 'Would you believe this woman? Prosecutorial screening for "credible" witnesses and a problem of justice', in Nicole Hahn Rafter and Elizabeth A. Stanko (eds), *Judge, Lawyer, Victim, Thief: Women, Gender Roles and Criminal Justice*, Boston, Northeastern University Press, 1982, pp.63–82.

17 Greer Litton Fox, 'Nice girl: social control of women through a value construct', *Signs*, vol.2, no.4, 1977, p.805.

18 For an explanation of the just world theory, see M. J. Lerner and C. H. Simmons, 'Observer's reaction to the innocent victim: compassion or rejection?', *Journal of Personality and Social Psychology*, vol.4, 1966, pp.203–20; M. J. Lerner, 'Evaluation of performance as a function of performer's reward and attractiveness', *Journal of Personality and Social Psychology*, vol.1, 1965, pp.355–60.

19 See for example, Kurt Weis and Sandra S. Borges, 'Victimology and rape: the case of the legitimate victim', *Issues in Criminology*, no.8, Fall 1973, pp.71–115; Julia R. Schwendinger and Herman Schwendinger, 'Rape myths: in legal, theoretical and everyday practice', *Crime and Social Justice*, no.13, Summer 1974, pp.18–26.

20 See also Cathaleen Jones and Elliot Aronson, 'Attribution of fault to a rape victim as a function of respectability of the victim', in Deanne R. Nass (ed.), *The Rape Victim*, Dubuque, Iowa, Kendall/Hunt, 1977, pp.27–34; Holmstrom and Burgess, op. cit., pp.157–236.

21 Ann Wolbert Burgess and Lynda Lytle Holmstrom, *Rape: Victims of Crisis*, Bowie, Maryland, Brady, 1974, pp.4–6.

22 Zsuzsanna Adler, 'The reality of rape trials', *New Society*, 4 February 1982, pp.190–1.

23 Carol Smart and Barry Smart, 'Accounting for rape, reality and myth in press reporting', in Carol Smart and Barry Smart (eds), *Women, Sexuality and Social Control*, London, Routledge & Kegan Paul, 1978, p.102, emphasis in original.

24 Julia Langdon, 'Rape trials reserved for senior judges', *Guardian*, 15 December 1982, p.1.

25 'Ordeal by Shame', *The Economist*, 23 January 1982, p.12; 'Asking for it?', *The Economist*, 16 January 1982.

26 The case was extensively reported in the *Boston Globe* and the *Worcester Telegram* in Fall 1981.

27 Ross Harper and Arnot McWhinnie, *The Glasgow Rape Case*, London, Hutchinson, 1983; 'Rape case Carol tells of new attack ordeal', *The Standard* (London), 25 August 1983, p.5.

28 Holmstrom and Burgess, op. cit., p.221.
29 Anna Coote, 'Warning to women who "asked for it"', *New Statesman*, 26 March 1982, p.2.
30 'Judge facing recall over sex case remark', *Worcester Telegram*, 1982.
31 Holmstrom and Burgess, op. cit., p.222.
32 *The Standard* (London), 16 June 1983.
33 'Double life of a triple rapist', *The Standard* (London), 19 May 1983, p.1.
34 'Sex horror video led to double rape', *The Standard* (London), 27 June 1983, p.9.
35 Diana E. H. Russell, *Rape in Marriage*, New York, Macmillan, 1982, p.84.
36 Psychological studies of rapists portray them as perverted and psychopathic or merely neurotic. See Rochelle Semmel Albin, 'Psychological studies of rape', *Signs*, vol.3, no.2, 1977, pp.423–35.
37 'Burglar "had sex drive of a Don Juan"', *The Standard* (London), 12 September 1983, p.5.
38 See Lucy Bland, 'The case of the Yorkshire Ripper: mad, bad, beast or male?' in Paul Gordon and Phil Scraton (eds), *Causes for Concern: Cases in Criminal Justice*, Harmondsworth, Penguin, 1984; Wendy Hollway, 'I just wanted to kill a woman? Why? The Ripper and male sexuality', *Feminist Review*, no.9, October 1981, pp.33–41; Joan Smith, 'Getting away with murder', *New Socialist*, May/June 1982, pp.10–12; The Press Council, *Press Conduct in the Sutcliffe Case*, London, Press Council Booklet no.7, 1983.
39 Smith, op. cit., p.12.
40 Ann Rule, *The Stranger Beside Me*, New York, Signet Books, 1980, p.135.
41 Robert M. Emerson, 'Holistic effects in social control decision-making', *Law and Society Review*, vol.17, no.3, 1983, pp.425–55.
42 See Joanna Shapland, J. Willmore and P. Duff, 'The victim in the criminal justice system', Final Report to the Home Office (England and Wales), October 1981; Deborah P. Kelly, 'Victims' reactions to the criminal justice response', paper delivered at the 1982 annual meeting of the Law and Society Association, June 1982.
43 Kelly, op. cit., p.12.
44 'Eight years for double rapist', *The Standard* (London), 13 September 1983, p.15.
45 Kelly, op. cit; Shapland et al., op. cit; Gerry Chambers and Ann Millar, *Investigating Sexual Assault*, Edinburgh, HMSO, 1983.

Chapter 9

1 For a discussion of discretion, see Kenneth Culp Davis, *Discretionary Justice: A Preliminary Inquiry*, Urbana, Illinois, University of Illinois Press, 1971, and Keith O. Hawkins, 'Thinking about legal decision-making', *Issues in Criminological and Legal Psychology*, no. 5, British Society for the Division of Criminological and Legal Psychology, 1983.

2 Common sense is rooted in the organisation as well as in the wider, social context of policing and prosecuting. See Egon Bittner, 'The police on Skid Row: a study of police keeping', *American Sociological Review*, vol.32, 1967, pp.699–715; Davis, op. cit.; Hawkins, op. cit.; Robert M. Emerson, 'Holistic effects in social control decision-making', *Law and Society Review*, vol.17, no.3, 1983, pp.425–55; Frank Miller, *Prosecution: The Decision to Charge a Suspect with a Crime*, Boston, Little Brown, 1970; S. R. Moody and J. Tombs, *Prosecution in the Public Interest*, Edinburgh, Scottish Academic Press, 1982. All the above examine discretionary decisions in the context of the criminal justice system and address the many practical features of these discretionary decisions. My approach throughout this chapter is grounded in an understanding of discretion as a legal decision maker's routine organisational task of 'doing' justice.

3 Erving Goffman, *Stigma*, Englewood Cliffs, New Jersey, Prentice Hall, 1963, p.2, notes that members of society become competent readers of others' behaviour, particularly deviant behaviour.

4 See Abraham Blumberg, *Criminal Justice*, Chicago, Quadrangle, 1967 (United States); Moody and Tombs, op. cit. (Scotland); and Michael King, *The Framework of Criminal Justice*, London Croom Helm, 1981 (England and Wales) for a discussion of the operations of the criminal justice system.

5 I have discussed this process in a preliminary way with respect to American prosecutors in Elizabeth Anne Stanko, 'Would you believe this woman? Prosecutorial screening for "credible" witnesses and a problem of Justice', in Nicole Hahn Rafter and Elizabeth A. Stanko, *Judge, Lawyer, Victim, Thief: Women, Gender Roles and Criminal Justice*, Boston, Northeastern University Press, 1982, pp.63–82.

6 Blumberg, op. cit.; Moody and Tombs, op. cit.; King, op. cit.; and George F. Cole and Andrew Sanders, 'Criminal prosecution in England: evolution and change', *Connecticut Law Review*, vol.14, no.1, Fall 1981, pp.23–39.

7 Jonathan Rubenstein, *City Police*, New York, Farrar, Straus & Giroux, 1972; Donald Black, *The Manners and Customs of the Police*, New York, Academic Press, 1980; S. Holdaway (ed.), *British Police*, London, Edward Arnold, 1979; Egon Bittner, *The Functions of Police in Modern Society*,

Rockville, Maryland, NIMH Center for Studies of Crime and Delinquency, 1972.

8 Black, op. cit.; Paul Ekblom and K. Heal, *The Police Response to Calls from the Public*, London, HMSO, 1982; Peter K. Manning, 'Queries concerning the decision-making approach to police research', *Issues in Criminological and Legal Psychology*, no.5, The British Psychological Society for the Division of Criminological and Legal Psychology, 1983, pp.50–60.

9 Manning, op. cit., p.53.

10 Morton Bard and Joseph Zacker, 'How police handle explosive squabbles', *Psychology Today*, November 1975, p.71.

11 Manning, op. cit., also found instances where callers were 'talked out' of their wish to have an officer sent.

12 Police Foundation, *Domestic Violence and the Police: Studies in Detroit and Kansas City*, Washington, DC, Police Foundation, 1976.

13 Harvey Sachs, 'Notes on police assessment of moral character', in David Sudnow (ed.), *Studies in Social Interaction*, New York, Free Press, 1972; a similar process is used by parole boards in determining a prisoner's chances of successful parole in Keith O. Hawkins, 'Assessing evil: decision behaviour and parole board justice', *The British Journal of Criminology*, vol.23, no.2, April 1983, pp.101–27.

14 Policing is male. For a discussion of masculinity and policing, see Jennifer Hunt, 'The development of rapport through the negotiation of gender in field work among police', *Human Organisation* (forthcoming): Jerome Skolnick, *Justice Without Trial*, New York, John Wiley & Sons, 1966; Nanci Koser Wilson, 'Women in the criminal justice professions: an analysis of status conflict', in Nicole Hahn Rafter and Elizabeth A. Stanko (eds), *Judge, Lawyer, Victim, Thief: Women, Gender Roles and Criminal Justice*, Boston, Northeastern University Press, 1982, pp.359–74.

15 Bittner, op. cit.; Rubenstein, op. cit.; Hawkins (1983), op. cit.

16 Lawrence W. Sherman, 'The specific deterrent effects of arrests for spouse assault: a field experiment', proposal submitted to National Institute of Justice, 1 April 1980.

17 Raymond I. Parnas, 'The police response to the domestic disturbance', in Leon Radzinowitz and Marvin E. Wolfgang (eds), *The Criminal in the Arms of the Law*, New York, Basic Books, 1972, pp. 206–36.

18 See Sherman, op. cit., on the United States; Margaret Borkowski, Merwyn Murch and Val Walker, *Marital Violence*, London, Tavistock, 1983; Val Binney, Gina Harkell and Judy Nixon, *Leaving Violent Men*, London, Women's Aid Federation, 1981, and R. Emerson Dobash and Russell Dobash, *Violence Against Wives*, New York, Free press, 1979 on police responses in Britain.

19 Donald Black, unpublished manuscript (1979), *Dispute Settlement by the Police*, cited in Sherman, op. cit., p.9.

20 Case example cited in study of male violence by Jill Radford, (London) Wandsworth Policing Campaign, November 1983. The police unit responding was probably the Instance Response Unit rather than the local street patrol.

21 Irving Piliavin and Scott Briar, 'Police encounters with juveniles', *American Journal of Sociology*, September 1964, pp.206–214 report juveniles are arrested more often if they challenge the authority of the police. I suspect a similar process works in situations of domestic violence.

22 Binney, Harkell and Nixon, op. cit.

23 M. E. Field and H. F. Field, 'Marital violence and the criminal process: neither justice nor peace', *Social Science Review*, vol.47, no.2, 1973, pp.221–40.

24 Criminal Injuries Compensation Board guidelines, 10–12 Russell Square, London, WC1B 5EN.

25 Frances Wasoff, 'Domestic violence and the police', conference paper 'Battered women and the state', Scottish Women's Aid, 13 December 1980.

26 See Susan Schechter, *Women and Male Violence*, Boston, South End Press, 1982, pp.160–1; Pauline W. Gee, 'Ensuring police protection for battered women: the Scott v. Hart Suit', *Signs*, vol.8, no.3, 1983, pp.554–67.

27 Philip M. Boffey, 'Domestic violence: study favors arrest', *The New York Times*, 5 April 1983, pp.C1–2.

28 Maureen McLeod, 'Victim Non-cooperation in the prosecution of domestic assault', *Criminology*, vol.21, no.3, August 1983, pp.395–416. Other US studies show similar findings; see Maria Roy (ed.), *The Battered Woman*, New York, Van Nostrand Reinhold, 1977, p.36.

29 Dobash and Dobash, op. cit.

30 Donald J. Black, 'Production of crime rates', *American Sociological Review*, vol.35, no.4, 1970 pp.733–48.

31 McLeod, op. cit., p.407.

32 On police production of crime figures, see A. K. Bottomley and C. A. Coleman, *Understanding Crime Rates*, Farnborough, Saxon House, 1981; Black, op. cit.; Skolnick, op. cit.; M. G. Maxfield, D. A. Lewis and R. Szoc, 'Producing official crimes: verified crime reports as measures of police output', *Social Science Quarterly*, vol.61, no.2, 1980; S. McCabe and F. Sutcliffe, *Defining Crime*, London, Blackwell, 1978.

33 As we saw in Part I, women's experiences of male violence are *not* taken seriously by others, including judges (chapter 8). All research in both

the US and Britain indicates the lack of police action in wife beating. Research is sorely needed in on-the-spot determinations by police in instances of men's violence to women. Taking women's experiences of men's violence seriously means questioning much of research on the production of crime reports by police.

34 Detectives, like police officers, make discretionary decisions regarding complaints. See William Sanders, *Detective Work*, New York, Free Press, 1977 and Richard V. Ericson, *Making Crime*, Toronto, Butterworths, 1981. Ericson presents a thorough examination of the research on detectives.

35 'Unfounding' or 'no criming' has been examined by Bottomley and Coleman, op. cit.; McCabe and Sutcliffe, op. cit.; Skolnick, op. cit.; Erickson, op. cit.; H. Pepinsky, 'Police decision-making', in D. Gottfredson (ed.), *Decision-Making in the Criminal Justice System: Reviews and Essays*, Rockville, Maryland, US National Institute of Mental Health, 1975; Gerry Chambers and Ann Millar, *Investigating Sexual Assault*, Edinburgh, HMSO, 1983, pp.35–44.

36 See Chambers and Millar, op. cit. (Scotland) and Richard Wright, 'Rape and physical violence', in D. J. West (ed.), *Sex Offenders in the Criminal Justice System*, Cambridge, Cropwood Conference Series, no. 12, 1980, pp.100–13 (England). Wayne A. Kerstetter, in 'Police response to sexual assault complaints', a paper presented at the 1982 Law and Society Association Meetings, Toronto, Canada, has found that unfounded rates vary by city. He is currently examining the process of sexual assault cases throughout the United States. He can be contacted at the American Bar Foundation, 1155 East 60th Street, Chicago, Illinois, 60637.

37 Loreen Clark and Debra Lewis, *Rape: The Price of Coercive Sexuality*, Toronto, The Women's Press, 1977.

38 Wright, op. cit., pp.101–2.

39 Vicki McNickle Rose and Susan Carol Randall, 'The impact of investigator perceptions of victim legitimacy on the processing of rape/sexual assault cases', *Symbolic Interaction*, vol.5, no.1, 1982, pp.23–36.

40 Ericson, op. cit., p.106.

41 Diana E. H. Russell, *The Politics of Rape*, New York, Stein & Day, 1975, p.203.

42 Chambers and Millar, op. cit., pp.85–6, emphasis in original.

43 Chambers and Millar, op. cit., p.125.

44 Chambers and Millar, op. cit., p.85.

45 Chambers and Millar, op. cit.; Rose and Randall, op cit.

46 Jalna Hanmer and Sheila Saunders, 'Blowing the cover of the protective male: a community study of violence to women', in Eva Gamarnikow,

David Morgan, June Purvis and Daphne Taylorson, *The Public and the
Private*, London, Heinemann, 1983, p.38. Confidence in the police is
undermined by fear of crime. Police treatment might affect a woman's
perception of the criminal justice system as a 'protector', but is unlikely
to ease women's fear about crime. As long as the structure of inquiry
throughout the legal process remains 'male', women's fear – of police
response, of male violence – will not be 'reduced'. See Mary Holland
Baker, Barbara C. Nienstedt, Ronald S. Everett and Richard
McCleary, 'The impact of a crime wave: perceptions, fear, and
confidence in the police', *Law and Society Review*, vo.17, no.2, 1983,
pp.319–35 and Catharine A. MacKinnon, 'Feminism, marxism, method
and the state: toward feminist jurisprudence', *Signs*, vol.8, no.4, 1983,
pp.635–58.

47 Ericson, op. cit., pp.101–2.

48 Robley Geis, Richard Wright and Gilbert Geis, 'Police surgeons and
rape: a questionnaire survey,' *The Police Surgeon*, Journal of the
Association of Police Surgeons of Great Britain, no.14, October 1978,
pp.7–14. See also Gerald D. Robin, 'Forcible rape: institutionalized
sexism in the criminal justice system', *Crime and Delinquency*, vol.23,
April 1977, pp.147–9.

49 In the United States, policing decision and prosecuting decisions are
made independently (Blumberg, op. cit.). Technically, those decisions are
separate in Scotland as well with the most serious cases forwarded to
the Lord Advocate's office (Moody and Tombs, op. cit.). In England and
Wales, police still determine which cases to prosecute, although the most
serious cases are forwarded to the Director of Public Prosecutions. Police
are still the most influential members of the criminal justice process;
their actions open the way for prosecution to be considered. Overall, the
process of prosecution decision-making is similar in England and Wales,
Scotland and the United States. While I refer to 'prosecutors' throughout
this section, I also include police who are making prosecution decisions
among 'prosecutors'. It is also possible that police decisions about
seriousness are different from prosecutors' decisions about seriousness;
see, Elizabeth A. Stanko, 'The arrest versus the case', *Urban Life*, vol.9,
no.4, 1981, pp.395–414.

50 Cole and Sanders, op. cit.; Miller, op. cit.; Blumberg, op. cit.; David
Neubauer, *Criminal Justice in Middle America*, Morristown, New Jersey,
General Learning Press, 1974; Arthur Rosett and Donald R. Cressy,
Justice By Consent, New York, J. B. Lippincott, 1976; John Baldwin
and Michael McConville, *Negotiated Justice: Pressures to Plead Guilty*,
London, Martin Robertson, 1977 address the process of prosecutorial
decision-making and the needs of negotiating the best 'deal' in
conviction. See also Carl J. Hosticka, 'We don't care about what

happened, we only care about what is going to happen: lawyer client negotiations of reality', *Social Problem*, vol.26, 1979, pp.599–610.

51 Emerson, op. cit.; Blumberg, op. cit.; Miller, op. cit.; Martha A. Myers and John Hagan, 'Private and public trouble: prosecutors and the allocation of court resources', *Social Problems*, vol.26, 1979, pp.439–51; Moody and Tombs, op. cit.; Lynn M. Mather, 'Some determinants of the method of case disposition', *Law and Society Review*, vol.8, Winter 1973, pp.187–216; Neubauer, op. cit.

52 Moody and Tombs, op. cit., pp.31–2. Moody and Tombs have also found that in approximately 8 per cent of the cases prosecutors decide not to proceed; it jumps to 30 per cent in cases of sexual assault. This is in contrast with the American experiences where more cases are not prosecuted.

53 Elizabeth A. Stanko, 'The impact of victim assessment on prosecutors' screening decisions: the case of the New York County District Attorney's Office,' *Law and Society Review*, vol.16, no.2, 1981–2, pp.225–39; Elizabeth A. Stanko (1982), op. cit.

54 Elizabeth A. Stanko, *These Are The Cases That Try Themselves*, unpublished PhD dissertation, City University of New York, 1977.

55 Stanko (1981–2), op. cit., p.231.

56 Lynda Lytle Holmstrom and Ann Wolbert Burgess, *The Victim of Rape: Institutional Reactions*, New York, John Wiley & Sons, 1978, p.143. Holmstrom and Burgess address the many problems arising during the prosecution of a case, see pp.121–259.

57 Personal communication, September 1983.

58 Holmstrom and Burgess, op. cit., note that allusions to women's sexuality as determining credibility are commonly addressed at trial. See also Chambers and Millar, op. cit.; and Zsuzsanna Adler, 'The reality of rape trials', *New Society*, 4 February 1982, pp.190–1.

59 Holmstrom and Burgess, op. cit., p.145.

60 Ross Harper and Arnot McWhinnie, *The Glasgow Rape Case*, London, Hutchinson, 1983.

61 A Crown office circular no.1779, dated 15 November 1982, now instructs procurators to inform victims when a case is marked 'no proceedings.' Chambers and Millar, op. cit., p.134, note 1.

62 Chambers and Millar, op. cit., p.10.

63 Chambers and Millar, op. cit., p.41.

64 *The Scotsman*, 30 November 1983, 1 December 1983.

65 Neubauer, op. cit., pp.201, 204.

66 Frank J. Cannavale and William D. Falcon, *Witness Cooperation*, Lexington, Massachusetts, D. C. Heath, 1976; McLeod, op. cit.

67 Stanko (1982), op. cit., p.77.

68 Lisa G. Lerman, *Prosecution of Spouse Abuse: Innovations in Criminal*

Justice Response, Center for Women Policy Studies, Washington DC, 1981; McLeod, op. cit.

69 Lerman, op. cit., p.19.

70 Emily Jane Goodman, 'Legal solutions: equal protection under the law', in Maria Roy (ed.), *Battered Women*, New York, Van Nostrand Reinhold, 1977, p.142.

71 Frances Wasoff, 'The need for legal protection: the role of the prosecutor and the courts in the legal response to domestic violence', paper presented to DHSS (Britain), *Seminar on Violence in the Family*, September 1981.

72 Moody and Tombs, op. cit., pp.67–8.

73 R. Emerson Dobash and Russell Dobash, *Violence Against Wives*, New York, Free Press, 1979.

74 Moody and Tombs, op. cit., p.68.

75 Ibid.

76 Ibid., p.69.

77 Wasoff (1981), op. cit.

78 Stanko (1981–2), op. cit., p.234.

79 Schechter, op. cit., pp.160–1.

80 Kirsten M. Williams, 'Few convictions in rape cases: empirical evidence concerning some alternative explanations', *Journal of Criminal Justice*, vol.9, no.1, 1981, p.37.

81 Myers and Hagan, op. cit.; Stanko (1982), op. cit.; Kirsten Williams, 'The effects of victim characteristics on the disposition of violent crimes', in William F. MacDonald (ed.), *Criminal Justice and the Victim*, Beverly Hills, California, Sage Publications, 1976; Kurt Weis and Sandra S. Borges, 'Victimology and rape: the case of the legitimate victim', *Issues in Criminology*, vol.8, Fall 1973, pp.71–115; Dobash and Dobash, op. cit.

Chapter 10

1 For Britain, see Nathalie Hadjifotiou, *Women and Harassment at Work*, London, Pluto Press, 1983; for the United States, see Catharine A. MacKinnon, *Sexual Harassment of Working Women*, New Haven, Connecticut, Yale University Press, 1979.

2 E. G. C. Collins and T. B. Blodgett, 'Sexual harassment – some see it – some won't', *Harvard Business Review*, vol.59, no.2, 1981, pp.76–95; Vicky Seddon, 'Keeping women in their place', *Marxism Today*, July 1983, pp.20–2; Ann Sedley and Melissa Benn, *Sexual Harassment at Work*, NCCL Rights for Women Unit, 1982.

3 See MacKinnon, op. cit.; Lin Farley, *Sexual Shakedown*, New York,

McGraw-Hill, 1978; Dierdre Silverman, 'Sexual harassment: working women's dilemma', *Quest*, vol.III, no.3, Winter 1976–7, pp.15–24.

4 See MacKinnon, op. cit.

5 MacKinnon, op. cit., pp.83–90.

6 'Employers act to curb sex harassing on the job: lawsuits fines fares', *Wall Street Journal*, 24 April 1981.

7 See Farley, op. cit., pp.183–207.

8 Hadjifotiou, op. cit., pp.7–26 gives details of the Alfred Marks Survey.

9 Robert Sam Anson, 'Unlimited partnership', *Savvy*, November 1982, p.34.

10 Anson, op. cit., p.37.

11 Ibid.

12 Ibid.

13 MacKinnon, op. cit., p.49.

14 Personal communication.

15 'Sexual harassment', *Spare Rib*, June 1983,p.25.

16 'Asking for it?', *Time*, 4 May 1981, p.29.

17 The first British case successfully arguing sexual harassment was decided on 8 September 1983. Elfrieda Walsh was fired after she slapped Jim Devine, a company accountant, after he persisted in 'fondling her'. She was awarded £2,255 compensation. Stated Ms Walsh, 'It is still on my mind now, and I think it will be for a long time.' *Daily Mail*, 9 September 1983, p.3.

18 Hadjifotiou, op. cit.

20 'It's a laugh', *The Standard*, 23 August 1983; *Daily Mirror* lead headline for 23 August 1983 reads, 'The sex commandments of the TUC'.

21 *Daily Mirror*, op. cit., p.1.

22 Personal interview conducted in December 1982 in London.

23 'Wog' is a derogatory and hence racist British term referring to a black person.

Chapter 11

1 Kathleen Barry, *Female Sexual Slavery*, New York, Avon Books, 1979, p.46.

2 Ann Wolbert Burgess and Lynda Lytle Holmstrom, *Rape: Victims of Crisis*, Bowie, Maryland, Brady, 1974.

3 Lin Farley, *Sexual Shakedown*, New York, McGraw-Hill, 1978; Sue Read, *Sexual Harassment at Work*, Feltham, Middlesex, Hamly, 1982; Leeds TUCRIC, *Sexual Harassment of Women at Work: A Study from West Yorkshire*, August 1983.

4 Del Martin, *Battered Wives*, New York, Dell, 1976; Val Binney, Gina Harkell and Judy Nixon, *Leaving Violent Men*, Women's Aid Federation

England, 1981; R. Emerson Dobash and Russell Dobash, *Violence Against Wives*, New York, Free Press, 1979.

5 Barry, op. cit., pp.138–62.

6 Linda Lovelace, *Ordeal*, New York, Berkley Books, 1981.

7 Gerry Chambers and Ann Millar, *Investigating Sexual Assaults*, Edinburgh, HMSO, 1983, p.90.

8 Andrea Dworkin, *Right-wing Women*, London, The Women's Press, 1983.

9 Diana E. H. Russell, *Rape in Marriage*, New York, Macmillan, 1982, p.108.

10 Mary Kay Blakely, 'Who were the men?', *MS*, July 1983, p.50. During the trial of the men charged with rape, the woman has been subjected to a variety of tactics aimed at discrediting her. In addition, the trial proceedings have been broadcast over cable television throughout the US. The four men were found guilty of aggravated rape; the two men who cheered were acquitted of all charges. The woman has since left the New Bedford area. As sentences were passed on the four convicted men (ranging from 6–8 years to 9–12 years in state prison), the woman's lawyer commented: 'There were five sentences in this case, one of them exile.' (*The Worcester Telegram*, 27 March 1984)

11 'Rape case girl "was no innocent",' *Sunday People*, London, 3 October 1982.

12 Albie Sachs and Joan Hoff Wilson, *Sexism and the Law*, Oxford, Martin Robertson, 1978.

13 'Scales tilted against women', *The New York Times*, 27 November 1983, p.6E.

14 Paul A. Engelmayer, 'Violence by students, from rape to racism, raises college worries', *Wall Street Journal*, 21 November 1983.

15 *Daily Record* (Scotland), 3 December 1983, p.1.

16 Russell, op. cit., Appendix II, pp.375–81.

17 Russell, op. cit.

18 This remark was made in a meeting I attended in September, 1980 in Worcester, Massachusetts.

19 Michelle Z. Rosaldo, 'Women, culture and society: a theoretical overview', in Michelle Z. Rosaldo and Louise Lamphere (eds), *Woman Culture and Society*, Stanford, California, Stanford University Press, 1974, pp.17–42.

20 See Jessie Bernard, *The Female World*, New York, Free Press, 1981 (USA); Elizabeth Whitelegg, Madeleine Arnot, Else Bartels, Veronica Beechey, Lynda Birke, Susan Himmelweit, Diana Leonard, Sonja Ruehl and Mary Anne Speakman (eds), *The Changing Experience of Women*, Oxford, Martin Robertson, 1982.

Bibliography

Adler, Zsuzsanna, 'The reality of rape trials', *New Society*, 4 February 1982, pp.190–1.

Albin, Rochelle Semmel, 'Psychological Studies of Rape', *Signs*, vol.3, no.2, 1977, pp.423–35.

Anson, Robert Sam, 'Unlimited partnership', *Savvy*, November 1982, p.34.

Armstrong, Louise, *Kiss Daddy Goodnight*, New York, Pocket Books, 1978.

'Asking for it?', *Time Magazine*, 4 May 1981, p.29.

Baker, Mary Holland, Nienstedt, Barbara C., Everett, Ronald S. and McCleary, Richard, 'The impact of a crime wave: perceptions, fear, and confidence in the police', *Law and Society Review*, vol.17, no.2, pp.319–35, 1983.

Baldwin, John and McConville, Michael, *Negotiated Justice: Pressures to Plead Guilty*, Oxford, Martin Robertson, 1977.

Bard, Morton and Zacker, Joseph, 'How police handle explosive squabbles', *Psychology Today*, November 1976.

Barry, Kathleen, *Female Sexual Slavery*, New York, Avon, 1979.

Beneke, Timothy, *Men on Rape*, New York, St. Martin's Press, 1982.

Benson, Donna J. and Thompson, Gregg, 'Sexual harassment on a university campus: the confluence of authority relations, sexual interest and gender stratification', *Social Problems*, vol.29, no.3, 1982, pp.236–51.

Bernard, Jessie, *The Female World*, New York, Free Press, 1981.

Binney, Val, Harkell, Gina and Nixon, Judy, *Leaving Violent Men: A Study of Refuges and Housing for Battered Women*, Leeds, England, Women's Aid Federation England, 1981.

Bittner, Egon, *The Functions of Police in Modern Society*, Rockville, Maryland, NIMH Center for Studies of Crime and Delinquency, 1972.

Bittner, Egon, 'The police on Skid Row: a study of peace keeping', *American Sociological Review*, vol.32, 1967, pp.699–715.

Black, Donald, *The Manners and Customs of the Police*, New York, Academic Press, 1980.

Black, Donald J., 'Production of crime rates', *American Sociological Review*, vol.35, no.4, 1970, pp.733–48.

Blakely, Mary Kay, 'Who were the men?', *MS*, July 1983.

Bland, Lucy, 'The trial of the Yorkshire Ripper: mad, bad, beast or male?' in Paul Gordon and Phil Scraton (eds), *Causes for Concern: Cases in Criminal Justice*, London, Penguin, 1984.

Borkowski, Margaret, Murch, Mervyn and Walker, Val, *Marital Violence*, London, Tavistock, 1983.

Bottomley, A. K. and Coleman, C. A., *Understanding Crime Rates*, Farnborough, Saxon House, 1981.

Bowker, Lee H., 'Women as victims: an examination of the results of L.E.A.A.'s National Crime Survey program', *Women and Crime in America*, New York, Macmillan, 1981, pp.158–79.

Box-Grainger, Jill, *Sentencing Rapists*, London, Radical Alternatives to Prison, 1982.

Breines, Wini and Gordon, Linda, 'The new scholarship on family violence', *Signs*, vol.8, no.3, 1983, pp.490–531.

Brownmiller, Susan, *Against Our Will: Men, Women and Rape*, New York, Bantam Books, 1975.

Burgess, Ann Wolbert and Holmstrom, Lynda Lytle, 'Rape: sexual disruption and recovery', *American Journal of Orthopsychiat*, vol.49, no.4, October 1979, pp.648–57.

Burgess, Ann W. and Holmstrom, Lynda L., 'Rape trauma syndrome', *American Journal of Psychiatry*, vol.131, 1974(a), pp.981–6.

Burgess, Ann W. and Holmstrom, Lynda L., *Rape: Victims of Crisis*, Bowie, Maryland, Brady, 1974(b).

Butler, Sandra, *The Conspiracy of Silence*, New York, Bantam Books, 1979.

Calhoun, Lawrence G., Selby, James W. and Warring, Louise J., 'Social perception of the victim's causal role in rape: an explanatory examination of four factors', *Human Relations*, vol.29, no.6, 1976, pp.517–26.

Cannavale, Frank J. and Falcon, William D., *Witness Cooperation*, Lexington, Massachusetts, D. C. Heath & Co., 1976.

Carlen, Pat, *Women's Imprisonment: A Study in Social Control*, London, Routledge & Kegan Paul, 1983.

Chambers, Gerry and Ann Millar, *Investigating Sexual Assault*, Edinburgh, HMSO, 1983.

Chesler, Phyllis, *Women and Madness*, New York, Doubleday, 1972; London, Allen Lane, 1974.

Clark, Lorenne and Lewis, Debra, *Rape: The Price of Coercive Sexuality*, Toronto, Canada, The Women's Press, 1977.

Cole, George F. and Sanders A., 'Criminal prosecution in England: evolution and change', *Connecticut Law Review*, vol.14, no.1, Fall 1981, pp.22–39.

Collins, E. G. C. and Blodgett, T. B., 'Sexual harassment – some see it – some won't', *Harvard Business Review*, 59:2, 1981, pp.76–95.

Connell, Noreen and Wilson, Cassandra, *Rape: The First Sourcebook for Women*, New York, Plume, 1974.

Cooper, Carey and Davidson, Marilyn, *High Pressure: Working Lives of Women Managers*, London, Fontana, 1982.

Coote, Anna and Campbell, Beatrix, *Sweet Freedom*, London, Picador, 1982.

Crocker, Phyllis L., 'An analysis of university definitions of sexual harassment', *Signs*, vol.8, no.4, 1983, pp.696–707.

Davis, Kenneth Culp, *Discretionary Justice: A Preliminary Inquiry*, Urbana, Illinois, University of Illinois Press, 1971.

Dobash, R. Emerson and Dobash, Russell P., 'The antecedents and nature of violent episodes', paper presented at the Annual Meeting, American Sociological Association, San Francisco, August, 1982.

Dobash, R. Emerson and Dobash, Russell P., *Violence Against Wives: A Case Against Patriarchy*, New York, Free Press, 1979.

Drapin, Israel and Viano, Emilio (eds), *Victimology: A New Focus*, Lexington, Massachusetts, D. C. Heath & Co., 1975.

Dworkin, Andrea, *Right-Wing Women*, London, The Women's Press, 1983.

Ekblom, Paul and Heal, K., *The Police Response to Calls from the Public*, London, HMSO 1982.

El Saadawi, Nawal, *The Hidden Face of Eve*, London, Zed Press, 1980.

Emerson, Robert M., 'Holistic effects in social control decision-making', *Law and Society Review*, vol.17, no.3, 1983, pp.425–55.

Ericson, Richard V., *Making Crime: A Study of Detective Work*, Toronto, Butterworth & Co., 1981.

Fairness Committee, 'The politics of sexual harassment', *Off Our Backs*, May 1982.

Farley, Lin, *Sexual Shakedown: The Sexual Harassment of Women on the Job*, New York, McGraw-Hill, 1978.

Feinman, Clarice, *Women in the Criminal Justice System*, New York, Praeger, 1980.

Field, Ann, 'Harassment on campus: sex in a tenured position?' *MS*, September 1981, pp.64–73.

Field, M. E. and Field, H. J., 'Marital violence and the criminal process: neither justice nor peace', *Social Science Review*, vol.47, no.2, 1973, pp.221–40.

Finkelhor, David, *Sexually Victimized Children*, New York, Free Press, 1979.

Fox, Greer Litton, 'Nice girl: social control of women through a value construct', *Signs*, vol.2, no.4, 1977, pp.805–17.

French, Marilyn, *The Women's Room*, London, André Deutsch, 1978.

Freud, Sigmund, *The Complete Psychological Works of Sigmund Freud*, vol.III, trans. James Strachey, Standard Edition, London, Hogarth Press, 1962.

Frieze, Irene Hanson, 'Investigating the causes and consequences of marital rape', *Signs*, vol.8, no.3, 1983, pp.532–53.

Gagnon, John, 'Female child victims of sex offenses', *Social Problems*, vol.13, 1956, pp.176–92.

Gee, Pauline W., 'Ensuring police protection for battered women: the Scott V. Hart suit', *SIGNS*, vol.8, no.3, 1983, pp.554–67.

Geis, Robley, Wright, Richard and Geis, Gilbert, 'Police surgeons and rape: A questionnaire survey', *The Police Surgeon*, Journal of the Association of Police Surgeons in Great Britain, no.14, October 1978, pp.7–14.

Gilligan, Carol, *In a Different Voice*, Cambridge, Massachusetts, Harvard University Press, 1982.

Goffman, Erving, *Stigma*, Englewood Cliffs, New Jersey, Prentice-Hall, 1963.

Goode, William J., 'Why men resist', in Thorne, Barrie with Yalom, Marilyn, *Rethinking the Family: Some Feminist Questions*, New York, Longman, 1982, pp.131–50.

Goodman, Emily Jane, 'Legal solutions: equal protection under the law', in Maria Roy (ed.), *Battered Women*, New York, Van Nostrand Reinhold, 1977.

Gordon, Margaret T., Riger, Stephanie, Le Bailly, Robert K., and Heath, Linda, 'Crime, women, and the quality of urban life', in Catharine R. Stimpson, Elsa Dixler, Martha J. Nelson and Kathryn B. Yatrakis, *Women and the American City*, Chicago, University of Chicago Press, 1980, pp.141–57.

Griffin, Susan, 'Rape: the all-American crime', *Ramparts*, September 1971, pp.26–35.

Griffin, Susan, *Rape: The Power of Consciousness*, San Francisco, Harper & Row, 1979.

Hadjifotiou, Nathalie, *Women and Harassment at Work*, London, Pluto Press, 1983.

Harmer, Jalna and Saunders, Sheila, 'Blowing the cover of the protective male – a community study of violence to women', in Eva Gamarnikow, David H. J. Morgan, June Purvis and Daphne Taylorson (eds), *The Public and The Private*, London, Heinemann, 1983, pp.28–46.

Hanmer, Jalna and Saunders, Sheila, *Well Founded Fear: A Community Study of Violence to Women*, London, Hutchinson, 1984.

Harper, Ross and McWhinnie, Arnot, *The Glasgow Rape Case*, London, Hutchinson, 1983.

Hawkins, Keith O., 'Assessing evil: decision behaviour and parole board justice', *The British Journal of Criminology*, vol.23, no.2, April 1983, pp.101–27.

Hawkins, Keith O., 'Thinking about legal decision-making', *Issues in Criminol-*

ogical and Legal Psychology, no.5, British Psychological Society for the Division of Criminological and Legal Psychology, 1983, pp.7–24.

Herman, Judith, Lewis, *Father-Daughter Incest*, Cambridge, Massachusetts, Harvard University Press, 1981.

Herman, Judith Lewis and Hirschman, Lisa, 'Father-daughter incest', *Signs*, vol.2, no.4, Summer 1977.

Holdaway, S., *British Police*, London, Edward Arnold, 1979.

Hollway, Wendy, '"I just wanted to kill a woman". Why? The Ripper and Male Sexuality', *Feminist Review*, no.9, October 1981, pp.33–41.

Holmstrom, Lynda Lytle and Burgess, Ann Wolbert, 'Rape: the husband's and boyfriend's initial reactions', *The Family Coordinator*, July 1979, pp.321–30.

Holmstrom, Lynda Lytle and Burgess, Ann Wolbert, 'Rapists' talk: linguistic strategies to control the victim', *Deviant Behaviour*, vol.1, 1979, pp.101–25.

Holmstrom, Lynda Lytle and Burgess, Ann Wolbert, *The Victim of Rape: Institutional Reactions*, New York, John Wiley & Sons, 1978.

Hosticka, Carl J., 'We don't care about what happened, we only care about what is going to happen: lawyer client negotiations of reality', *Social Problems*, vol.26, 1979, pp.599–610.

Hough, Mike and Mayhew, Pat, *The British Crime Survey*, London, HMSO, 1983.

Hunt, Jennifer, 'The development of rapport through the negotiation of gender in field work among police', *Human Organisation* (forthcoming), 1984.

James, Jennifer, 'The prostitute as victim', in June Roberts Chapman and Margaret Gates (eds), *The Victimization of Women*, Beverly Hills, California, Sage Publications, 1978, pp.175–202.

Johnson, Allan Griswold, 'On the prevalence of rape in the United States', *Signs*, vol.6, no.1, 1980, pp.136–46.

Jones, Ann, *Women Who Kill*, New York, Fawcett Columbine Books, 1981.

Jones, Cathaleen and Arnson, Elliot, 'Attribution of fault to a rape victim as a function of respectability of the victim', in Deanna R. Nass (ed.), *The Rape Victim*, Dubuque, Iowa, Kendall/Hunt Publishing Co., 1977, pp.27–34.

Kelly, Deborah P., 'Victim reactions to the criminal justice response', paper delivered at the 1982 Annual Meeting of the Law and Society Association, June, 1982.

Kerstetter, Wayne A., 'Police response to sexual assault complaints', paper delivered to the 1982 annual Law and Society Meetings, Toronto.

King, Michael, *The Framework of Criminal Justice*, London, Croom Helm 1981.

Kinsey, Alfred C., Pomeroy, Wardell B., Martin, Clyde E. and Gebhard, Paul H., *Sexual Behaviour in the Human Female*, Philadelphia, Saunders, 1953.

Klein, Dorie, 'The dark side of marriage: battered wives and the domination of women', in Nicole H. Rafter and Elizabeth A. Stanko (eds), *Judge, Lawyer, Victim, Thief: Women, Gender Roles and Criminal Justice*, Boston, Northeastern University Press, 1982, pp.83–107.

Landis, Carney, *Sex in Development*, New York, Harper & Brothers, 1940.

Landis, Judson, 'Experience of 500 children with adult sexual deviance', *Psychiatric Quarterly Supplement*, vol.30, 1956, pp.91–109.

Leeds TUCRIC, *Sexual Harassment of Women at Work: A Study from West Yorkshire*, August 1983.

Lerman, Lisa G., *Prosecution of Spouse Abuse: Innovations in Criminal Justice Response*, Center for Women Policy Studies, Washington, DC, 1981.

Lerner, M. J., 'Evaluation of performance as a function of performer's reward and attractiveness', *Journal of Personality and Social Psychology*, 1, 1965, pp.355–60.

Lerner, Melvin and Simmons, C. H., 'Observers' reaction to the innocent victim: compassion or rejection?', *Journal of Personality and Social Psychology* 4, 1966, pp.203–20.

Lovelace, Linda with McGrady, Mike, *Ordeal*, New York, Berkley Books, 1981.

McCabe, S. and Sutcliffe, F., *Defining Crime*, London, Blackwell, 1978.

McDermott, M. Joan, *Rape Victimization in 26 American Cities*, Washington DC, US Government Printing Office, 1979.

McGuire, Mike, *Burglary in a Dwelling*, Cambridge Studies in Criminology, XLIX, London, Heinemann, 1982.

McLeod, Maureen, 'Victim noncooperation in the prosecution of domestic assaults', *Criminology*, vol.21, no.3, August 1983, pp.395–416.

MacKinnon, Catharine A., 'Feminism, marxism, method, and the state: an agenda for theory', *Signs*, vol.7, no.3, 1982, pp.515–44.

MacKinnon, Catharine A., 'Feminism, marxism, method, and the state: toward feminist jurisprudence', *Signs*, vol.8, no.4, 1983, pp.635–58.

MacKinnon, Catharine A., *Sexual Harassment of Working Women*, New Haven, Connecticut, Yale University Press, 1979.

Manning, Peter K., 'Queries concerning the decision-making approach to police research', *Issues in Criminological and Legal Psychology*, no.5, British Psychological Society for the Division of Criminological and Legal Psychology, 1983, pp.50–60.

Martin, Del, *Battered Wives*, New York, Dell, 1976.

Martin, Susan E., 'Sexual harassment in the workplace: from occupational hazard to sex discrimination', paper delivered at Law and Society Annual Meeting, Amherst, Massachusetts, 1981.

Mather, Lynn, 'Some determinants of the method of case disposition', *Law and Society Review*, vol.8, Winter 1973, pp.187–216.

Maxfield, M. G., Lewis, D. A. and Szoc, R., 'Producing official crimes:

verified crime reports as measures of police output', *Social Science Quarterly*, vol.61, no.2, 1980.

Mendelsohn, Beniamin, 'The origin of the doctrine of victimology', *Excerpta Criminologica*, vol.3, May-June 1963, pp.239–344.

Meulenbelt, Anja, *The Shame is Over*, London, The Women's Press, 1980.

Miller, Frank, *Prosecution: The Decision to Charge a Suspect with a Crime*, Boston, Little Brown, 1970.

Miller, Jill, Moeller, Deborah, Kaufman, Arthur, Di Vasto, Peter, Pathak, Dorothy and Christy, Joan, 'Recidivism among sex assault victims', *American Journal of Psychiatry*, vol.35, 1978, pp.1103–4.

Moody, Susan R. and Tombs, Jacqueline, *Prosecution in the Public Interest*, Edinburgh, Scottish Academic Press, 1982.

Mullard, Judith, 'Death of a librarian', *New Statesman* (London), July 9 1982, pp.3–4.

Myers, Martha A. and Hagan, John, 'Private and public trouble: Prosecutors and the allocation of court resources', *Social Problems*, vol.26, no.4, 1979, pp.439–51.

Neubauer, David, *Criminal Justice in Middle America*, Morristown, New Jersey, General Learning Press, 1974.

Oakley, Ann, *Sex, Gender and Society*, New York, Harper & Row, 1972.

Ortner, Sherry B. and Whitehead, Harriet, *Sexual Meanings: The Cultural Construction of Gender and Sexuality*, London, Cambridge University Press, 1981.

Parisi, Nicolette, 'Are females treated differently?' in Nicole Hahn Rafter and Elizabeth A. Stanko (eds), *Judge, Lawyer, Victim, Thief: Women, Gender Roles and Criminal Justice*, Boston, Northeastern University Press, 1972, pp.205–20.

Parnas, Raymond I., 'The police response to the domestic disturbance', in Leon Radzinowitz and Marvin E. Wolfgang (eds), *The Criminal in the Arms of the Law*, New York, Basic Books, 1972, pp.206–36.

Pepinsky, H., 'Police decision making', in D. Gottfredson (ed.), *Decision-Making in the Criminal Justice System: Review and Essays*, Rockville, Maryland, US National Institute of Mental Health, 1975.

Perkins, T. E., 'Rethinking stereotypes', in Michèle Barrett, Philip Corrigan, Annette Kuhn and Janet Wolff, *Ideology and Cultural Production*, London, Croom Helm, 1974, pp.135–59.

Piliavin, Irving and Briar, Scott, 'Police encounters with juveniles', *American Journal of Sociology*, September 1964, pp.206–14.

Pizzey, Erin and Shapiro, Jeff, *Prone to Violence*, Feltham, Middlesex, Hamlyn Paperbacks, 1982.

Pleck, Elizabeth, 'Feminist responses to "crimes against women", 1868–1896', *Signs*, vol.8, no.3, Spring 1983, pp.451–70.

Police Foundation, *Domestic Violence and the Police: Studies in Detroit and Kansas City*, Washington DC, The Police Foundation, 1976.

Press Council, *Press Conduct in the Sutcliffe Case*, London, Press Council Booklet, no.7, 1983.

Quina, Kathryn, 'Long-term Psychological Consequences of Sexual Assault,' unpublished manuscript, University of Rhode Island, Kingston, RI, 1979.

Radford, Jill, 'Womanslaughter: a licence to kill? The killing of Jane Asher', in Paul Gordon and Phil Scraton (eds), *Causes for Concern: Cases in Criminal Justice*, Harmondsworth, Penguin, 1984.

Rafter, Nicole H. and Stanko, Elizabeth A., 'Introduction', *Judge, Lawyer, Victim, Thief: Women, Gender Roles and Criminal Justice*, Boston, Northeastern University Press, 1982.

Read, Sue, *Sexual Harassment at Work*, Feltham, Middlesex, Hamlyn Paperbacks, 1982.

Renvoize, Jean, *Incest: A Family Pattern*, London, Routledge & Kegan Paul, 1982.

Rich, Adrienne, 'Compulsory heterosexuality and lesbian existence', in Catharine R. Stimpson and Ethel Spector Person (eds), *Women: Sex and Sexuality*, Chicago, University of Chicago Press, 1980, pp.62–91.

Robin, Gerald D., 'Forcible rape. Institutionalized sexism in the criminal justice system', *Crime and Delinquency*, vol.23, April 1977, pp.147–9.

Rosaldo, Michelle Zimbalist, 'Women, culture and society: a theoretical overview', in Michelle Zimbalist Rosaldo and Louise Lamphere (eds), *Women, Culture and Society*, Stanford, Connecticut, Stanford University Press, 1974, pp.17–42.

Rose, Vicki McNickle and Randall, Susan Carol, 'The impact of investigator perceptions of victim legitimacy on the processing of rape/sexual assault cases', *Symbolic Interaction*, vol.5, no.1, 1982, pp.23–36.

Rosett, Arthur and Cressey, Donald R., *Justice by Consent*, New York, J. B. Lippincott, 1976.

Roy, Maria, *Battered Women*, New York, Van Nostrand Reinhold, 1977.

Rubenstein, Jonathan, *City Police*, New York, Farrar, Straus & Giroux, 1972.

Rule, Ann, *The Stranger Beside Me*, New York, Signet Books, 1980.

Rush, Florence, 'Freud and the sexual abuse of children', *Chrysalis*, no.1, 1977, pp.31–45.

Rush, Florence, 'The sexual abuse of children: a feminist point of view', in Noreen Connell and Cassandra Wilson (eds), *Rape: The First Sourcebook for Women*, New York, New American Library, 1974, pp.65–75.

Russell, Diana E. H., *The Politics of Rape*, New York, Stein & Day, 1975.

Russell, Diana E. H., *Rape in Marriage*, New York, Macmillan, 1982.

Russell, Diana E. H. and Howell, Nancy, 'The prevalence of rape in the United States revisited', *Signs*, vol.8, no.4, 1983, pp.688–95.

Sachs, Albie and Wilson, Joan Hoff, *Sexism and the Law*, Oxford, Martin Robertson, 1978.

Sachs, Harvey, 'Notes on police assessment of moral character', in David Sudnow (ed.), *Studies in Social Interaction*, New York, Free Press, 1972.

Sanders, William, *Detective Work*, New York, Free Press, 1977.

Schafer, Stephen, 'The beginning of victimology', in Burt Galaway and Joe Hudson (eds), *Perspectives on Crime Victims*, St. Louis, Missouri, C. V. Mosby Company, 1981, pp.15–26.

Schafer, Stephen, *The Victim and His Criminal*, New York, Random House, 1968.

Schechter, Susan, *Women and Male Violence: The Visions and Struggles of the Battered Women's Movement*, Boston, Massachusetts, South-End Press, 1982.

Schwendinger, Julia R. and Schwendinger, Herman, 'Rape myths: in legal, theoretical and everyday practice', *Crime and Social Justice*, 13, Summer 1974, pp.18–26.

Seddon, Vicky, 'Keeping women in their place', *Marxism Today*, July 1983, pp.20–2.

Sedley, Ann and Benn, Melissa, *Sexual Harassment at Work*, London, NCCL Rights for Women Unit, 1982.

Shapland, Joanna, Willmore, J. and Duff, P., 'The victim in the criminal justice system', Final Report to the Home Office, October 1981.

Sherman, Lawrence W., 'The specific deterrent effects of arrests for spouse assault: a field experiment', proposal submitted to National Institute of Justice, 1 April 1980.

Silverman, Dierdre, 'Sexual harassment: working women's dilemma', *Quest*, vol.III, no.3, Winter 1976–7, pp.15–24.

Skolnick, Jerome K., *Justice Without Trial*, New York, John Wiley & Sons, 1966.

Smart, Carol, *Women, Crime and Criminology*, London, Routledge & Kegan Paul, 1976.

Smart, Carol and Smart, Barry, *Women, Sexuality and Social Control*, London, Routledge & Kegan Paul, 1978.

Smith, Joan, 'Getting away with murder', *New Socialist*, May/June 1982, pp.10–12.

Stanko, Elizabeth A., 'The arrest versus the case', *Urban Life*, vol.9, no.4, 1981, pp.395–414.

Stanko, Elizabeth Anne, 'The impact of victim assessment on prosecutors' screening decisions: the case of the New York County District Attorney's Office', *Law and Society Review*, vol.16, no.2, 1981–2, pp.225–39.

Stanko, Elizabeth A., *These Are the Cases That Try Themselves*, unpublished PhD dissertation, City University of New York, 1977.

Stanko, Elizabeth Anne, 'Would you believe this woman: prosecutorial screening for "credible" witnesses and a problem of justice', in Nicole Hahn Rafter and Elizabeth Anne Stanko (eds), *Judge, Lawyer, Victim, Thief: Women, Gender Roles and Criminal Justice*, Boston, Northeastern University Press, 1982, pp.63–82.

Stark, Evan, Flitcraft, Ann and Frazier, William, 'Medicine and patriarchal violence: the social construction of a "private" event', *International Journal of Health Services*, 9, no.3, 1979, p.466.

Steinmetz, Suzanne, *The Cycle of Violence: Assertive, Aggressive, and Abusive Family Interaction*, New York, Praeger Publishers, 1977.

Straus, Murray, Gelles, Richard J. and Steinmetz, Suzanne, *Behind Closed Doors*, New York, Doubleday, 1980.

Tsai, Mavis and Wagner, Nathaniel, 'Therapy groups for women sexually molested as children', *Archives of Sexual Behaviour*, vol.7, 1978, pp.417–29.

Von Hentig, Hans, *The Criminal and His Victim*, New Haven, Connecticut, Yale University Press, 1948.

Walker, Ian, 'The double killing of Mary Bristow', *Observer*, 19 June 1973, pp.20–3.

Walkowitz, Judith R., 'Jack the Ripper and the myth of male violence', *Feminist Studies*, vol.8, no.3, 1982, pp.543–74.

Walkowitz, Judith R., *Prostitution and Victorian Society*, Cambridge, Cambridge University Press, 1980.

Walmsley, Roy and White, Karen, *Supplementary Information on Sexual Offences and Sentencing* (Research Unit Paper 2;), London, HMSO, 1980.

Wasoff, Frances, 'Domestic violence and the police', conference paper, 'Battered women and the state', Scottish Women's Aid, 13 December 1980.

Wasoff, Frances, 'The need for legal protection: the role of the prosecutor and the courts in the legal response to domestic violence', paper presented to DHSS (Britain), *Seminar on Violence in the Family*, September 1981.

Weeks, Jeffrey, *Sex, Politics and Society*, London, Longman, 1981.

Weis, Kurt and Borges, Sandra S., 'Victimology and rape: the case of the legitimate victim', *Issues in Criminology*, 8, Fall 1973, pp.71–115.

Wilbanks, William, 'Murdered women and women who murder: a critique of the literature', in Nicole Hahn Rafter and Elizabeth A. Stanko (eds), *Judge, Lawyer, Victim, Thief: Women, Gender Roles and Criminal Justice*, Boston, Northeastern University Press, 1982, pp.151–81.

Williams, Kirsten M., 'The effects of victim characteristics on the disposition of violent crimes', in William F. MacDonald (ed.), *Criminal Justice and the Victim*, Beverly Hills, California, Sage, 1976.

Williams, Kirsten M., 'Few convictions in rape cases: empirical evidence concerning some alternative explanations', *Journal of Criminal Justice*, vol.9, no.1, 1981, pp.29–40.

Wilson, Nanci Koser, 'Women in the criminal justice professions: an analysis of status conflict', in Nicole Hahn Rafter and Elizabeth A. Stanko (eds), *Judge, Lawyer, Victim, Thief: Women, Gender Roles and Criminal Justice*, Boston, Northeastern University Press, 1982, pp.359–74.

Wright, Richard, 'Rape and physical violence', in D. J. West (ed.), *Sex offenders in the Criminal Justice System*, Cropwood Conference Series, Cambridge, no.12, 1980, pp.100–13.

Index

205